上海高等学校一流本科建设引领计划系列教材

U0366767

社会科学
任务型学术英语写作

Task-based: Academic Writing of Social Sciences

主　编　王春岩

副主编　邵严毅

编　者（以姓氏拼音为序）

李梅青　鲁瑶　孟娇娇　申琳

上海交通大学出版社
SHANGHAI JIAO TONG UNIVERSITY PRESS

内容提要

  本书为"上海高等学校一流本科建设引领计划项目系列教材"。教程针对社会科学专业的大学生进行"项目式"学术英语写作的指导。教程采用广义专门用途英语概念,同时关注写作认知过程和学术英语的语言特征,引导学生分步完成研究选题、数据收集分析、报告写作和展示活动,并提供 Endnote 使用方法、APA 格式讲解、小组互评、写作能力评价等实用的教学与研究工具。本书适合大学本科生及研究生使用。

图书在版编目(CIP)数据

  社会科学任务型学术英语写作/王春岩主编.—上海:上海交通大学出版社,2021.12
  ISBN 978-7-313-25596-9

  Ⅰ.①社… Ⅱ.①王… Ⅲ.①英语—写作 Ⅳ.①H315

  中国版本图书馆 CIP 数据核字(2021)第 203625 号

社会科学任务型学术英语写作
SHEHUIKEXUE RENWUXING XUESHU YINGYU XIEZUO

主　　编:王春岩			
出版发行:上海交通大学出版社		地　　址:上海市番禺路 951 号
邮政编码:200030		电　　话:021-64071208
印　　制:上海新艺印刷有限公司		经　　销:全国新华书店
开　　本:787mm×1092mm　1/16		印　　张:15.5
字　　数:347 千字		
版　　次:2021 年 12 月第 1 版		印　　次:2021 年 12 月第 1 次印刷
书　　号:ISBN 978-7-313-25596-9		
定　　价:56.00 元		

版权所有　侵权必究
告读者:如发现本书有印装质量问题请与印刷厂质量科联系
联系电话:021-33854186

❖ 前　言 ❖

《大学英语教学指南》(2020 年版)把专门用途英语(ESP)列为大学生外语能力培养的核心内容之一,ESP 中一个重要的分支是学术英语(EAP)。学术英语写作培养学生用英语写作研究性论文的能力,然而在目前 EAP 写作教程中,未有适合社会科学专业领域大学生的专用教程。在这样的背景下,我们编写了《社会科学任务型学术英语写作》。

教程目的

本教程为三类学习者准备,分别为进行研究性学术英语学习的社会科学(文科)专业大学生、进行毕业论文写作的英语专业大学生以及从事国际期刊发表写作的社会科学专业研究生。我们的总体目标和具体目标如下:

(1) 总体目标。训练并提高社会科学专业大学生进行学术研究、学术英语写作、学术英语展示和学习管理的能力。

(2) 具体目标。培养学生进行学术文献查找和批判阅读的能力,培养学生观察分析和解决社会问题的创新思维能力,培养学生使用国际通用语言进行学术写作和学术展示的能力。在研究性任务的探索过程中,培养学生任务管理、情绪管理、团队合作的能力,树立学生的学术研究道德和社会责任感。

内容安排、教程特色与教学建议

本教程包括五个部分,共 27 个单元。

第一部分介绍了社会科学研究性写作的基本知识、学习管理和研究道德,包括设立目标、确立问题、查阅文献、分析问题、运作团队、恪守道德等 9 个单元。

木书该部分区别与其他教程之处为:我们把研究过程和学术写作紧密结合,认为好的写作建立的基础是扎实的阅读、思考和分析。本教程依托课程组积累的教学经验,用学生的日志、课堂观察和往届学生的研究选题为案例,对研究过程中的认知误区和情感困难进行梳理,并提供解决方案。

教学建议：这部分涉及文献查找、研究方法、研究选题等跨学科能力,对语言教师挑战度极高,教师在提高自己研究素养的同时,应当寻找图书馆馆员、社会科学专业教师和数据分析教师共同完成课堂讲座,同时培养学生借助网络资源进行探索学习的能力。

第二部分介绍了社会科学研究性写作中各个部分的结构和语言。借用功能语言学的发现,详细讲解引言、方法、结果、讨论、标题和摘要部分的表达功能和语言特征。这部分也包括了初稿的修改、同伴互评和 APA 引用方法,共 10 章内容。我们选择社会科学中的经济学、管理学、文化学等学科的期刊样文,标注样文中的功能和语言搭配,并配有练习题目,提供课堂分析教学素材。

本书在该部分区别与其他教程之处为:在样文选取上,紧紧依托社会科学,充分考虑学生的知识框架;在初稿修改上提供了自查和同伴互评两种方式;提供了文内和文后引用格式、Endnote 的使用介绍和最新(第七版)APA 格式。

教学建议：本部分可以采用归纳法和演绎法结合进行。虽然本教程聚焦社会科学,但是即使在社会科学内部,研究性写作的语篇结构也差异极大。教师应充分关注各个学科的特征,引导学生归纳自己学科的写作结构,并进行一般性的修辞指导。

第三部分介绍了研究性报告的展示和如何参加学术会议,共四章内容。分别为:陈述报告准备、PPT 和发言准备、展板设计,以及会议摘要写作。

本书在该部分区别与其他教程之处:我们提供了详细的展板对比样例和会议摘要。展板样例和会议摘要来自教学真实案例,可直观指导学习。我们详细分析了书面报告和会议展示的目标、对象、语言和策略差异。

教学建议：模拟学术会议和专题论坛是展示学术研究的有效方式。

第四部分介绍了社会科学研究性写作的特殊文体:案例分析写作、社会调查报告和商务策划书,共三章内容。每一章提供了语篇结构、语言特点和样文。

本书在该部分区别与其他教程之处:本部分突出社会科学写作的特质性文体,为选择特殊文体写作的作者提供样文参考。

教学建议：本部分独立于前面的一般社科研究性写作,仅供个性化教学参考。

第五部分介绍了如何进行反思和自我评价,有一章学习内容。本部分还包括了参考文献、学生写作样文等内容。

本书在该部分区别与其他教程之处:很少有写作教程介绍如何做学习反思和自我评价。我们综合研究性写作能力培养要素,提出了 6 维度评价表,并提供反思写作的方法和样文。

教学建议：反思和评价是提高自我调控学习能力的重要手段,可以分教学阶段进行,也可以只在最后一单元进行反思。

教程总体特色

（1）提供研究方法。本教程采用广义专门用途英语概念（Widdowson，1983），认为写作思想和写作过程同样重要，提供浅显的社会科学研究方法指导，减少学生进行研究性写作的认知负荷和心理焦虑。

（2）提供学习指导。任务型写作过程不仅是研究和写作的过程，更是一般学习能力的培养过程，本教程提供目标管理、进度反思、成果反思、团队合作等内容，培养学生的学习能力。

（3）培养科学精神。本教程考虑中国学生引用意识不强、引用能力缺乏的短板，以从提高做笔记、写综述的能力到寻找自己的原创思想为路径，培养学生创新能力。

（4）囊括最新知识。本教程融入前沿内容，如 Endnote 的使用方法、APA 格式第七版讲解、研究性写作评价维度、小组互评方法、学生能力自评表、学生反思写作指导等。

教学使用说明

本教程主要针对社会科学专业的大学生进行研究性学术英语写作学习，建议采用任务型教学法（PBL）和在研究中学习的方式，完成研究和写作。教师可以在一个学期内，引导学生从研究选题和设立学习目标开始，逐步完成团队建设、文献查阅、研究选题、数据收集、数据分析、引言写作、文献写作、方法和结果写作、文本修改、提交和展示等环节。本教程也适合英语专业本科学生进行毕业论文写作时自学使用，以及社会科学研究生进行国际论文发表时作为参考使用。

本教材为"上海高等学校一流本科建设引领计划项目系列教材"。教材出版受到该项目全额资助，特此感谢。本书编写过程中，我们充分参考了国内外的学术写作教程和文章，并得到了经济学、法学、管理学专业教师在期刊范围和期刊特征方面的指导，得到了往届学生在学习日记、范文写作、展板等方面的支持。在此我们对所有帮助本教程写作的老师和同学表示感谢。

由于时间和能力限制，本教程中必然存在需要改进的地方，欢迎读者提出宝贵意见。联系邮箱：Wangchunyan@suibe.edu.cn。

编者

2021 年 11 月

❧ Contents ❧

Part 2　The Journey of Writing

Part 5   Conclusion

❧ **Introduction** ❧

> 在高等教育国际化背景下，使用国际通用语言进行专业学术交流的必要性不容忽视。本教程为社会科学类本科生和学术英语写作教师提供写作体裁、语言、心理和学习管理上的支持。本章介绍教程的目标读者、社会科学常用研究方法、学术报告写作过程、学习所需的能力和学习结果的评价方式。

I. Who is the book for?

This is a book for college students of social sciences in general, and business studies in particular, to learn to write academic reports. Against the background of internationalization, it is common for college students to learn around the world, and thus they need to know how to write properly in their disciplines. Many universities in China provide academic writing (AW) courses for this purpose, and if you are a student learning social science, or an English teacher searching for a book for an AW course, congratulations! This is your book.

The book focuses on writing a report or a long essay based on research. Writing a report is an exciting, wonderful, rewarding, frustrating, and unfortunately, sometimes desperate experience. We will show the ins and outs of the process, giving you all the help that you need and ensuring success in the end.

II. What is social science, exactly?

Broadly speaking, social sciences are the observation of society and the people that make it up. Throughout the book, we use examples from more commonly studied social science subjects, such as economics and sociology, but the ideas apply equally to other disciplines including anthropology, education, history, law, linguistics, political science, psychology, sociology, and others.

III. Researching social science

Social scientists explore open-ended but focused questions in systematic ways. They explore the social behaviors of human beings, their relationships, and institutions (Melzer, 2011, p.394). They review the research of other social scientists, and collect data by making observations, conducting interviews and analyzing social artifacts.

Generally speaking, sociology is an empirical discipline, which means that the research of sociology is based on documented and collected data. These data usually draw upon observed patterns and information from collected cases and experiences. Social science research methods, generally speaking, can be divided into two kinds: empirical and non-empirical.

Empirical research means that the data used to support writing are collected by yourself. For example, to gather the views of patients in hospitals, volunteers in community service, or students in universities, you will have to ask these people about their attitudes about the issues that they are involved in. You can use questionnaires, observations, or interviews to collect your data, or you may collect data by analyzing existing data from various institutions.

Some students like spending time in the library, reading, thinking, and discussing theories. The non-empirical research method is common for politics, law, history, literature, and sociology. Key theories in some disciplines such as feminism or pragmatism can be carried out with non-empirical methods.

IV. The process of writing a report

Fisher (2010) uses a beautiful figure to show the steps of research-based report writing as shown in Figure 0.1. Three dimensions can be seen. The time dimension is vertical: the height of the cube is to show the time needed from planning the project to finishing doing it. The right-side dimension shows the thinking process: from choosing a topic to finding out the result of the research question. And the left side of the cube shows the mental process from confusion to confidence. This is how writers go through the process of writing: it is not only the cognitive activity of formulating and analyzing a problem, but also a psychological course from the feeling of confusion to gaining the insights, confidence, or self-efficacy after solving the problem.

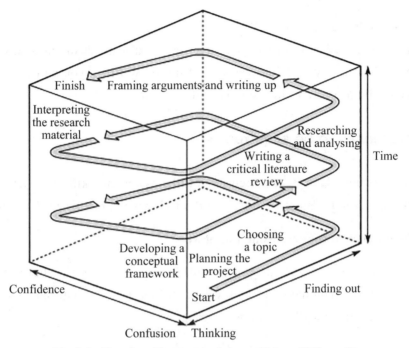

Fig.0.1 Report writing process (source: Fisher, 2010, p.5)

Stage 1—Choose a topic and design your research

At this stage, you might be confused about what to do. Formulating a research problem and finding a method to work out the problem are the first mountain for you to conquer. The main activities in this stage are to read widely and discuss with your team members or tutors the research problem. You would be very confused at this time till you come up with a clearer research idea.

Stage 2—Write a literature review

This is the second mountain to be crossed and is extremely hard for undergraduate students. With more time devoted to reading around the topic, taking notes, and comparing the literature, you will gain a clearer picture of the research problem and be more confident to carry out the research.

Stage 3—Collect and analyze data

Conducting interviews, dispatching questionnaires, or downloading information online are dominant activities in this stage. The main activity of this stage is about finding out the results. When working out the research results, your confidence will be boosted.

Stage 4—Interpret research material

This can be a daunting task and initially, there can be an increase in confusion as you think about what the data mean. But hard thinking and interrogation usually result in exciting findings.

Stage 5—Write and edit

In the final stage, you formulate your arguments and shape them into a dissertation. If everything goes well, by the time you have finished writing, you will have had more confidence in the project, in the report, and yourself.

V. Competences to be acquired

Report writing requires an extension of the academic skills that are related to English skills, but much more than it. See the following competences you can acquire.

1. Competence to find academic literature

As an undergraduate student, this is probably the first time you have searched for academic resources. You have to know where to look for the material related to your research and find them efficiently and thoroughly.

2. Competence to read efficiently and critically

Understanding academic articles, summarizing the main ideas, comparing different views and evaluating them are required when choosing a research topic and forming a research outline. Note-taking is the basic skill to avoid plagiarism, and a critical reading skill that determines the quality of topic choice. Fast reading and deep reading competencies are expected to be cultivated.

3. Competence to research

Academic writing is the process of inferring knowledge out of facts, and these facts are out of first-hand research based on a reliable research method. Learning to write is learning to think scientifically and conclude logically. Original ideas and methods are favored by all teachers.

4. Competence to write

Report writing has its comparatively set structure, vocabulary and expression. For traditional academic writing books, this is the main part. In our book, this is also very important knowledge. You must utilize multiple theories, incorporate relevant materials with your data, and write in a complex disciplinary genre. The road from an apprentice to an insider in a major is struggling.

5. Competence to learn

There are some important qualities we want to cultivate in this book: plan learning tasks, choose time to do it, choose a place to avoid distraction, find social help, and reflect on the challenges and solutions. We see the process of learning to learn as important as the process of learning to research and learning to write.

6. Competence to cooperate

Task-based report writing needs a team to carry out the research. Team members have to support each other not only intellectually, but also spiritually while learning to research and write.

VI. The assessment criteria

At the completion of this course, you will be able to write a clearly structured, adequately expressed, and well-presented report. The following marking rubric by Good et al. (2012) is for teachers and students to refer to.

The five dimensions include focus, idea development, organization, style and language convention. The first dimension shows students' understanding of writing purpose, audience, focus and tone. The second dimension, content and idea development, is based on research quality. The organization dimension is of great importance for report, and especially so for empirical research, which has a long history of Introduction-Method-Discussion-Conclusion structure. The last two dimensions are vocabulary choice and grammatical correctness. This is similar to general English writing requirement, but a more formal and academic style is expected.

VII. Summary of the chapter

Academic writing is not all about writing. We concern about the competence of doing research and learning strategies as well. That is why the first chapter of the book is not "how to use the library" or "how to take notes", but to make your learning plan. Wish you enjoy the researching, writing, and learning journey with us.

Table 0.1　Writing assessment rubric template

Writing Dimensions	1: Inadequate	2: Marginal	3: Acceptable	4: Good	5: Excellent
Focus: Discipline-Based Written Product	Student demonstrates a lack of awareness of purpose and audience; unclear focus; inappropriate tone.	Student demonstrates minimal awareness of purpose and audience; marginal ability to provide a clear focus; borderline ability to convey appropriate tone.	Student demonstrates acceptable awareness of purpose and audience; somewhat clear focus; indication of understanding of appropriate tone in writing.	Student demonstrates accurate awareness of purpose and audience; mostly clear focus; satisfactory use of tone in writing.	Student demonstrates perceptive awareness of purpose and audience; clarity of focus; deep understanding and ability to create appropriate tone.
Content: Idea Development	Student provides no explanation and illustration of key ideas; no attempt to incorporate primary concepts of the discipline or to analyze and weigh differing facts and ideas; no synthesis of content-area materials or facts.	Student provides vague explanation and illustration of key ideas; inconsistent incorporation of primary concepts of the discipline; weak effort to analyze and weigh differing facts and ideas; incomplete synthesis of material.	Student provides explanation and illustration of most key ideas; incorporation of some primary concepts of the discipline; analysis of differing facts and ideas and an effort to synthesize all materials, although possibly inconsistent	Student provides detailed explanation and illustration of key ideas; incorporation of several primary concepts of the discipline; accurate analysis of different facts and ideas and a clear synthesis of all material.	Student provides extensive explanations and illustrations of key ideas; thorough incorporation of primary concepts of the discipline; sophisticated ability to analyze and weigh different facts and ideas and synthesize all material.
Organization	Student does not use transitions or headings; student writing is absent of logical and clear arrangement of ideas; writing lacks unity and coherence of paragraphs.	Student minimally uses transitions or headings; provides inconsistent and sometimes unclear logic and arrangement of ideas; creates borderline unity and coherence of paragraphs.	Student uses some of transitions or headings; provides fairly logical and clear arrangement of ideas; creates adequate unity and coherence of paragraphs.	Student appropriately uses transitions or headings; provides mostly logical and clear arrangement of ideas; creates consistent unity and coherence of paragraphs.	Student efficiently uses transitions or headings; provides highly logical and clear arrangement of ideas; creates comprehensive unity and coherence of paragraphs.

(Continued)

Writing Dimensions	1: Inadequate	2: Marginal	3: Acceptable	4: Good	5: Excellent
Style	Student's ability to use discourse and language appropriate to their academic discipline is weak with several redundancies; student does not use appropriate word choice and/or vocabulary of field; student does not demonstrate an understanding of specific style guide for documentation (i.e., APA, MLA, etc.)	Student uses minimal discourse and language appropriate to their academic discipline with some redundancy; inconsistently uses vocabulary of field and some inappropriate word choice; student makes several errors in using discipline-specific style guide for documentation (i.e., APA, MLA, etc.).	Student sometimes uses discourse and language appropriate to academic discipline with some redundancy; attempts to use appropriate word choice that is specific to vocabulary of field; makes an effort at following discipline-specific style guide for documentation (i.e., APA, MLA, etc.), although some errors occur.	Student mostly uses discourse and language appropriate to academic discipline; avoids redundancy; demonstrates good use of appropriate word choice and vocabulary of field; demonstrates competence in following discipline-specific style guide for documentation (i.e., APA, MLA, etc.).	Student demonstrates an ease in using discourse and language appropriate to academic discipline; is not redundant; selects sophisticated word choice and masters accurate use of vocabulary in field; demonstrates accurate ability to use discipline-specific style guide for documentation (i.e., APA, MLA, etc.).
English Language Conventions	Student writes with many patterns of errors in grammar, and frequently includes comma splices, run-ons, and/or fragments; writing exhibits patterns of usage and grammatical errors; numerous misspellings.	Student writes several grammatically incorrect sentences, comma splices, run-ons, and/or fragments and a pattern of errors begins to emerge in any one error type; several misspellings.	Student writes some grammatically incorrect sentences, and has some comma splices, run-ons, and/or fragments but not a clear pattern in any error type; some misspellings.	Student writes mostly grammatically correct sentences, with few comma splices, runons, and/or fragments; writing has few to no misspellings.	Student writes grammatically correct sentences with an absence of comma splices, run-ons, fragments; writing is absent of usage and grammatical errors and maintains accurate spelling.

Part 1

The Journey of

Researching

Chapter 1

Design Your Plan

学术写作是复杂的认知活动,写作过程中会遇到阅读、选题、数据收集、数据分析、小组合作、语言、修辞等各个阶段的问题。理解写作的心理、保持积极的写作心态、制订写作计划是顺利完成写作的必要条件。本章介绍成功的学习者所使用的学习策略,为课程学习做好准备。

Learning objectives

When learning this chapter, you are expected:

- to understand the feelings of report writing,
- to learn the keys to keep positive writing experiences, and
- to design your plan for submitting your paper.

It sounds strange for a writing book to begin the first chapter with "design your plan" instead of "how to the library" or "how to take motes". In our eyes, designing a plan, keeping a learning diary, and committing to the task are decisive strategies for successful academic writing. We have been teaching the course for years and we found many students unable to sustain their original motivation, and ended up with sloppy papers. The following notes taken from an author's teaching journal show the challenges felt by her students:

At noon four girl students stopped me and mentioned their interview experience. Last night they met a governor of the university town who did not provide any useful information for their research data. They lack time, knowledge, and connection to carry out the project and feel depressed.

Four boys went to another city to investigate how a company adopted traditional Chinese culture in its management. The dirty and mysterious atmosphere there frightened them and they escaped with almost no data.

These frustrating experiences are not rare. When we collected students' feelings about academic writing, they handed in notes like this:

I feel depressed when thinking about writing. . . I feel knowing little about research. . . I cannot read English research articles quickly enough and have to translate Chinese writers' articles into English. . . I just cannot find anything new to explore. . . I am too busy to read and write. . .

However, we never failed to meet successful students. They wrote intelligent reports with deep theoretical thoughts, accurate statistical calculation and academic language. They told us how they enjoyed the writing process and the secrets of overcoming difficulties:

I have a deadline that forces me to sit down and write. . . I have a friend who is encouraging. . . I read an article that inspires me to go on. . . The topic is very important and I must write about it. . . I meet my teacher twice a week and that forces me to do something new. . .

Interestingly, happy writers are all alike, to paraphrase Tolstoy. Successful writers share similar attitudes and writing habits. There are keys to successful writing.

I. Keys to successful writing

We find the following three important points leading to successful writing.

1. Successful students read in volume

A boy student we taught 4 years ago took part in the National College Academic Forum and won the Best Writer Award. He told us he chose the topic after reading more than thirty related articles. The number we heard from other students was often three, instead of thirty. Extensive reading is essential. The inspiration of research and writing would not come to your brain intrusively without dogged pursuit.

Make reading and writing a habit of learning. It is not easy for undergraduates to open the Web of Science, choose an article of 10,000 words and finish reading in 30 minutes. Two mountains block your way: one is discipline knowledge and the other is the terms used by scholars. Magazines and journals such as *Economists* and *Nature* are good choices for college students. These resources are useful to tackle cognitive and affective problems before reading pure research articles.

Another suggestion for undergraduates is to follow textbooks. Some boy students we taught in the past questioned the theory of income hypothesis taught in their economic course, then they read related articles and came up with a good report after testing the theory in Shanghai.

2. Successful students solicit social support

Academic writing is not a solo activity. When the idea of collaboration is lost, writing problems arise, such as the difficulty to get useful data or the confusion of handling statistics. You can always find some partners who are good at communicating with others and getting interview data you want so much. You can always find a math talent who can help you with a good story out of messy data in your hands.

Our recent research on the relationship between writing strategy and writing performance showed that those students who frequently ask for social support write better than those who do not. The story of an Indonesian writer, Pramoedya Ananta Toer, is inspiring. Toer stayed in prison for years, creating stories and sharing with other prisoners, who attributed their survival to listening to interesting stories. Toer published these stories and won the Nobel Prize in Literature many years later. The story shows that writing is a social activity created collectively.

Make your writing social instead of solitary by starting a writing group. Teamwork time and tutorial time are the best chances to have a hearing. Writing course teachers should also construct a communicating environment to help students lessen their anxiety. Fortunately, when stating your problems, you can always find someone rich in solutions, and that you are not a big idiot as you think.

3. Successful students persist and overcome obstacles

To learn how to undertake a project and report your findings provides more chances of losing than persisting and winning. The writing process includes:

(1) Finding an interesting and important issue;

(2) Reading on till you find the research method;

(3) Undertaking effective and competent primary or secondary research;

(4) Observing and analyzing data in hand;

(5) Incorporating data in your hand with a critical review of the literature;

(6) Writing your report on solid analysis;

(7) Writing in proper academic English: structure, vocabulary, and grammar.

This is a daunting task considering the poor discipline knowledge background for undergraduate students and it is more demoralizing if you take an academic writing course in the first two years before you have much substantial knowledge of your disciplines. What learning strategies can make the academic journey less thorny?

One method of making those tasks less demanding is finding an article and **replicating its research method**. One boy group replicated the research method of a published article on the relationship between urbanization and pollution index. The original research was done in Europe and theirs was in China, and they compared their findings with those of the original one. Replication research is good for undergraduates who lack both disciplinary and language skills by providing them with a chance to learn and create at the same time. Besides that, students learn how to avoid plagiarism and organize their own literature review to justify their replication at the same time.

Talking to oneself is another method to overcome difficulties. It is interesting to note that some students have sites to get themselves in a positive writing mood before moving to their writing spot. One student would enter the bathroom, close the door and talk aloud to herself about the writing plan, facts or logic till she got clear thought and focus of the writing.

Having a customary writing site helps to form the habit of writing regularly. Many students have a variety of writing sites, including library stacks, reading rooms, coffee shops and dining tables. Your writing site should be comfortable, convenient and without any distraction.

Choosing an interesting research topic is also important so that you have the passion to continue. Successful writers do not write primarily for their teacher or their classmates. Rather, they focus on the questions that fascinate them. You are more likely to have positive writing experiences if you follow your deepest interests rather than passing fads in the fast-changing world.

Our last suggestion to overcome obstacles is **getting ready to pick up new knowledge** by yourself. It is not rare that even Harvard University cannot open all courses needed by its students. Learn to learn. You will have to pick up new skills in your life and it is especially so when you are graduated. One favorite example is a girl student who graduated from our university as an event management major and ended up working as a software engineer at Google. She learned programming all by herself.

II. Setting a realistic writing goal

We designed the workbook to help to keep up with writing till you submit it. If you meet twice a week with your tutor, adjust your timetable accordingly. That is to say, basically, the book suits courses of 16 sessions in a semester and 8 sessions as well. You can decide the deadline that will keep you disciplined, such as the end of the semester or some conference date. Once the firm completion date is set, time can be planned accordingly. Important subtasks and suggested time for doing these tasks are:

(1) Preparing reading and writing proposal time: the first four weeks;

(2) Data collection and analysis: the 5th to the 8th week;

(3) Introduction section writing time: the 9th week;

(4) Body (literature review, method, and results) section writing time: the 10th to the 12th week;

(5) Discussion and Conclusion section writing time: the 13th week to the 14th week;

(6) Reviewing and submitting work: the 15th week to the 16th week.

Table 1.1   16-week calendar for academic writing schedule

Week	Task	Mon	Tues	Wed	Thu	Fri	Sat	Sun
1	planning							
2	reading for ideas							
3	reading for methods							
4	proposal writing							
5	data collection							
6	data collection							
7	data analysis							
8	data analysis							
9	write introduction							
10	write literature review							
11	write method							
12	write results							
13	write discussion							
14	write conclusion							
15	review and submit							
16	conference and reflection							

III. Summary of the chapter

Begin a research-based writing journey with the following tools: a learning plan to control your speed, a resolute heart to swallow books, and a supporting team to cry with several times and to laugh with in the end.

Chapter 2

Get an Exciting Idea

学术研究中的"创新"是对前人研究的继承发展。学习者基于中英文文献或专业课本的阅读思考,结合对日常生活的观察进行研究选题。选题是否恰当直接关系到后续写作的学习动机和任务完成的质量。阅读选题的过程也是培养快速阅读和批判思维能力的过程。本章讲述什么是好的选题,如何找到恰当的选题,以及如何做文献阅读笔记。

Learning objectives

Chapter 2 will help you know where to get academic resources and how to read analytically. When learning this chapter, you are expected:
- to find an exciting research idea, and
- to write annotated bibliography.

We want to clarify a misunderstanding here about what is original research. The notion that research must be completely original is a misconception. All research is based on the work of others to some extent. *Original* implies some novel twist, fresh perspectives, or innovative methods that make the research worthwhile reading.

I. Where is the exciting idea?

All new knowledge begins with new questions. If you have a clear academic pursuit, it may not be hard to select a research topic. If you do not have, the following sources may be helpful:

Textbooks that you are currently using in your courses or that you have used in previous courses can be a source of ideas for broad topic areas. Often, the authors of textbooks point out areas of controversy or gaps in the research on specific topics.

There are reliable **media** such as CCTV or local TV that provides a deep analysis of economic, social, or political problems. These programs are often good resources for you to gain inspiration of research.

Every university subscribes to large **databases** for research, such as CnKi or EBSCO host. Use keyword search to find articles on your topic. Your database search should generate lists of citations and brief descriptions of articles. At this point, study the results and do the following:

- Refine the search by narrowing or expanding it.
- Download specific articles to read.
- Follow references for further information.
- Use effective keywords when searching. Keywords are words or phrases that the search engine looks for across the web. The more specific a keyword or phrase is, the more tightly a search will be focused on. Here is a set of keywords for the research topic of "games used to simulate real-world".

general	Game	This general term will produce a very unfocused list of millions of websites.
	Simulation	This more specific term will narrow the search considerably and will show topic sites such as suppliers of simulated products.
	Simulation game	This set of keywords is much more specific, but the engine will also find sites using both words but not in combination.
Specific	" Simulation game"	The quotation marks for this search will turn out the sites that use the exact phrase "simulation game".

Suppose you have done your search and have several options at hand. Discuss and brainstorm with your partner to share ideas, and you may compare these ideas and complete with a satisfactory research topic at last.

Then you may visit your thesis adviser. Do not go to your thesis adviser with an empty head. If you or your research team has come up with a broad topic, your thesis adviser would be happy to give further advice on how to refine it or make it more suitable for your ability.

See the following research questions chosen by our students. The first idea came from their economic textbook. The second idea came from their observation of the fashion market. The third idea came from their daily life and the last came from the searching of database.

(1) Feasibility of Permanent Income Hypothesis in Shanghai

(2) An Analysis of the Advantages and Disadvantages of Fast Fashion Brands Based on University Students Consumption Tendency

(3) Analysis Report on the Utilization of Library Resources by University Users

(4) Detailed Analysis of the Negative Relationship between Urbanization and Pollution in Chinese Cities

II. Find the topic that suits you

No topic is a good topic if it does not suit the doer. Let's have a game and see what kind of research suits you. This is taken from Winstanley (2010, p. 29). Questions in the following will help you audit your research skills. Think about each question and rate from 1 (little knowledge and experience) to 5 (plenty of knowledge and experience). After finishing this exercise you're likely to have pinpointed the areas in which you feel confident and areas that need improving.

√ **Research skills and techniques**
- ☐ I can recognize problems in my field.
- ☐ I can demonstrate original, independent and critical thinking.
- ☐ I have the ability to develop theoretical ideas.
- ☐ I understand relevant research methodologies.
- ☐ I'm able to critically analyze and evaluate research findings.
- ☐ I can summarize, document and report my findings.
- ☐ I can reflect constructively on my progress.

√ **Background to research field**
- ☐ I've a reasonable grasp of the national and international context in my field.
- ☐ I have some knowledge of recent ideas within my field.
- ☐ I've thought about how people may be affected by my work.
- ☐ I've considered ethical and health and safety concerns from my research project.

√ **Managing research**
- ☐ I'm good at setting myself short-term and long-term goals.
- ☐ I can prioritize activities effectively.
- ☐ I'm good at planning ahead.
- ☐ I know where to find appropriate bibliographical sources and archives (in hard copy and electronic format).
- ☐ I'm confident at using IT to manage my work.

√ **Personal effectiveness**
- ☐ I'm keen to learn new techniques.
- ☐ I'm willing to acquire new knowledge.
- ☐ I'm good at finding creative solutions to problems.
- ☐ I'm flexible and open-minded.
- ☐ I have self-awareness.

- [ ] I'm well-disciplined.
- [ ] I'm well-motivated.
- [ ] I know when to ask for help.
- [ ] I'm an independent worker.

√ **Communication skills**
- [ ] My writing is clear and informative.
- [ ] I can write for a target audience.
- [ ] I can construct coherent arguments.

This is an interesting test to discover yourself. How is your performance? Are you good at communicating? Are you more efficient at work? The following research methods match different students.

Interviewing—if you are good at talking to people.
Case-study—if you are good at building relationships without being too involved.
Reviewing existing data—if you like doing your research in a library.
Number-crunching—if you like handling numbers.
Statistical analysis—if you have an analytical mind.
Qualitative research—if you prefer concentrating on focused samples of research.

Besides your strength, your interests and experiences are also very important. Your interest is the best guarantee to guide you through long and hard research. If you are interested in practical market research, or theoretical economic probe, follow your interest.

III. Process of generating ideas

Social science is the study of society, people, and how people live their lives. To help you find a research question, think about the following broad topics:
- What is society like? Are there social problems in your life?
- What do people need? What comes slowly and what is in short supply?
- How do people behave? Do you hate people who misbehave around you?
- What do people think? Where do their thoughts come from?
- What do people say? What is media reporting?
- What institutional system can help people? How does a system match a society?

Starting from the broad topic to a researchable question, you need to take the following steps:

Step 1: Narrow the topic to one that you can investigate thoroughly in a given time. Question: "TV program" or "Entertaining program", which is manageable?

Step 2: Choose a topic which you can find practitioners, or which is well documented. Question: "Information security" or "student canteen problem", which might be more documented?

Step 3: Discuss with others about your research idea and find a research angle. Question: "What are some different angles on these issues?"

Step 4: Identify possible outcomes, theoretical or practical; refine the topic until they become clear.
Question: "What problems are connected with the topic? How might they be solved?

Step 5: Write and re-write the question or working title, examining thoroughly the implications of each phrase or word to check assumptions and ensure you mean what you write. Question: "Have I made clear the research issue in the topic?"

IV. What is a good research topic?

A good research topic should:

- raise an answerable question;
- be narrow enough to be covered within the required pages;
- be broad enough that actually you can find information;
- be abstract enough that it requires analysis.

Do not make your research question

- too broad that you cannot make an effective argument;
- too specific that you cannot find any published literature.

In-class activity

Study the following topics. Some are too narrow or broad. Can you provide proper topics?

Too broad	Just right	Too narrow
Reality TV Show		Race Problem in Reality TV Show Big Brother in 2013
Bullying		Consequences and Prevention of Bullying in No. 1 Elementary School
Campus Safety		Numbers of Robberies Prevented by Installing Lights on campus

V.　Read academic articles skillfully

One secret to guarantee a top-level report is reading deeper and further. The following are our suggestions on how to read.

1.　Skimming

Skimming an article is to get a general sense of the suitability of the text for your topic as well as its readability. Skim the title, keywords, and abstract of an article to explore if it is related to your concern. At the same time, if the language of the article is too theoretical and beyond your concern, neglect it and hook your fish.

2.　Deep reading

Reading in depth is to keep your mind on the work and paying attention to details. After finding the perfect text for your research by skimming, the next step is to read it deeply.

Firstly, read for the research method. For academic writing learners, a good research method is a basis for a good writing product. Working out how to collect data and how to apply different statistical analyses needs thorough scrutiny. Think about if you can follow or extend this method in your research. Secondly, read for meaning. To understand what a book or journal article is about, you need to read the text word by word, letting the meaning thoroughly sink in.

Ask yourself the following questions to make sure you are reading effectively:

(1) Is the article worth reading?
(2) What is the research question of the article?
(3) What research method is used by the author?
(4) Can I follow this research method?
(5) What are the limitations of the article?
(6) How can I refer to the article in my writing?

3.　Take notes freely

College reading is critical reading, and critical reading is active reading. Successful college readers annotate the text as they read, underline key terms and concepts, and write questions and responses in the margins. Successful college readers are not afraid to reread when they are struggling to understand a difficult text.

Read with a pen, or mark with an electronic pencil while reading. If you are reading an indigestible text, read through the text once without taking notes, and then read it a second time and annotate it. Pay close attention to the introductory paragraph or paragraphs, read these parts carefully, and underline important information, such as "Four reasons why zoos have been ignored by scholars".

Keep in mind that in most academic texts, each paragraph has a central focus. Underline the topic sentence and its supporting evidence. Write down your feelings when reading, such as "What does she mean by high-context and low-context culture?" and "I think I agree with this view...most zoos still have the animals behind bars like a prison!"

4. Write annotated bibliography

You may take notes and write annotated bibliography for your reading by describing the main contents and evaluate the literature. See the following sample of an annotated bibliography. An annotated bibliography includes the main idea of the literature and how you may use it in your own research. We also encourage undergraduate students like you to build vocabulary through reading. The following is a sample of an annotated bibliography.

Annotated bibliography

Archard, D. (1995) Children: Rights and Childhood. London, Routledge. (General information of the book)

Synopsis:

Archard examines the rights of children from a legal and moral perspective looking philosophically at children and childhood. Archard analyses the work of John Locke and Philippe Ariès in part one of the text, where he looks at the conception of childhood. Part two of the book concentrates on children's rights and part three examines the roles of children, parents, family and the state. (Summary of the main idea)

Archard's comprehensive approach combines philosophy with everyday practice and highlights the connections. (Comment of the book)

Rationale:

I consider this work to be very important as it is a multifaceted examination of the children's rights debate and looks at the roles of the family and state critically. One of the main reasons for the inclusion of Archard is that his book challenges contemporary thinking surrounding the "proper" roles of the state and the family in the upbringing of children. I suggest this should be essential in the examination of the ideology behind most policy and legislation on children.

> **After-class task**
>
> **Questions to consider after class:** What is your research interest? What strong points do you have? What research topics do you like to begin with? Search library academic databases, read related articles, and write annotated bibliographies.

VI. Summary of the chapter

In chapter 2, we learned how to get an exciting research idea. We began by providing environments or outside sources for you to find a research idea—media, library, partner, textbook and your teacher are all at your service. The second issue to consider when getting a good idea is to know your strength and interests. Then we provide a small reading skill: how to do annotated bibliography. Reading and choosing the topic is a very dark, tiring, and confusing psychological moment of the whole journey. You will feel a little relieved when finding out a suitable one for you.

Chapter 3

Choose Research Methods and Write Research Proposals

研究可以分为实证研究和非实证研究。实证研究可以进一步分为基于一手材料的研究和基于二手材料的研究。根据研究方法中数量化的程度,研究又可以分为质性研究和量化研究,或者两种方法兼用的混合研究。开题报告用来描述研究的背景、问题、方法和重要性。好的开题报告能帮助学习者对研究问题、方法和任务的价值有一个清晰的理解。本章讲述社会科学常用的研究方法以及研究过程中应遵守的道德准则,并介绍开题报告的写作。

Learning objectives

Chapter 3 will help you know more about report types according to different research methods. Then you are to learn to write a research proposal. When learning this chapter, you are expected:

● to have a general understanding of the research methods,
● to know ethical issues in research, and
● to learn to write a research proposal.

I. Report types in brief

As mentioned in the Introduction part, a report can be based on an empirical or non-empirical investigation. This division is not absolute in practice because you can always find a mix of the two in one report.

Your research question governs the method of research. Make sure that you are clear about the nature of your research question so that you know where to look for help and how to plan and carry out your work. The sort of data you need to gather is closely linked to the type of question you are asking:

1) A case study?

If your study is about a specific case or a person's particular experience, you will need data about the case or the person's views and ideas.

2) A general phenomenon?

If your study is about what is happening generally, you need to make a survey and need statistics or information covering a wide range of people.

3) A policy?

If your study involves examining a policy, this is an evaluation. You will need evidence of the policy in practice or at least the views of experts in the area of study to find out if the policy is successful.

4) A comparison?

Are you trying to decide which of the two methods is better suited to a specific problem? Your data will be centered on the results of each approach and perhaps the underlying principles.

Here we want to explain some research-related terms: primary data, secondary data, qualitative research method, and quantitative research method.

5) Primary data and secondary data

Generally, data are divided into primary and secondary, according to whether the data are gained by first (primary) hand, or by second hand. Primary data include information from observations, tests, interviews or questionnaire surveys.

Secondary data are collected by other researchers for other purposes. For example, a company's annual reports or statistics released by a government agency are often used as secondary data by researchers. If you are to review policy, analyze statistical data, or compare national concerns, you need to collect secondary data.

6) Quantitative approach and qualitative approach

There are, basically, two kinds of research approaches: quantitative and qualitative. A quantitative approach is likely to be associated with a deductive approach to testing theory, often using numbers or facts and an objectivist view of the objects studied.

A qualitative approach is likely to be associated with an inductive approach to generate theory. Using an interpretive model allows the existence of subjective perspectives. We can summarize the two research approaches in the following table.

Table 3.1 Comparison of quantitative and qualitative research

	Quantitative research	Qualitative research
Form of data	numbers	Words
Sources of data	questionnaire survey & secondary economic report	case study; observation; interviews; participant diaries
Sample size	large	Small
Data quality	hard & reliable	rich & deep
Tools for data analysis	mathematical & statistical tools	interpretation & categorization of meanings
Function	theory testing	theory emerging

As shown in the above table, the quantitative research method uses data in the form of numbers. These data are from the large-scale survey or secondary big data pools. These data are solidly reliable and need statistical tools to do the analysis. Quantitative research is often used to test a theory that has already existed. On the other hand, data of qualitative research are in the form of words. These data are from small-scale interviews, observations, diaries or case studies. These data are rich, deep, and their meanings are derived from interpretation. In social science research, you are likely to find a mix of both methods when investigating the messy reality of people and organizations.

II. Ethical issues are important

In carrying out research it is unavoidable to meet some moral traps. Here is a brief list of the kinds of ethical issues, which can arise at different points in the research process. More detailed ethical issues can be found in Chapter 9 of this book.

- Access—just getting at the appropriate people can be frustrating and tempt researchers to cut corners. Do not be tempted.
- Convenience sampling—asking people you know to take part could produce participants who simply want to please you with their answers or with excluding troublesome views.
- Cheating in analysis when results do not fit—this can affect both quantitative and qualitative research methods. Remember that provided the process was justified and conducted ethically and professionally, a not very exciting outcome does not matter. We cannot all discover gravity or relativity, but we can all design sound research plans and carry them out professionally.
- Participants have the right to refuse to take part in and their need for anonymity

should be respected.

- Full information about the purpose of the study and researcher's status and role should be given.
- Gain informed consent of the participants of the research.

Social science studies are about people and societies. Make sure that the interests of those who help you are protected. Show your appreciation to them when writing the report and show them the research results if you do a case study. For a researcher and writer, social responsibility should go ahead of your personal consideration.

(In-class activity)

Students share literature they read in small groups and the whole class. Pay special attention to the research method used by the author, and consider how the method can be used for different research contexts.

III. Write your research proposal

For research-based writing, proposal writing is a good start. It provides a chance for the writer to think of a problem systematically and practically. A research proposal is usually about 500 or 1,000 words in length, and consists of the following basic components:

1) Research title

The title of your research presents the theme of your research in a compact phrase. At this stage, the title is tentative, subject to change and refinement later.

2) Introduction or background

It sets the research in its social and academic context, such as why this research is worth doing, what related research has been conducted, and so on.

3) Research problem

It indicates what your research is about and what it intends to achieve.

4) Research objective

Objectives provide a list of goals that will be achieved through the proposed research.

5) Research methodology

This part gives what methods you will use to carry out your research.

6) Timetable

This session helps you manage your research time. But this part is selective and can be omitted.

7) References

Undergraduate students do not need to follow a specific style such as APA or Harvard. See a proposal sample from a student with comments in the following table:

Table 3.2 Sample proposal with comments

Sample proposal text	Comments
Title: The Contrastive Study of Water Protection Legislation Among China, Japan, and Russia	Provide a brief and meaningful title
1. Introduction ① **The problem** of water pollution is one of the most important environmental problems in China and the whole world. The Chinese government has long been putting efforts into water protection problem. ①**Nevertheless**, the implementation and application of protection actions **don't work in an efficient way** on account that the delay and ignorance of water pollution by water users, despite that governments of different levels advocate coordinated and sustainable development. ①According to a study on drinking water safety released by the environmental protection department in March 2014, 280 million people in China use unsafe drinking water (Liu Ding, 2015). ②As a result, **perfecting the legislation of water pollution crime is imminent.** ②To keep the balance between the rapid development of industrial civilization and environmental protection, as fundamental and limited resource, **water should be** protected as urgently as air and land. ③**This research project will** investigate the legislation of foreign countries including Japan and Russia, to facilitate establishing a holistic legal system of water protection in our country.	● Background for introduction section provides a description of the basic facts and importance of the research area: What is your research area and the motivation of research? How important is it to solve the problem? ● Important moves of the part are blackened: ① background of the project; ② significance of the study; ③ research object.
2. Problem Statement The water pollution problem aroused from industrial production **has long been recognized** by the government. ① However, currently Chinese Criminal Law does not take water resources as an independent resource to be protected, and so it is difficult to give full play to the role of the Criminal Law in water resources protection. ② In law enforcement, water pollution enforcement is soft; arbitrary violations of planning and non-implementation of planning are more prominent; the supervision method and supervision system are not perfect and unpractical, causing these laws cease to exist except in name (Zhou Ming, 2009). ③ **In summary, there is a need** to borrow ideas of water protection law in other countries, and better the legislation of water pollution crime in our country. ④**More specifically, the following research questions need to be addressed:** (1) What are the differences between domestic and foreign laws on pollution of industrial sewage? (2) What can we learn from other countries' advanced law enforcement and legislation on pollution of industrial sewage?	● Problem statement provides a clear and concise description of the issues that need to be addressed. ● Important moves are blackened: ① problem in brief; ② problem in detail; ③ research necessity; ④ research questions.

(Continued)

Sample proposal text	Comments
3. Objectives ①**The long-term goal** of the research is to provide a comprehensive analysis and suggestions to relevant departments in terms of the impact of water pollution on economy. Since the pollution and environmental degradation have become increasingly serious issues, and have greatly influenced the sustainable development of economy and the safety of people in city and countryside as well. ② **The objective of the current study is to** find out the water pollution condition in China and what we can use for reference from foreign countries by comparing the laws at home and abroad. ③**Particularly, the study has the following sub-objectives:** (1) To provide a comprehensive review of the Chinese current situation of water pollution and relevant laws. (2) To provide a series of data of foreign countries' laws of controlling water pollution. ④**The result of this study will** not only be valuable to the government and national resource protection departments but could also give an alarm to some industries which ignore the environment and pollute the rivers, thus avoiding making further destruction to our economy and life standard.	● Objectives provide a list of goals that will be achieved through the proposed research and the benefits that will be generated if the research problem is answered. ● Important moves are blackened in the part: ① long term goal; ② short term goal; ③ objective in detail; ④ research value.
4. Preliminary Literature Review ①**A preliminary literature review shows that past studies primarily focused** on differences between Chinese and Western countries' standard and laws of industrial sewage emission rather than the relationship between efficiency of execution through laws and water quality. ②Though **several researches have studied** water protection issue from water right system (Wang 2017; Cui 2002) and unified water managing system (Fan 2007), ③ **not many studies till now have** compared water protection law from diversified cultural backgrounds, so that the understanding of the connection between water protection law and people's perspective of the meaning of water, or nature elements, is not clear. ③**More importantly, what is missing from the past studies is** a comprehensive comparison of water protection legislation and regulation systems between China and developed countries.	● Preliminary literature review provides a summary of previous related research on the research problem and their strength and weakness, and a justification of your research: What is known/what has been done by others? And, why your research is still necessary? ● Important moves are blackened: ① general review; ② achievements; ③ research gap.
5. Methodology ①**The primary research method** for this study is literature review and interview. ②Having a total image on current solution of industrial sewage emission in China by reviewing the past studies **is the very first step.** Based on this understanding, collection and further analysis of data will be developed to categorize different factors which lead to the gap between Chinese and Western countries' effects on water treatment, especially in the aspect of industrial sewage emission. ② **In the second stage** of this study, several interviews towards the officials in the relevant departments will be held to explore further reasons triggering a series of affairs of illegal industrial sewage emission under the laws seemingly severe enough.	● Research methodology defines the research methods and logic steps: What to do and how to solve the problem and achieve proposed objectives? Which research methods (e.g., survey, modeling, and case study) will be used? ● important moves are blackened: ① research method; ② research process; ③ research schedule.

(Continued)

Sample proposal text	Comments
② **Finally,** once data analysis and summarization of interviews are completed, a conceptual framework for sewage emission in China will be outlined, where available solutions can be raised to settle the problems still existing in the procedure. ③**This study will be conducted between** September 2017 and May 2018.	
References (Omitted)	• Any idea that is not original with you must be accompanied by a reference to its source.

Tutorial & after-class task

Tutorial in groups is a chance for teachers to support students' learning. Tutorial contents vary depending on the learning process. After the third teaching section, students are to search online thoroughly for related literature, refine the research topic, method, and write a research proposal.

IV. Summary of the chapter

In this chapter, we learned that research can be either empirical or non-empirical. Empirical research can be further divided into research based on primary data and research based on secondary data. Research can be carried out with qualitative, quantitative, or mixed methods.

A research proposal is used to draw a scenario of the research background, questions, method, and significance. When a research proposal is clearly written, you will feel much more relieved and will see a little hope for the success of the writing task.

Chapter 4

Get Data for Your Research

确立研究问题和研究方法之后,学习者需要收集数据。本章讲述如何获取质性研究和量化研究所需的数据,重点讲述发放问卷和访谈的方法及要避免的问题。

Learning objectives

From now on you will consider how to gather information to solve problems raised or to propose hypotheses. Getting your hands on useful and thorough resources is quite a task in itself. In this chapter, you are expected:
- to learn how to get desired data;
- to learn how to avoid mistakes when going on with research.

This chapter seems very long, but actually, you need not read all the parts. Only focus on the research method that you are using. For example, if you are doing non-empirical data collection, the first part is yours.

I. Getting non-empirical data

For all researchers, whatever research method you have chosen, make the most use of your library is the first step for getting data. You have explored academic data websites since the beginning of the course as introduced in the second chapter. Besides this, there must be many important journals related to your major in your school library. Local archives are useful for historical researchers and should not be overlooked.

One skill of searching data online is to find proper keywords. For example, if the keyword such as "part-time job" cannot show substantial information, try using "internship". Narrow your search by selecting the scope of searching in "ABSTRACT, KEY WORDS and TITLE". Limit your finding to full articles, and the published time within 3 or 5 years.

II. Get empirical data

Research is formalized curiosity. It is to poke and pry with a purpose. To satisfy the curiosity in the name of writing might be the reason for students to love empirical data. This part is to introduce how to get empirical data through frequently used research methods for undergraduate students.

1. Key issues in qualitative research

Qualitative methods are used when your question cannot be expressed by numbers but can be better answered with language or pictures. Principal qualitative methods include action research, case study, ethnographic observation, interviews and participant diaries. In the following part we will introduce some of these qualitative methods.

1) Action research

Action research is often used by educators or managers when they work in an institution or an organization. They are involved in a project, take action, observe the running of the project, reflect and take action again.

2) Case study

Case study involves more than one way of deriving data, such as observing the organization, talking to people, analyzing the document, taking pictures and surveying. Case study is often used in business and management lines for a deep understanding of a special issue.

3) Observation

Observation comes from the study of anthropology, where "tribes" living in a certain environment are observed for purposes of the research. Observation can be very open in which the researcher sits around the participants, watching and listening to them. At the end of the study, they would write a research diary.

Before observing research, the researcher should know the research goal, consider possible perspectives and plan the observation. The following checklist is a sample observation plan.

Table 4.1　Sample of observation checklist

Things to look when approaching the building
1. What does the building look like? And what does it make you think of?
2. How do you feel about the surroundings of the building?
3. Have you made attempts to improve its surroundings?
. . .

The visual impression of the building
1. What's your impression of the reception area?
2. What sorts of furniture are used?
3. How clean is it?
. . .

Watching and listening to people
1. How do people greet or ignore each other as they pass by?
2. How do the staff speak to you, or to each other?
. . .

When doing observation, you should be both focused and flexible. Take notes on specific details and your impressions, review your notes, and list your conclusions before the ideas disappear.

4) Participant diaries

Keeping diaries is a favored technique of the observers. Diaries can be both qualitative descriptions of events and thoughts, or a quantitative record of the frequencies of doing something.

5) Interview

Interview is the most often used qualitative method among all choices. Tips for conducting interviews are shown in this part.

(1) Build relationships with your interviewees

A researcher needs to develop skills to build relationships with interviewees so that key informants can provide broad background. Find appropriate people for your interview and give you all support needed.

For example, a group of our students wanted to know hygienic conditions in small restaurants around their living community. They paid visits to those restaurants and formed a very good relationship with the staff working in those bars and stands. These staff received their interview and showed the true hygienic conditions there.

(2) Choose among structured, semi-structured, and unstructured interviews

A fully structured interview is similar to a questionnaire if the interview is administered strictly. This is not easy to be realized since interviewing is a social communicating process. The advantage of a structured interview is its being efficient and focused, so that important questions can be covered in as short a time as possible.

A semi-structured interview has a question guide. However, since it is not fully structured, the interviewees are allowed to go where they want to and to divert to other things which interest them. The focus of a qualitative interview is the interviewee, not the interviewer.

An unstructured or in-depth interview provides chances to discover much more about the interviewees through what they say and think. The interviewer's role is to manage the process and keep the conversation going broadly around the research question. The interviewee is subjected to very few constraints.

(3) Behave properly when interviewing

a. Subtasks to do

An interviewer should be knowledgeable, sensitive, flexible and critical. They should open the interview, raise questions, listen attentively, test or summarize their understanding, and record data. After the interview, the interviewer should transcribe the interview from the recording as quickly as possible.

b. Communication skills

The social skills of empathy, attentiveness, and humor are important. Use active listening techniques such as repeating back "Wow! Tell me more about that!", or "That sounds interesting. What happened later?"

c. Use silence

Don't be afraid of silence. You can use it to get deeper answers. Follow the respondent's tempo of thinking.

(4) Types of questions which should be used in interviews

You may find the following list of questions helpful when preparing your interview questions.

- **Introduction questions** such as: Would you like to tell me about...?
- **Follow-up questions** to know more about an issue, such as: Could you say more about...?
- **Specifying questions** such as: How did you do that...?
- **Structuring questions** such as: Now let's move to another question...
- **Silence** to encourage reflection
- **Interpreting questions** such as: Do you mean that...?

(5) Write interview questions step by step

- Write down the larger research questions of the study.
- Develop questions within each of these major areas.
- Adjust the language of the interview according to the respondents (child, professional, etc.).
- Word questions carefully so that respondents are motivated to answer honestly.
- Ask "how" questions rather than "why" questions to get stories, such as "How did you come to join this group?"

- Begin the interview with a "warm-up" question—something that the respondent can answer easily. This activity will put you more at ease with one another.
- Think about the logical flow of the interview: What topics should come first? What follows naturally?
- Difficult or potentially embarrassing questions should be asked toward the end of the interview.
- The last question should provide some closure for the interview. Leave the respondent feeling empowered, listened to, or feeling glad that they talked to you.

Here is an interview guide sample.

Interview Guide Sample

Introduction to key components: ● Thank you ● Your name ● Purpose ● Confidentiality ● Duration ● How interview will be conducted ● Opportunity for questions ● Signature of consent	I want to thank you for taking the time to meet with me today. My name is ＿＿＿＿＿ and I would like to talk to you about your experiences participating in the African Youth Alliance (AYA) project. Specifically, as one of the components of our overall program evaluation, we are assessing program effectiveness in order to capture lessons that can be used in future interventions. The interview should take less than an hour. I will be taping the session because I don't want to miss any of your comments. Because we're on tape, please be sure to speak up so that we don't miss your comments. All responses will be kept confidential. We will ensure that any information we include in our report does not identify you as the respondent. Remember, you don't have to talk about anything you don't want to and you may end the interview at any time. Are there any questions about what I have just explained? Are you willing to participate in this interview? ＿＿＿＿＿＿＿　＿＿＿＿＿＿＿　＿＿＿＿＿＿＿ Interviewee witness date ＿＿＿＿＿＿＿＿＿＿＿＿＿＿ Legal guardian (if the interviewee is under 18)
Questions ● No more than 15 open-ended questions ● Ask factual information before opinion ● Use probes as Needed	1. What strategies (e.g., facility assessment and quality improvement process), interventions (e.g., pre-service training, facility strengthening, or training of facility supervisors), and tools were used (e.g., facility assessment tool or curricula)? Please list. 2. Which of these strategies would you consider to be key program elements? Please explain. 3. To what extent did participation in the project advance or hinder the organization's development? Please explain. 4. What worked well? Please elaborate. 5. What would you do differently next time? Please explain why. 6. What strategies (interventions, tools, etc.) would you recommend be sustained? Please provide a justification. 7. What were the barriers, if any, that you encountered? Staff turnover? Lack of technical assistance? Or others? 8. How did you overcome the barrier(s)?

(Continued)

	9. What effect do you feel the AYA project had on the community in which you work? Increased use of services by youth? Increased knowledge of youth friendly services by clinic staff? Or others? 10. What recommendations do you have for future efforts?
Closing key components ● Additional comments ● Next steps ● Thank you	Is there anything more you would like to add? I'll analyze the information you gave me and submit a draft report to the organization in one month. I'll be happy to send you a copy to review at that time, if you are interested. Thank you for your time.

In-class activity

Students who will use interview research method prepare interview questions.

2. Key issues in quantitative research

Quantitative methods emphasize objective measurements and the statistical, mathematical, or numerical analysis of data collected through questionnaires or by manipulating pre-existing statistical data. The questionnaire-based survey is most frequently used by students. We will consider sampling, size, preparation and distribution issues.

1) Sampling

Sampling is about choosing data from a random group to find out what's going on in the population as a whole. The responses you get from the sample group should effectively represent the views you're likely to find among a large population.

The size of your sample is important, but you're not expected to carry out an enormous investigation as professionals. The people that you select for your sample is more important than the size.

There are two main ways of selecting samples: randomly (in a haphazard fashion), and non-randomly (where samples are selected using a strategy). Both ways have pros and cons.

(1) Random sampling

If you have an enormous population and a sizeable sample, it's a great way of getting a reliable representation of the views of the entire population. But sometimes random sampling results in an uneven set of views.

(2) Non-random sampling

Selecting a sample non-randomly cuts down the generalizability, or, general principles, of your findings. However, it may be used where you're not focusing on generalizability, but are more concerned with the representation of a typical sample, such as college students. You may also be looking for a quota, where you select equal numbers from different groups.

For undergraduate research, students often have to be satisfied with **accidental** or **convenience** sampling. Accidental or convenience sampling is non-random. There is limited generalizability from accidental or convenience sampling, but there's a greater chance that you are going to get a pleasing return size.

A number of aspects of a research question need to be taken into account if the research is serious. Some of the aspects have implications for your choice of population and how sampling is carried out. Your investigation needs to be:

- **Valid:** Well-founded, convincing and justifiable, demonstrated through using consistent and objective research methods.
- **Transferable:** The principles you talk about can be translated to different contexts.
- **Replicable:** If someone follows your methods, they can recreate your work.

(3) Sample size

The first question that worries people's designing a questionnaire is "How many should I send out?" The answer depends on a statistical number known as the limit or margin of error. The size of the sample you need depends in part on the size of the margin of error you are prepared to accept and the size of the population from which you are going to take the sample. If there were 1,000 employees that you wanted to sample, and if you were prepared to accept a margin of error of $+/-5$ percent, then according to Table 4.2, 278 questionnaires would be necessary. If I choose 10 students randomly to check the rate of class (of 50 students) attendance, all of them are present, can I safely conclude that all students are present? No, I cannot. I have to count 44 noses before saying that with 95 percent probability, all students attend my class.

Table 4.2   Estimating margin of error on sample survey results

Margin of error				
Population	5%	3%	2%	1%
50	44	48	49	50
100	79	91	96	99
150	108	132	141	148
200	132	168	185	196

(Continued)

Population	5%	3%	2%	1%
250	151	203	226	244
300	168	234	267	291
400	196	291	343	384
500	217	340	414	475
750	254	440	571	696
1 000	278	516	706	906
2 000	322	696	1 091	1 655
5 000	357	879	1 622	3 288
10 000	370	964	1 936	4 899
100 000	383	1 056	2 345	8 762
1 000 000	384	1 066	2 395	9 513
10 000 000	384	1 067	2 400	9 595

Note: At 95 percent level of certainty means that 95 out of 100 times the true result will be within the range of the margin of error. There is, however, a 5 percent chance that the true value will be outside of the range. If a 99 percent confidence level were needed, then many more completed questionnaires would be necessary. Source: Saunders et al. (2015, p. 156)

2) Issues on preparing a questionnaire

There are a number of general issues to bear in mind when designing a questionnaire:

● Keep the questionnaire as short as possible.

● Give it a logical and sequential structure.

● Divide the questionnaire into parts.

● Ask the easy questions first and the hard ones last.

● Keep personal questions (as long as they are justified) until last.

The next step in designing a questionnaire is to choose the question formats that are appropriate to the information being sought. A number of formats will be rehearsed here.

◆ *Dichotomous questions*

These are questions that offer the respondent only two alternatives to choose between. The examples given below are dichotomous questions.

Are you

　　Male ＿＿＿　　Female ＿＿＿

The law requires all employees to have a contract of employment.

True ＿＿＿＿　False ＿＿＿＿

◆ *Multiple choice questions*

These questions normally provide respondents with a choice of three to five options and ask them to choose one. There is normally a final ***Other*** option. These questions have to be mutually exclusive.

What sort of domestic animal would you choose as a pet?
Dog ＿＿＿　Cat ＿＿＿　Bird ＿＿＿　Fish ＿＿＿　None ＿＿＿

◆ *Checklists*

These are the same as multiple-choice questions, but the respondents are allowed to tick as many items as they wish：

What aspects of the service do you think are unsatisfactory?
Menu choice ＿＿＿　Prices ＿＿＿　Quality of food ＿＿＿　Style and design ＿＿＿

◆ *Rating scales*

These questions ask respondents to rate or evaluate a service, policy or option according to a graduated scale. For example：

What is your opinion of the service provided by the call center?
Excellent　　　　　　　　　　　Poor
1　　　　2　　　　3　　　　4　　　　5

◆ *Likert scales*

These are a form of rating scale that is commonly used to ask people about their opinions and attitudes. The basic structure is to ask the respondent to choose a position on a 5 – 10 point scale between choices of "strongly agree" and "strongly disagree". It is a scale that Rensis Likert invented. For example：

Statements	Strongly disagree	Disagree	Uncertain	Agree	Strongly agree
1. Training in office management improves one's promotion					

◆ *Open questions*

Open questions are vital when the researcher is interested in new ideas or novel points of view or cannot anticipate the likely answers. But it is suggested that no more than two open questions be used in your questionnaire.

The smallest, simplest error can result in failing to generate any useful responses. Ask the following questions to avoid pitfalls:

- Is the purpose of the questionnaire clear and apparent?
- Is the questionnaire simply enough?
- Is the data produced from the questionnaire easy to interpret?
- Are the questions clear and unambiguous?
- Is the questionnaire valid? Does the questionnaire actually measure what it sets out to measure?
- Is the questionnaire reliable? If the questionnaire is used within a similar group, will it generate comparable results?

To avoid these problems, you are suggested to use a small-scale pilot study before handing out your questionnaire formally. Ask your respondents about language problems, length acceptability, and any other confusions.

Secondly, hand out your questionnaire at the end (or the start) of a class or a meeting to avoid a low response rate. However, other problems can come up, such as people not having enough time to fill in the questionnaire and feeling inhibited by being surrounded by others in the class or meeting.

Distributing some small gifts is suggested to avoid sloppy answers, but for student researchers, it brings about financial problems.

In-class activity

Review the following fictitious questionnaire and identify as many mistakes and inappropriate aspects as you can. Treat it as a first draft.

Survey into staff attitudes concerning the performance appraisal scheme

The organization's Investors in People (IiP) are coming up for renewal. As part of the preparation for the visit of the inspection team, this questionnaire is being sent to all staff to complete. The questionnaire is anonymous. When the results have been analyzed, it will provide the information necessary to show that the organization's appraisal scheme is effective and supports our investment on you, our employees.

It takes just a few minutes to fill in the questionnaire and the managing director is looking for a very high response rate. Please tick the boxes with appropriate choices.

Part 1

1. What is your role in the organization?

   Top management team ☐   Senior manager ☐

Upper middle manager ☐　　Middle manager ☐
Senior team leader ☐　　Team leader ☐
Core worker ☐　　　　　Casual worker ☐
Blue-collar worker ☐

2. What is your age?
Under 12 ☐　13 to 15 ☐　15 to 21 ☐　22 to 30 ☐　30 or over ☐

3. Are you　male ☐　female ☐

4. How would you describe your ethnic and cultural origins?
UK ☐　　　　　Indian ☐
European ☐　　Pakistani ☐
African ☐　　　Other Asian ☐
Caribbean ☐
Other (please specify). . . . .

5. Have you applied for a job outside the organization within the last year?
Yes ☐　No ☐

Part 2

6. How many days' absence have you had in the past two years?　＿＿＿＿　days

7. Do non-work related interests take up much of your time?　Yes ☐　No ☐

8. Have you had an appraisal this year?　Yes ☐　No ☐

9. My appraisal was:
Exceedingly helpful and beneficial ☐
Quite helpful ☐
A complete waste of time ☐

10. Did you find. . . ?
The preparatory documentation
very satisfactory ☐　　satisfactory ☐　　acceptable ☐
The appraisal interview
very satisfactory ☐　　satisfactory ☐　　acceptable ☐
Your performance ratings
very satisfactory ☐　　satisfactory ☐　　acceptable ☐

How often do you. . . ?
11. Review your performance against targets and objectives
frequently ☐　　sometimes ☐　　occasionally ☐

12. Review your personal development with your manager
regularly ☐　　frequently ☐　　sometimes ☐

13. Discuss your career ambitions with your manager
often ☐　　occasionally ☐　　rarely ☐

Part 3

Please read the statements below; decide whether you strongly agree, agree, disagree or strongly disagree, and then circle the number to indicate your choice.

	Strongly disagree	Disagree	Agree	Strongly agree
14. An effective appraisal scheme improves the organization's performance.	1	2	3	4
15 The performance pay element of the appraisal scheme is fair and motivates me to perform better	1	2	3	4

16. Without an appraisal interview my staff development needs would not be met.　　1　　2　　3　　4

17. If a peer mentoring scheme were introduced it would help me become better at my job and I would take part in it with enthusiasm.　　1　　2　　3　　4

Part 4

18. The appraisal system benefits me and the organization because...

(Please complete the sentence in no more than 50 words)

19. What changes would you like to see made to improve the appraisal system?

(**Tutorial & after-class activity**)

Tutorial time is for teachers to meet students to solve problems they meet and give guidance for the following research. After learning this chapter, students will carry out research according to their plan. They will collect data and prepare for analyzing the data in the next section.

III. Summary of the chapter

Chapter 4 provides the guidance of collecting data. If you are carrying out non-empirical research, make good use of online data, books, journals, and newspapers in the library, or local archives. If you are doing empirical research, qualitative or quantitative, you are to prepare interview questions, observation lists or questionnaires. Read the related part when preparing questions or lists to do.

Planning enough time for collecting data is important. Generally, an informal pre-test of a questionnaire needs one day; learning to use SPSS needs three days; preparing interview costs one day; transferring interview data into words needs one week... We mention this to remind you that it is important to plan enough time for data collection and leave some to enjoy your life.

At this research stage, you might feel fully pressured with three mountains on the researching journey: unable to find related literature, unable to read quickly enough, and unable to understand research methods used by other researchers. Scaffolding from teachers is in great need. Search for social support from your teachers, and make good use of tutorial time for help.

Chapter 5

Analyze Your Data

　　描述和分析是不同层次的思维,分析能力是大学课程的培养核心。学术报告的价值在于显示分析和批判思维的能力。本章介绍如何做简单的数据分析,如何对数据进行系统的解释,如何解决遇到的数据分析问题。从写作心理上讲,克服对新知识的恐惧,对提高分析能力至关重要。

Learning objectives

Contents in this chapter will help analyze the data in hand, whether it is non-empirical or empirical materials. When learning this chapter, you are expected:

● to know how to analyze data in hand;

● to learn to interpret your data systemically; and

● to learn to solve the problems you meet.

After strenuously collecting data, empirical or non-empirical, it is time to do data analysis. In this chapter we talk about the best approaches for analyzing data.

I. Understanding analysis

University courses put analytical ability at the center. The gist of the matter is that you need to go beyond description of facts to show how the facts link to your research question. Analysis is related to the action of classification, investigation, breakdown and scrutiny. Analysis is the process of reviewing, interrogating, assessing, appraising and evaluating.

II. From description to analysis

Analyzing is a different activity from describing. An analysis is about evaluating the data, while the description is objectively presenting facts such as the research process. The value of an academic report is to show analytical or critical thinking competence. The writing of piling facts is not worth reading. Keep smiling. With this lesson in mind, you can shift from a descriptive approach to the analysis side. Follow these suggestions:

- After saying what research method you used, explain why the method is good to solve the problem.
- After describing the information you got, discuss the value of the data.
- Do not report what is happening, explore the consequences, and the causal relationships among these happenings.
- Do not just say that some ideas are similar to others. Show how these ideas link or how they differ.

III. How to analyze critically

Critical analysis is a thinking pattern. In the following we list some of the practices of doing critical analysis. It applies to all kinds of data in your hand, empirical or not.

The first practice is keeping some distance from the data. Look at the data objectively and from different angles. Read and search for related literature and see if you can find something hidden in your data.

Looking for gaps or missing data is also helpful. When comparing your data with the known theory, check if the argument has logic leaps or jumps, also whether it is illogical and incoherent.

After examining the data in hand for some time, take a break and go back with your fresh eyes and mind. You are bound to spot something new.

When you analyze theories, you need to question what you're reading or hearing by keeping the following in mind and asking:

- What's the source of this information or idea?
- How reliable is the source?
- How consistent is this theory?
- What is missing?
- What makes the theory or idea persuasive?
- How can the theory or idea be improved?

• Is the theory or idea applicable to a particular context?

The following table provides the reliability and depth of information. Use Table 5.1 to assess the quality of the sources you are gathering.

Table 5.1 Quality of the sources from high to low

reliable sources	1) Scholarly books and scholarly articles: largely based on careful research; written by experts for experts; address topics in depth; involve peer review.
	2) Specialized magazines: largely based on careful research; written by experts for an educated general audience, such as *Nature, Economic Study*.
	3) Government Resources: reports, web pages, guides, statistics developed by experts at government agencies, such as Statistical Yearly Report.
	4) Reviewed official online documents: internet resources posted by legitimate institutions— colleges and universities, research institutes.
unreliable sources	5) Reference works and textbooks such as encyclopedia entry.
	6) Blog articles, talk radio discussions.
	7) Unregulated Web Material: personal sites, chat room.

IV. How to do analysis for non-empirical research

For most non-empirical reports, evaluating ideas is obviously your main concern. Your analysis needs to be concerned with:

• Comparing and contrasting;
• Considering different or multiple perspectives;
• Evaluating the cause and effect of an action;
• Speculating about the consequences of different ideas;
• Understanding that ideas are open to be challenged;
• Showing the strength and weakness of an argument.

Analyzing qualitative data is to collect evidence, observe and reflect on the data. In qualitative data, analysis is iterative, which means you have to return to your argument again and again. Analyze with the following steps.

1. Organizing your data

You need to arrange and sort your data so that it is manageable and indicates you are showing connections and themes. You can start by reducing your data and leaving out the least important aspects and highlighting the aspects that are likely to be the most significant, and then coding your data to help you spot patterns.

2. Reducing your data

Data reduction is to simplify the raw data into something that is going to be intelligible. Start reducing your data by summarizing. For example, create a file noting the important details such as name of your interviewee, length of talk, location and other basic details. Find a method suitable for organizing your data.

3. Coding your data

Before writing you need to take out the usable information. The process is coding. It includes identifying themes and dividing these data into units. Coding can be done manually or with software.

Coding audio-recorded interviews is hard. The process can be especially slow if there is no proper equipment. You will not have the time to transcript. In this case, it is perfectly possible to write a set of notes on each interview based on listening to the taped interviews. If you have transcripts of the interviews, you can go through the sheets using a highlighter pen, or by marking the margins to identify the themes that you think will be useful.

The process of coding is also the process of finding patterns and themes that can connect your data with ideas. This process is exciting because you see the idea in your mind emerging more and more clearly. You find the patterns taking shape. You can use pens of different colors to mark your data: one color for one idea.

4. Seeing themes and patterns in your data

What is meant by patterns or themes depends on the data you have had. The following examples show how my students have their expectations on the one hand and the patterns shown on the other hand. This is the most interesting part of the research because students are either very thrilled with their discovery, or very confused and disappointed.

- **Project 1:** Questionnaire asking students what they think of government censorship of film market. **Pattern:** Data showed it was acceptable because they were more safely protected against wrong thoughts. Student researchers were surprised to see this pattern.
- **Project 2:** Setting up an online free platform for peer teaching and running the platform for three months. **Pattern:** very indifferent reception among universities. Student researchers felt that college students now did not really care about learning.
- **Project 3:** Interviews with students attending English mediated courses and

teachers responsible for the module, in expectation to complain about their working load. **Pattern**: both students and teachers are happy to be loaded. Student researchers were surprised with the findings.

When the pattern shown by data agrees with your expectation, we congratulate you on smooth research. But if the pattern does not prove the idea or theory, we congratulate you more, because you are on the brink of finding new theories or coming up with new ideas. Disagreement is the chance of further exploration. Use critical analyzing tips listed in the chapter, read widely, check the flaw when collecting data and explain the data with your fresh eyes.

There are several computer packages on the market you can use for analyzing qualitative data, such as Ethnography and NUDIST. But because the sample size in undergraduate research is small, using software is not very necessary.

5. Content analysis

Content analysis is an additional step you can take when you have finished coding the material. It adds a quantitative element to the analysis of qualitative material. In a content analysis, the frequency with which issues or themes appear in the material is measured.

V. Analyzing quantitative data

"No statistics!" I hear you say. Do not be frightened by the thought of statistics. Actually, you are using statistical thinking every day. Any time you say "On average I walk 5 miles a week" or "We expect snowing at this season" or "The earlier I start work, the more efficient I am", you are making a type of statistical statement.

The examples of statistical thinking described above reveal two different types of statistical thought. The statement "On average I walk 5 miles a week" is descriptive. The statement "The earlier I start, the more efficient I am" infers what is likely to happen in the future. How safe is it to make generalizations from a part to a whole? This is what statistics is all about: quantifying the probability of error. It is this issue that is covered below.

Authors of the book major in linguistics. We picked up statistics learning while doing research. We mention this only to encourage young people with quick minds to confront statistical problems courageously. Take a breath. It's not that hard. But here we only introduce very basic statistic ideas. If you are to use statistics for your research, much more knowledge have to be learned. Open your mind to numbers now. Most of the following parts came from Rowntree (2018) and Lunenburg and Irby

(2007).

1. Types of variables

Samples are made up of individuals. These individuals have different characteristics. For example, some young men are tall, rich and handsome. The characteristics of being tall, rich and handsome differentiate them from others. Such characteristics are called variable characteristics or, **variables**.

Suppose you are considering purchasing a second-hand car. You would consider the following variables: price, make (e. g. Peugeot, Fiat, Rover, Toyota), type (e. g. estate, four-wheel drive, soft top), color, age, mileage, transmission type (automatic or manual), and size of engine.

Among these variables, price, age, mileage and size of engine are quantity variables. Such variables can be either *discrete* or *continuous*. A *discrete* **variable** is one in which the possible values are clearly separated from one another. Take family size for example, a family can have one child, or two or three, etc., but it cannot have 2.5 or 3.75 children. *Continuous* **variables**, however, do have possible values between them. Take the variable of height as an example. A child may be three feet high this year and three feet six inches next year.

In this case, "age" of a car could be considered as a discrete variable. Size of engine is also a discrete variable—1.4 litre engines are not 1.6 litre engines. Mileage, on the other hand, is *continuous*.

Variable such as "make of car" shows categories. This type of variable is called a **category variable**. Other variables listed above include "type of car" "color" and "transmission type", and these are also category variables.

Different variable types require different statistical analysis. However, it is important to note that data about quantity variables *can* be converted into category data.

2. Summarizing quantitative data

The techniques for summarizing quantitative data include the methods of determining measures of **central tendency**, as well as measures of **dispersion**. Statistical packages will calculate these measures for you. Measures of central tendency include the **median** and **mean**, while measures of dispersion include the range and standard deviation. Let's look at these a little more closely, without going into too much mathematical detail.

The **median value** indicates the center of a distribution. The median is the value that splits the distribution of data into half. There should be as many observed values greater than the median as there are less. Thus, if the following were the number of miles driven by seven students per week:

　0　16　18　20　33　48　68

The median here would be 20 (miles per week). That is the value with equal numbers of observations greater and lesser. When the number of observed values is even, the median is quoted as the value halfway between the two middle values. Thus, if our sample looked like this:

　0　16　18　20　33　48

the median here would be halfway between 18 and 20 (18 + 20)/2 = 19; and 19 is thus the value that has equal numbers on either side of it (even though no student actually drove just 19 miles).

The **range**, the difference between the highest and the lowest, is the simplest measure of **dispersion**. Range may be deceiving however, if some cases are extremely high or low. A better measure of dispersion is the *standard deviation*. Standard deviation is a way of indicating a sort of "average" amount by which values deviate from the mean. The greater the dispersion, the bigger the standard deviation. For example:

　(a) 6　　24　　37　　49　　64　　(mean = 36)
　(b) 111　114　　117　　118　　120　　(mean = 116)

The values in group (a) are more dispersed (i. e. they deviate more from the mean) than those in group (b), and so it is possible that the standard deviation is larger in group (a). Let us calculate how each value in (b) differs from the mean of 116:

　Value:　　　　　　　111　114　117　118　120
　Deviation from 116: − 5　− 2　+ 1　+ 2　+ 4

We cannot take an average of these deviations, since there are negative values. In order to overcome this, we square each deviation, and thus get rid of the minus signs:

　Deviations:　　　　　− 5　− 2　+ 1　+ 2　+ 4
　Squared deviation:　25　4　1　4　16

The mean of these squared deviations is called the **variance**:

　Variance = (25 + 4 + 1 + 4 + 16)/5 = 50/5 = 10

The **variance** is a measure with some good uses. However, if the original values were, say, "heartbeats per minute", then the variance would be so many "square heartbeats per minute"! So, in order to get the measure of dispersion back into the same units as the observed values, we take the square root of the variance—and this is termed the **standard deviation**: Standard deviation of distribution (b) = 10 = 3. 16

The same process of calculation for (a) above reveals a standard deviation of 20. We can thus comment that the distribution of (a) is much more dispersed.

3. Comparing samples and tests of significance

When comparing samples, researchers want to arrive at a safe conclusion: "The difference between the two samples is significant." How do they do this? They begin by assuming there is *no* real difference between the two groups. This hypothesis is named as the **null hypothesis**. If the difference turns out to be too big to be explained as chance variation, then they reject the null hypothesis, and explain it by an alternative. The alternative hypothesis is: **there is a difference**. But How big does a difference have to be, in order to be regarded as against null hypothesis?

The two common cut-off points in statistical analysis are the 5 percent level and the 1 percent level (written as 0.05 level and 0.01 level). This type of information will be displayed in the results of your computer analysis on your statistical software. A difference is less significant at the 0.05 level than at the 0.01 level. Any result of a test of significance greater than 0.05 would result in acceptance of the null hypothesis (i.e. there is no difference between the samples). A difference at 0.05 is called "significant", while a difference at 0.001 is called "highly significant".

4. Comparing two means—the t-test

If you have two groups and you would like to test the difference in their mean scores, t-test is appropriate. Suppose that you want to test the different levels of job satisfaction between permanent and casual employees. Your computer will provide you with a t-statistic and a significance level. Remember, if the significance level is 0.05 or less, you can reject the null hypothesis, and conclude that one group differs from the other.

5. Comparing several means—ANOVA (F-statistic)

Let us say you want to compare three groups in terms of their job satisfaction-permanent employees, fixed-term contract employees and casual employees. In this case, with more than two groups, the t-test cannot be used. Instead, you should use what is called an analysis of variance test (or ANOVA). Your computer will do all this for you! The ANOVA test results in what is called the F-statistic (named after the British statistician R. A. Fisher). The larger the ratio of variance, the greater the value of the F-statistic. A high F-statistic usually indicates that the results are significant. Once again, however, your computer will provide you with significance levels. Remember, if the significance level is 0.05 or less you can reject the null hypothesis, and conclude that the groups differ in terms of job satisfaction.

6. Analyzing relationships—correlations

Correlation analysis is a measure of relationship between two or more variables. There are three kinds of correlations: positive, negative and zero. With **positive correlation** changes in one variable are accompanied by changes in the other variable and in the *same direction*. In other words, larger values in one variable tend to go with larger values in the other. This is illustrated in the scatter diagram shown in Figure 5.1.

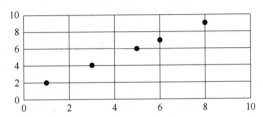

Figure 5.1   Diagram sample for positive correlation

However, in equally strong relationships, the two variables change in the *opposite* directions. Larger values in one will tend to go with smaller values in the other. This is called a **negative correlation**. For example, there may be a negative correlation between age and willingness to learn about statistics.

If there were no clear tendency for the values on one variable to move in a particular direction (up or down) with changes on another variable, then it could be said that we are approaching a **zero correlation**.

The computer can calculate the strength of the relationship, which is called the **correlation coefficient**. It is represented by the letter r. The correlation coefficient (r) lies within the range between -1 and $+1$. When $r=0$, there is no correlation at all. The closer the correlation gets to $+1$ or -1, the stronger the correlation; the closer it gets to 0, the weaker it is. Table 5.2 is a guide to interpreting correlation coefficients.

Table 5.2   Interpreting correlation coefficients

Correlation coefficient	Strength
0.0 to 0.2	Very weak, negligible
0.2 to 0.4	Weak, low
0.4 to 0.7	Moderate
0.7 to 0.9	Strong, high, marked
0.9 to 1.0	Very strong, very high

(Source: Rowntree 2018)

A serious word of caution needs to be included here: correlation does *not* imply causation. If variables X and Y are correlated, this may be because X causes Y. For those students who are interested to learn inference relationship, that is, if Y is caused by X, regression analysis is needed, but regression analysis is beyond the length of the chapter.

7. Final words

This section has attempted to cover a lot of material in a fairly short space. But as the saying goes, "There are lies, damned lies, and statistics." When reading statistics, act with caution; as a user of statistics, act with integrity.

Learning to use software like SPSS or AMOS is helpful for your study. Website as Wen Juanxing provides useful tutorial lessons for students. We suggest learning simple statistics for the academic writing task, because you have a task to do, a teacher to support you, and a deadline to submit a report. There is no better time than now.

Tutorial & after class activity

Tutorial time is for teachers to meet students to solve problems they meet and give guidance for the following research. After learning this chapter, students will go on collecting data or analyze the data and prepare for writing.

VI. Summary of the chapter

Two parts are included in the chapter. One is the importance of analysis and how to do critical analysis. This is important for all researchers. The second part is about how to analyze qualitative data and quantitative data. For the former, the coding data method is introduced. For the latter, simple statistics are given to chase away the sense of scare.

Psychologically speaking, this is the darkest moment when you are doing academic writing. You will find things starting to go against your expectation. There is no correlation between variables. Few people answer your questionnaire. Your respondents misunderstood a particular question. This is why we are to check if you are on the right track till now in the next chapter.

Chapter 6

Stay on the Right Track

在前 5 章中,我们一起学习了研究选题、文献阅读、数据收集和简单的数据分析。本章我们调整节奏,对过去的学习进展进行总结,并重点介绍如何应对现有的困难。

Learning objectives

If you followed our steps of the past 5 chapters, you have learned to find a research topic, read literature on the topic, use some methods to collect data, and are probably observing or analyzing the data. Reviewing your work is necessary at this moment. When learning this chapter, you are expected

● to check your progress, and

● to learn to find support strategies when things do not go well.

Writing a report is a long process and you need to stand back and take stock from time to time, to make sure that you're moving in the right direction towards your goal. In this chapter we give you tips for reviewing your progress and checking that you're keeping on track.

I. Reviewing your progress

You need to consider honestly how you're getting on with your work. It's not just a question of how many words you've written or how many books you've read. What you need to review is how to use remaining time to ensure that you can do a great job in completing your report.

Whatever you decide, make sure that you can easily see your plan from your desk. Use color to mark the progress of your work, showing where you've got to and what you've achieved. More specific to-do lists (with all those smaller tasks listed) are best kept in your notebook or diary.

Some people find having a plan of campaign staring them in the face a bit threatening and overpowering. If you feel this way, rely on your to-do lists for a while, and mark each item off boldly when it is completed. Seeing the mountains taken away bit by bit will give you confidence and stronger motivation to keep on climbing.

II. Moving in the right direction

If you find that the direction which you're moving in isn't matching up with your plans, you need to stop and take stock. Does any of the following situations strike a chord?

- **Topic confusion.** You are confused about what you are supposed to be researching and not sure how to go about things.

- **Emphasis confusion.** The emphasis of your research is changing because you've found a new area of interest or your data/reading is leading you to new ways of thinking about your topic.

- **Confusion about methods.** You probably need to go back to your original objectives, defining exactly what you're trying to find out. Once you're quite clear about what you want to achieve, your methods are likely to fall into place.

- **Shift in interests.** If your new interest is related to your original objectives, that's fine because your ideas are likely to be covered by the work you've already done in your literature review.

- **More practical approach.** Taking a more practical approach is usually fine and normally means cutting down your original plan that is rather over ambitious.

- **Loss of interest.** It's hard to keep motivated when you aren't really interested in what you're doing. Having enough time to pursue your new idea depends on how far away the topic is from what you've already covered in your research and how much time you've got until the submission date.

At all costs avoid submitting a half-hearted and poorly thought-through paper. Instead, face up to your change of direction and set about thinking through how you can overcome the difficulties involved in taking a new approach. Most tutors are pleased to support a student who is facing up to a shift in plans, especially when the student is coming up with ideas for a new approach to his or her work.

III. Backing up your work

Regularly backing up your work is as necessary as breathing. You need to be aware of two important activities: one is keeping track of different versions of your work (keeping the drafts clearly labelled), and the other is keeping copies of your work in case the original version is lost or damaged.

As you write more and more texts without having a system in place for keeping your work in order, safe and secure, you can easily become overwhelmed. Having too many piles of paper on your desk or too many files to keep track of on your desktop means trouble. The best place to save your work is online: your e-mail box, or cloud disk.

Don't name all your files "Academic Report", because you are going to end up lost and confused. A simple system is to save things chapter by chapter and each time you make substantial revisions to your work add a number. When you are happy with your final version, call it "final version".

If you have lots of notes that you need to include, it can be handy to put the notes in separate files so that you can delete as you go (or better still move the notes to named folders). For example, create a folder for your literature review and put all the versions of your review into the folder together with notes or items you want to keep. Your folder may end up looking like the following:

Folder—Literature Review
File—Lit rev notes: Web
File—Lit rev notes: Library
File—Lit rev notes: Other
Folder—Literature Review Notes: (finished)
File—Lit rev: 1
File—Lit rev: 2
File—Lit rev: Bibliography
File—Lit rev: Extras
File—Lit rev: Final

To keep a firm grip of your work, copy your files to more than one memory stick, keeping each memory stick updated with the latest version of your work. This may seem a bit troublesome, but just think how you are going to feel if one and the only memory stick of your computer gets corrupted.

IV. Strategies to lift up your spirit

Try keeping your goals in mind at all times while you are working on your report writing, and fix your eyes firmly on the finishing post. Researchers like Winstanley (2012) and Zimmerman (1997) gave practical suggestions for regulating writing motivation.

1) Read something

First try reading a text linked to your study and see if it gives you a flash of inspiration. If that is no good, try reading something totally different but well written. It can be the excellence of the writing that enlightens you.

2) Look at your writing as a whole

Rather than focusing on the bit that has left you stuck, you can benefit from looking at the bigger picture.

3) Get up and do something else

Go and wash your face, brush your teeth or make a cup of tea, or put away the dried dishes or tidy up your shoes from the hallway. Doing something minor or trivial for a short time can help you get moving again on the real task in hand.

4) Have a complete break

Just switch off and try thinking about anything except your work for a few hours. Obviously, this isn't going to work if you've only a few days before submission, but can be reviving if you still have a bit more time in the bank.

5) Just write anything

Try writing something else, such as a thank you card, or answer some e-mails, and return to formal writing gradually.

6) Go chat with someone

Someone in your support group is your best choice. If it fails, anyone who is willing to listen will help! Call your mum and chat about all things totally unconnected with your work. Escape from your own problems, and return refreshed.

7) Swear

We know you are confused whether or not this is the "swear" in your understanding. Yes, swear as a thug. Pour out the anguish. Tell the world what is blocking your writing, pour the feeling out of your system, and start anew.

8) Seeking help from your supervisor

From the beginning of the course, we gave tutorial the same important position as lecturing, and remind teachers to arrange as much tutorial time as possible to support students at different writing stages. For students who need special help in idea creating or data analysis, seeking help from your tutor is necessary. Do not worry about busy schedule of your tutor, make a date and visit him or her with your problems.

9) Networking with friends

Besides teachers, anyone who is ready and willing to have a chat and listen to your hopes and fears will be a great help. Tell them how miserable you are because your supervisor is a difficult middle-aged woman!

Try focusing on some positive aspects of your work, and while you are getting things off your chest, keeping things in perspective is a must. No matter how awful your questionnaire has turned out, it is not the end of the world. You must want your friend to sympathize and have a giggle with you. Having the mutual support of fellow students who are likewise writing report is ideal. After letting out your disappointment, you will find you are not the only one on the brink of breakdown.

V. Summary of the chapter

In this chapter, we take a break from the research process, reflect progresses, problems, and make sure that the research is on the right track slowly, hard but promising.

If you meet problems of changing or losing the research direction, or cannot deal with data collection, adjusting your emotion is suggested.

As far as we know, if you follow the advices in this book, all is going to come right in the end. When you find patterns out of your data, or find new ideas from statistic conclusion, you will be eager to go into the writing section, and will find a better self.

Chapter 7

Work Well in a Team

基于任务的学术写作往往采取团队合作的方式。本章学习如何建立一个高效的团队,发挥团队成员的作用,达到 1 + 1>2 的作用。

Learning objectives

When learning this chapter, you are expected:
- to learn how to build a strong team, and
- to learn how to deal with a poor-performer or an uncooperative team member.

In task-based writing, students are expected to complete written tasks as part of a group of three to six. This chapter explains the best way to approach group work in order to achieve the maximum benefit from the process.

I. How to build a strong team

During your academic study, just like in a workplace or professional sports, team building requires a keen understanding of people, their strengths and what gets them excited to work with others. It also requires the management of egos and their constant demands for attention and recognition. It is far more than finding a group of people with the right mix of professional skills. Sounds pretty challenging. You need to, therefore, practice it instead of avoiding it because a group could do much bigger things than a single person, no matter how powerful he/she is.

On the way to successful team work, there would be conflicts happening now and then within a team. The most common causes of conflicts are:

- team members refuse to do their share of the work;
- a domineering team member tries to force others to do everything in a specific way;
- a team member refuses to participate;
- uneven workload or free-riding;

Deeper reasons of conflicts are:

- poor communication;
- poor task management;
- unfair work allocation;
- unequal treatment;
- being egocentric and lack of sense of responsibility.

Therefore, how to solve conflicts and achieve successful team work? Here are several rules about what you can do to make sure your team is as strong as possible.

1. Have a team leader

You need a team leader to make things go efficiently, allocate work, make decisions and urge the poor performers.

2. Get to know the rest of the team

If the team leader has not chosen the team members he/she wants, it is still a good opportunity to work with someone new. Make the time to get to know your team and form good fellowship to maximize your performance and result. As for the leader, it is important to understand how your team members think and what is required to motivate them to excel beyond what is expected from them.

Try to gather intelligence from each member and find out their respective strengths and capabilities—the real assets that each member brings to the table, those they leave behind and those yet to be developed. It is like a SWOT analysis: SWOT refers to strengths, weaknesses, opportunities and threats, by which the team's internal and external resources are estimated.

3. Clearly define roles and responsibilities

Break a large task down into smaller, more manageable pieces. Define the roles and responsibilities of your team members clearly. Let each member have roughly equal share of the work. Do not overwhelm individuals with too much work while leaving other members with tons of free time.

Each of your team member's responsibilities must be interconnected and dependent upon one another. This is exactly like team sports, where some players are known as "system players"—meaning that although they may not be the most talented person in the team, they know how to work best within the "system". That's why each of you needs to be a team player. One student reflected in her learning journal that "Our research went on efficiently because the team leader divided tasks into subtasks, made deadline, and we did accordingly". Here are two tips for dividing a task:

- Write down task division clearly and fix the deadline for each phase of the work. Double check if each one of you is 100% clear about this.
- When you discuss the task division together, that means all of you together and make sure each of you agrees on it. If someone could not make it, change to another available time. Don't inform anyone of their role after the discussion he/she hasn't taken part in.

4. Flawless communication

Communication is vital to successful team work. Please ensure smooth communication during each phase of your team work. Whenever someone has a question or gets an idea, he/she should be able to communicate it. For instance, during task division, each member should express freely their opinions on it: their doubts, different ideas, etc. Only by doing so can your work be done effectively.

When every team member takes the time to evaluate a decision and form an opinion, they're attached to the outcome. Allowing this gives people a feeling of ownership over their work, thus leading to better performance.

Let constant feedback be your team's greatest stimulus for continuous improvement. It is the key to assure any team is staying on track as well. As a leader or even just a team member, when you find someone does a great job at something, give him/her a shout out in front of the rest of the team so that every effort is seen and appreciated.

II. Deal with a poor-performer or an uncooperative team member

After trying your best to follow the above rules, what if you still face a poor performer or an uncooperative team member?

1. Have a private talk

Have a talk with him/her personally instead of publicizing anything. Please remember the purpose of the talk is to make him/her a better performer. If you point out his/her problem publicly, his/her energy will be focused on defending his or her dignity, not on improving the performance.

Purpose of the talk	
1. Prove him/her wrong	×
2. Prove you correct	×
3. Strengthen your relations	√
4. Catch up with the schedule and meet the original goal	√

2. Have the talk immediately

When you spot any unsatisfactory things happening, please remember to point it out immediately, rather than to wait till a bigger problem arises.

If you point out the problem immediately on the spot, your target is the problem, not the person who causes it. If you try to avoid the conflicts to achieve the temporary harmony and bear it until you couldn't, the talk then becomes blame instead. Your relations will be tense.

3. Get down to the point directly

If you want to give negative feedback to someone, do it directly. Don't use "praise sandwich" (start with a positive comment on performance, then provide negative feedback which is the key and finally close the sandwich by offering a final positive comment). Although popularly used, it is misleading, making the listener get lost in your real purpose. Get down to it directly instead. For instance: "I want to talk with you about your share of work because you have delayed for two days". Don't talk through the phone or type through WeChat or QQ. Have a face-to-face talk would be much better and more effective.

4. Get things clear

After the opening sentence mentioned above, ask the question: "**What's going on?**" Then listen carefully to the description of the fact from his/her perspective. The facts from different angles could be different. Maybe you think it is due to poor attitude but it is actually because of lack of information which he/she didn't get. Maybe you think the reason is lack of information but it is actually misunderstanding.

5. Get back on track

Ask the next question: "**If you want to finish your share and meet our partial goals, what help do you need?**" This could redirect the talk to your goal and the settlement of the problem. The key is not why it is wrong, but how it could be corrected.

6. Set the further feedback point

After you reach agreement on how to settle the problem, readjust the schedule and plan. For example, "You will get three more days to finish your share of work."

All in all, when tackling conflicts, please remember not to throw anyone under the bus or turn a damage-control discussion into a blame game. This never helps anybody. Instead, give your team equal responsibility to put your heads together and figure out the next steps or pivots.

III. Summary of the chapter

In this chapter, we learned how to build a strong and successful team. First of all, don't be afraid of conflicts because the optimum level of them could lead to effective decision making and high performance. Follow the basic rules to achieve good teamwork: have a team leader, get to know the rest of your team, clearly define roles and responsibilities, and ensure flawless communication throughout the whole process. When you meet a poor-performer or an uncooperative member in your team, have a private talk immediately when you spot the problem. During your talk, get down to the point directly and get to know what really happened. After that, get things back on the right track by finding a solution and set the further feedback point.

Chapter 8
Reject Plagiarism and Find Your Voice

学术研究均以前人的研究为基础。学术写作的作者应对前人的贡献表示尊重，并区分自己的贡献和他人的贡献。中国学生由于文化、修辞上差异以及外语能力限制，较为缺乏防止剽窃的意识和能力。本章讲述什么是剽窃，如何做好引用，以及在防止剽窃的过程中发出自己的学术声音。

Learning objectives

When learning this chapter, you are expected
- to understand the importance of citation, and
- to know what is plagiarism, and how to avoid it.

Academic research is based on the knowledge of previous researchers. To show the writer's credit to these contributions and tell your readers where to get further extensive information, citation is used. Avoiding plagiarism and keeping academic integrity matter, especially for undergraduate students. Chinese students are often criticized for not obeying academic norms. There is no space in the chapter to discuss the causes of the impression. We hold that besides different cultural and rhetorical tradition, lacking language competence to avoid plagiarism explains parts of the impression. Here we focus on explaining the necessity of avoiding plagiarism before explaining how to avoid it.

I. What is plagiarism

Plagiarism refers to giving the reader the impression that you have written or thought something that you have in fact borrowed from someone else (Gibaldi, 2013). In other words, it is to steal knowledge from others and own it.

There are, basically, three forms of plagiarism based on the method of stealing. The most direct plagiarism is to download someone's paper, and hand in with the stealer's name; The second kind of plagiarism is to copy the original text, change some expressions to avoid software duplicate checking, and pretend to be yours; The third kind is to put the writer's ideas with your original ideas without separation, so that your reader does not know where your thinking begins or ends. All the three forms are against the rule that your assignment should include your ideas and words. The words or ideas that do not belong to you should be indicated by citations, and if you are quoting, indicate the citation by quotation marks.

II. How to avoid plagiarism

The best way to avoid plagiarism is to be overt. Tell the reader the sources in the text of your paper, not just in bibliographies at the end of your paper. But of course, for common knowledge and facts that you can find in any encyclopedia, you need not give citation. For example, the people's Republic of China was established in 1949 is a fact everyone knows and no citation is needed. But this distinction is sometimes tricky for undergraduates. You need to stay in one discipline long enough to know what is common sense for people around. But our suggestion to this tricky problem is: when you are not sure if a citation is needed, cite.

Besides being overt, you are suggested to have good learning habits, such as taking notes carefully when reading, summarizing and paraphrasing the original idea, keeping a full record of the sources you read, which makes plagiarism unnecessary. By the way, do not leave your writing homework to the last minute.

III. Do not bury your voice in citations

Suppose you are an undergraduate who has no knowledge at all about a question, and all your paper is based on various sources. Is it proper for you to hand in a paper with 10 pages and 100 citations? We feel it a pity to say: yes, you may hand in a summary as this when you document clearly these borrowings. But often your tutor expects something more than summary. He or she wants to see your ability to compare, contrast and evaluate these sources. When you devote some of your thoughts into the matter, you can cite actively, make these sources into your knowledge, and, in effect, make dialogues with the scholars you are citing. The result? You hear your voice.

IV. How to facilitate your progress by rejecting plagiarism

One shortcut loved by lazy students is to borrow literature review articles for summarizing a topic. For example, for the topic "How fast do brands survive in local Chinese market", some students read one literature review article, which divided the strategies into three categories, and they followed this division in their writing. What teachers intended was that they should read 30 articles instead of one secondary source. This is also cheating in a way that not only ruins the intention of the assignment, but more seriously, it slows down the speed of their progress. Depending on others' ideas will deprive students of their confidence of searching for ideas themselves.

As mentioned in this part, it is not only for your readers' convenience to keep track on sources of information and attribute credit to the owner of ideas. Also, rejecting plagiarism benefits your own growth in logical thinking and improves your efficacy as a writer.

V. How to integrate citations into your writing

There are two ways to acknowledge the sources when you borrow others' ideas: one is summary and citation; the other is quotation and citation (Bailey 2020: 29).

a. Summary and citation, for example:

Breza et al. (2018) found that pay inequality could have a necessary effect on employees, unless it could be justified in their terms.

b. Quotation and citation, for example:

According to Breza et al. (2018): "relative pay enters utility function, with the potential for sizable negative impacts on labor supply and group cohesion. However, our findings indicate that pay inequality in itself is not necessarily problematic..." (p.623).

These in-text citations are linked to references at the end of the text, which includes the author's name, title of the article, journal title, and other publication details. Good citation will help your paper stand firmly in theoretical background and experimental conclusion. Following are some suggestions to follow.

(1) Include sources in your text. Include the source clearly in your text, not just in a citation. This is called a strong citation. When citing strongly, much emphasis is

given to the writer. Use the phrases 'according to Max' or 'as Sinclair argues.' Strong citation as this clearly distinguishes your idea from the cited one. Useful verbs for introducing attributions include *notes, observes, argues, comments, writes, says, reports, suggests,* and *claims*. For example:

Max (2018) noted that paying inequality could have a negative effect on employees, unless it could be justified in their terms.

(2) Cite sources after quotations. Put citations in parentheses after the quotation and before the final period. This is a weak citation version, which gives more strength to the cited idea, rather than the original writer. The information of the source is at the end of the sentence, but before the final period of the sentence. For example:

A recent article on the best-selling albums in America claimed that pop musicians were the main challenge to the moral standards of older generation (Hornby, 200).

(3) Use ellipses when citing. Use ellipsis points to indicate that you have omitted some of the language from within the quotation. Ellipses can be shown with three dots (periods), or four dots to indicate that the omission continues to the end of the sentence. For example:

The album "OK Computer"... pictured the onslaught of the information age and a young person's panicky embrace of it (Rose, 1999, p.85).

But it is the writer's responsibility to keep the original meaning when selecting information. Do not distort it.

(4) Use square brackets to alter or add information within a quotation. Square brackets are used when it is necessary to slightly change the original wording so that the text is more fluent, or you are inserting explanatory information. For example:

Popular music has always "[challenged] the morals of the older generation" according to Hornby (2000, p.25).

VI. Summary of the chapter

In this chapter, we learned that plagiarism is to borrow words and ideas and pretend that they are yours. Plagiarism is not only against academic norms, but slows your speed of making progress. By rejecting plagiarism, comparing and evaluating ideas, you can learn to find your own voices. Then we gave suggestions on how to cite beautifully when writing by using strong citation, weak citation, ellipsis and square brackets.

Chapter 9

Be an Ethical Researcher

对社会科学研究者而言,研究数据来源于对他人信息的收集。本章讲述学术道德的含义,给出研究过程中的 10 个道德建议。对研究者而言,学术道德比成功更加重要。

Learning objectives

When learning this chapter, you are expected
- to have a general understanding of research ethics, and
- to learn to do research ethically.

As student researchers, you are unable to conduct proper research successfully if you don't receive the help of other people. They give up their time to help and are willing to disclose personal information during your research. You are bound to act with respect towards the participants. This is called **research ethics**.

This chapter explores ethical issues in detail through the whole research process. In addition, a number of fictional "ethical dilemmas" and "ethical dialogues" are integrated with the text to give you a deeper understanding. Dawson (2009) and Oliver (2010) have more detailed discussion on research ethics, and the ideas in this chapter are inspired by them.

I. Ethical issues before the research starts

We want to mention three issues in this stage: finding potential respondents, informing research purpose, and investigating vulnerable subjects.

1. Finding potential respondents

Researchers should allow respondents to choose to participate or not. Students usually send questionnaires in WeChat groups or QQ groups. If people there know you, for example your friends or classmates, they may feel obliged to help with the research, even though they would prefer to decline your invitation. Here comes the issue that unwilling participants may not be truly helpful for the research program. Let people decide themselves whether to do the questionnaire or not. No pressure should be given.

When you approach people in person to ask if they would like to be interviewed, they, especially those whom you are familiar with, may find it difficult to refuse your request. Therefore, the key point is that people should be given sufficient time to make up their minds. One suggestion is as follows: you could explain the main aspects of your research and you could express your hope for them to take part, but leave them some time and contact them later for a reply. Some people could decide not to take part with an excuse, but at least you will know that those who do accept your offer have thought about the research, and taken a positive decision to help.

2. The principle of informed consent

The principle that participants should be fully informed about a research project before they agree to take part in the research is called informed consent. It is necessary because it seems not fair to expect people to make a decision when they don't know the relevant facts. They have the "right to know".

One difficulty may arise when some technical aspects or terms of the research are difficult to be explained. You should try to put it in simple language but not distort the ideas.

There may be difficulties with informed consent in situations where participants are part of a hierarchical work structure, like social organizations or companies. That means you need to get the organization's approval before you approach potential participants.

Let us look at how this problem might occur in practice. In the following table, the discussion is taking place between two student researchers who are planning some research on management styles in an organization. The cases in this chapter were taken from Oliver's book on students' ethic study (2010).

Table 9.1 Ethical dialogue: informed consent in an organizational context

A: What we are really trying to uncover here are the private views of people in the offices on the management style of the organization.

B: OK, but they will never talk to us, I mean really talk to us, unless they feel absolutely empowered to do so, and also that **confidentiality** is absolutely assured.

A: Well, we can deal with confidentiality. If we explain our systems for handling data, hopefully there will be sufficient reassurance. But we also need to get the approval from the senior management, saying that people can participate.

B: Right, we basically need an e-mail to all staff from the chief executive, saying that she has approved our research, and is willing to let people get involved.

A: And she could also say that she has asked us to ensure the **anonymity** of all participants. Oh, and we really want some sort of statement that staff are encouraged to discuss with us any management issues which we raise in the interviews.

B: Clear.

A: Good. Once this e-mail has gone round, we should be able to ask people to take part, and get a reasonable response.

Source: Oliver 2010

The researchers above are rightly sensitive to the feelings of the workers in the organization. The confidentiality and anonymity of the information the workers released should be reassured. This is a necessary part to get consent from participants in an organization.

3. Investigating vulnerable groups of people

Broadly speaking, these vulnerable groups are people who may not have the required degree of understanding to give their informed consent to participate in the research. A fairly obvious category is children. Other groups are socially or economically vulnerable, such as unemployed or homeless people. They may feel uncertain, lacking in confidence, anxious about their social situations. In this frame of mind, they may not react in the manner in which they would normally react when participating in the research. You could try to get consent from an appropriate third party. For example, if your research participants are school pupils or left-over children, you need to obtain third-party consent. It may be possible to explain the research roughly to the children, whereas the fully informed consent should be obtained from their parents, guardians or teachers.

You need not try to reach a full and final decision about an entire research project, but proceed gradually, reaching decisions about small aspects of the research. You could start with a small pilot study for instance, in order to judge any effects of the research on the respondents.

Case study

Case: A sociologist would like to investigate the health problems of homeless people. The sociologist is concerned that as a group they may have a wide range of health problems, some of which could be treated easily and this would improve their quality of life. The sociologist hopes to use the research to publicize the health needs of such people, and to encourage the relevant authorities to establish a program of regular intervention. Some colleagues remind the sociologist of the possibility that some of the homeless people may be opposed to the idea of getting help from authorities. They may even feel the research process is a threat to their independence. Several initial interviews conducted by the sociologist suggest that regular medical checks may possibly disturb the research respondents' lifestyle. **Solution:** The sociologist is experiencing something of a dilemma, by wanting to provide better health care for the homeless people, but not wishing to disturb their lifestyle. Therefore, it may be decided that the research is inappropriate. The sociologist could find ways in which the health authorities are able to respond when requested by homeless people.

II. Ethical issues during the research

1. The ethics of recording data

During data-collection phase, the researcher and the respondent interact with each other more frequently. Therefore, ethical issues may arise more often.

The first thing is about tape recording, whether video or audio, the informed consent of the participant should be obtained. The researcher should explain to participants the reason for recording, the way in which the recordings will be used, the way in which the tapes will be stored, and the procedure for destruction of the records when all the data have been transcribed. Participants should also be informed of the way in which they will be identified on the tape. Don't mention their names or use fictional ones during recording. It may take some time to fully inform the prospective interviewees, but it is necessary to do so before getting their consent.

During recording, some respondents may feel nervous and uneasy no matter how they are reassured about anonymity and confidentiality. There are two strategies to make them more relaxed.

● **First strategy**

Place the recording machine within easy reach of the interviewee, and explain to them before the interview starts that they may press the pause button at any time in order to let them have time to reflect. Let the interviewee have absolute control.

● **Second strategy**

Offer interviewees the opportunity to play back the record at the end of the interview. If at that stage they feel some details or the whole answer should be changed to fully express what they really want to mean, they could edit it or redo it again. This could reassure the worried ones and could obtain data which reflect accurate views.

2. Minimizing the risks of research

"Minimal risk" means that during research, participants will encounter no harms or discomforts greater than those in their daily lives. The risk of your research should not be greater than that. If not, you must seek the advice of your teacher.

What risks can arise in or result from research and how to minimize them?

Emotional or psychological trauma is a risk when respondents are asked to describe a painful event or a humiliating identity that they do not usually discuss otherwise. Personal experiences of being assaulted, or of serious illness or injury are among the many potentially traumatizing topics of interview.

One risk-minimizing strategy is to interview individuals who have already talked publicly or talk frequently about a past trauma or a stigmatized identity. Students with limited experience and training in sensitive interviewing are strongly discouraged from trying to do it.

Potentials for other types of greater than minimal risks arise if individuals are asked to do anything that they would not normally do in the course of daily life which could jeopardize:

- their physical safety
- their emotional well-being
- their academic standing
- their legal standing
- their financial or employment security
- their reputation in any context

Note that if the risk of an intended project might be greater than minimal risk, you must seek the advice of your teacher.

The participants should feel free to withdraw at any time of the research. Even when participants give their informed consent, they are not necessarily expected to anticipate their feelings when participating. They could simply walk away without giving any explanation whenever they feel not safe or comfortable enough.

3. Sensitivity to the research field

The ethnographic approach to research usually involves collecting data on social phenomena in a natural environment. It is often termed the "field". You may imagine fieldwork being conducted in a remote Tibetan village, or among a community of one national minority, for instance the Miao nationality.

As a researcher, you need to cultivate a sensitivity to the research field. One can think of the researcher as an intruder into a social context. Therefore, you have a responsibility to disturb that environment as little as possible.

For example, you may be conducting a study of a school, or you may witness what you regard as a rather inefficient system. Such may be the situation where you feel that you would like to intervene between staff and students. Yet you are suggested simply to observe and not to engage in any formal interaction.

4. Respecting other people's ideas and views

When you're doing interviews and carrying out questionnaires, it's important to keep your thoughts to yourself. Hiding your feelings can be hard, and you can express mild surprise if someone says something really strange. Anyhow, you're asking for the person's opinion, so you need to let him express his opinion without feeling stupid.

5. The use of inducements to provide data

Sometimes student researchers feel it is appropriate to provide inducements to participants, like a little cash as compensation to show appreciation for the time and effort participants spent for their research.

With inducement, however, you may not find the participant who are really willing to participate. Thus, the nature of the data may be changed. Meanwhile, you may not explain details about the research as carefully as before. Therefore, as a green hand, if it is possible, it is preferable to avoid the introduction of inducements, and keep the relationship between researcher and respondent simple and original (help requestor and helper).

III. Ethical issues when data collection has been completed

After collecting data, the following ethical issues are to be considered:

1. Reporting research results to respondents

Some respondents may be interested in the research results. If it is intended to be published in an academic journal, or to be a research paper for your academic class, there will be no difficulty. You could send them an offprint of the article or paper.

2. Arrangements for the disposal of raw data

For a single project in our academic course, you may collect a comparably large quantity of raw data. You could destroy them right away after you finish your research and academic paper writing. Of course, you could keep them for some period after the completion of the thesis or the research report, in case there are questions raised about some of the analysis.

Concerning the confidentiality of the data, all precautions should be taken to ensure that irrelevant individuals cannot gain access to the database by accident.

IV. Summary of the chapter

When you are doing research, you are bound to look at an issue that involves people. Therefore, you need to sort out any ethical matters connected with your research. Try to use the tips in this chapter to lead you through the whole research and settle problems popping up along the way. Please remember the essence of all the suggestions: show respect to participants and others' ideas, assure anonymity and confidentiality, get informed consent from your participants. For a researcher, being ethical values more than being successful.

Part 2

The Journey of

Writing

Chapter 10

Write Introduction

我们希望学习者已经完成了研究问题的选题、数据的获取和分析,从数据中找到了研究问题的答案,开始进入引言部分的写作。本章我们讲述引言部分的修辞功能和结构,学习引言的语言特征,以及其他修辞方法,以便达到有效的书面交际目的。

Learning objectives

In this chapter, you will learn how to write an Introduction for a research report. When learning this chapter, you are expected:

- to learn the functions and structure of the Introduction section,
- to learn the language features of the Introduction section, and
- to be able to produce effective Introduction writing by the end of this week.

Research reports are very common assignments in many academic disciplines. While essays are often concerned with abstract or theoretical subjects, a research report is a description of a situation or problem that you have examined or investigated. Research report writing is characterized, at a very basic level, by three main features: a pre-defined structure, independent sections, and reaching unbiased conclusions. The fundamental rule for writing research reports is informing the reader about all relevant issues in a simple and objective manner.

A research report is a highly structured piece of work. But the structure is not decided by the writer. Instead, writers should follow a pre-defined structure and are only allowed some flexibility and freedom in deciding on the organization of subsections which comprise the report's main sections.

Research reports may include some or all of the following components:

- Introduction (What question was asked?)
- Methods (How was it studied?)
- Results (What was found?)
- Discussion (What do the findings mean?)
- Conclusion (Summary of the work)

The Introduction section is the beginning part of a research report. It provides an orientation to the research. However, in practice, you will find that you need to be certain about what you have done and what you have found to write the Introduction, so the best time to write it will be after you have collected and analyzed data.

In the Introduction section, you begin by establishing the importance of the research topic. Then you provide a background of the research and a definition of key terms used in your research. This is followed by a review of previous research in the area and a research gap you have identified. Next, you move on to describe your own research. You first introduce the purpose of your research and the specific problem you will deal with, and then you provide a synopsis of the theoretical framework undergirding your research, which is followed immediately by the research questions or research hypotheses. If there are any limitations and delimitations of the research, also address them. Finally, an overview of the contents of each chapter of the report is presented.

In summary, to write an effective Introduction you must know your audience, tell them why you have done the study, explain why it's important to do the research, and convince readers that your research is better than what has been done before.

I. Functions of an Introduction section

As the first part of a report, the Introduction section has the following three main functions: making the purpose of the report clear, preparing the reader for the contents, giving a framework on which to build an understanding of the report, and sometimes providing a roadmap to the content of the report.

II. Structural features of an Introduction section

The structure of the report sections will be analyzed and described in terms of "move" which is a unit of the text's content. A move indicates the communicative purpose of a particular part of the text and may sometimes consist of several sub-moves.

Conventional Introduction sections are composed of three moves, as is shown below.

---

1. Introduce the research area
1.1   Establish the significance of the research topic
1.2   Provide background information
1.3   Define the terminology in the title/key words
1.4   Review items of previous research in the area
2. Establish the motivation of the research
Indicate the gap(s) in the previous research or extend previous knowledge in some way
3. Describe the present research
3.1   State the purpose or the nature of the present research
3.2   List research questions or hypotheses
3.3   Present main findings
3.4   State the value of the present research
3.5   Indicate the structure of the research report

Read the following Introduction section taken from a published research report. Numbers are added in front of the sentences to facilitate the analysis. Useful sentence patterns and phrases are highlighted in bold.

International Marketing Ethics: A Literature Review and Research Agenda

Rajshekhar G. Javalgi and La Toya M. Russell

(Published in *Journal of Business Ethics*, 2018)

Introduction

①**The importance of international marketing ethics has gained attention** due to the dismantling of trade barriers, the rise of multinational enterprises, and the globalization of markets (Leonidou et al., 2010; Iyer, 2001; Carrigan et al., 2005). ②As more firms expand business internationally, ethics and ethical practices **have become major topics of interest** in both academic and practitioner circles. ③**Undoubtedly,** international marketing is a field where questions about ethics are often raised since more and more companies expand operations into foreign markets which differ by culture, values, norms, behavior, rule, and regulations (Murphy & Laczniak, 1981; Alsmadi & Alnawas, 2012). ④Business behavior that is deemed ethical in one culture may be viewed as unethical in another culture. ⑤Therefore, it is important for international marketing marketers to understand why the variance exists. ⑥International marketing marketers need to be well-rounded and should not rely on their understanding of ethical judgments and practices used domestically to understand international marketing ethical practices. ⑦When conducting business abroad, ethics needs to be understood on a cross-cultural basis because ethical behavior varies from country to country and culture to culture. ⑧For example, when discussing ethical problems, **Armstrong and Sweeney(1994) find that** managers from China perceive ethical problems less frequently and less important than Australian managers. ⑨**The findings also show that** the culture of the manager has the greatest effect on perceptions of ethical problems.

⑩**Smith (1995) argues that** we are now living in the "ethics era", whereby expectations of marketers have changed and consumers have become more educated and better informed. ⑪**Furthermore,** the emergence of new competitors, especially from emerging markets, **has created a new set of challenges in** conducting business abroad. ⑫ Some of the challenges in arriving at a consensus on ethics in marketing stem from the lack of uniform philosophical discussions of what is "good" and "ethical", and whether "good" and "ethical" have equivalent meaning and interpretation (Carrigan et al., 2005). ⑬Given that ethical decision-making is very complex, **Sheth et al. (1988) note that** "allegedly guilty marketing practitioners have quite sincerely stated that they honestly did not realize that their actions could possibly create ethical problem". ⑭ Today, as the field of international marketing develops stronger ethical concepts, international marketers are finding that it is harder to ignore the "ethics gap" between what society expects and what marketing practitioners are delivering (Laczniak 1993; Carrigan et al., 2005).

⑮Scholars are actively researching the dilemmas faced by international marketers when dealing with marketing ethics in cross-cultural settings (Rawwas et al., 1995; Singhapakdi et al., 1999; Carrigan et al., 2005). ⑯Although the research in international marketing ethics has increased in the last two decades, **a comprehensive understanding of this growing topic is lacking.** ⑰Therefore, **it is timely to conduct** a state-of-art review of the literature on international marketing ethics.

⑱**The paper aims to** review existing research, and, based on this review, we examine the research in terms of conceptual definitions, theoretical frameworks used, statistical methods employed, the number of countries studied, and finally discuss limitations and directions for future research. ⑲ **To accomplish these objectives,** we review the articles from 1960 through 2013 from various journals. ⑳We chose 1960 as a starting point for our review because the first journal that covered marketing ethics was the *Journal of Marketing* in the early 1960s. ㉑However, the field truly emerged in the late 1980s owing to the rise of international business and international marketing.

㉒**We contribute to the literature by** reviewing and assessing the current state of research on international marketing ethics and by delineating where gaps exist and further suggesting opportunities for future research.

㉓ **The remainder of the article is organized as follows.** ㉔ **The first section discusses** the methodological approach in international marketing ethics research. ㉕**The second section gives** a brief overview of the process pursued in the selection of journals. ㉖ **The third section discusses** the definitions, concepts, and theories in international marketing ethics research. ㉗**The fourth section discusses** the dominant topics discussed. ㉘ **The fifth section discusses** the countries studied in international marketing ethics research. ㉙**The sixth section discusses** the statistical methods used in research for international marketing ethics. ㉚**The final section presents** a discussion, the limitations, and future research.

Move 1: Sentences ①~⑭ introduce the research area. Sentences ①~② form Move 1.1, establishing the significance of the research topic. Sentences ③~⑭ form Move 1. 2 and Move 1. 4 which provide background information and present a brief review of relevant research.

Move 2: Sentences ⑮~⑰ indicate the gap in the previous research.

Move 3: Sentences ⑱~㉚ describe the present research. Sentences ⑱~㉑ form Move 3.1, outlining the aim of the present research. Sentence ㉒ forms Move 3.4, stating the value of the present research. Sentences ㉓~㉚ form Move 3.5, indicating the structure of the research report.

III. Language features

Moves are realized in phrases and sentence patterns. The following sentence patterns and phrases are frequently and typically used as signals of different moves of the Introduction's structure.

1. Establishing the significance of a research area

- A growing body of literature has been undertaken on...
- A large body of research shows...
- A large number of investigations have described...
- It is generally accepted that...
- It is widely recognized that...
- Much research in recent years has focused on...
- Numerous experiments have established that...
- The importance of...has been demonstrated by...
- The importance of...has gained attention due to...
- There has been an increasing awareness of...
- There is a growing interest in...
- ...are attracting widespread interest in fields such as...
- ...has attracted widespread attention.
- ...has generated considerable recent research interest.
- ...have become major topics of interest.
- ...have gained increasing attention.
- ...is vital for two important reasons: ...
- ...plays an important role in...

2. Review relevant studies in the area

- An alternative approach was developed by...
- As Smith (1995) noted that...
- Early data was interpreted in the study by...
- In recent years, researchers have claimed...

- Initial attempts focused on. . .
- Previous literature has provided evidence of. . .
- Prior studies have developed. . .
- Recent research has shown that. . .
- Research conducted in recent years has shed light on. . .
- Smith (1995) argues that. . .
- The results on. . . were reported in. . .
- Their study suggested a possible cause for. . .
- This phenomenon was demonstrated by. . .
- . . . has been proposed for these applications. . .

3. Indicate a gap in previous research

- A comprehensive understanding of this growing topic is lacking.
- An alternative approach is necessary.
- Few researchers have addressed the problem of. . .
- Few studies have examined. . .
- However, . . . has been largely unsuccessful to date.
- However, previous research has not examined. . .
- However, . . . was far from optimal.
- Little attention has been devoted to. . .
- Previous work has focused only on. . .
- There remains a need for an efficient method that can. . .
- Unfortunately, these methods do not always guarantee. . .
- We know relatively little about. . .
- We still have a limited understanding of. . .
- . . . have rarely been taken into account.
- . . . remains unclear.

4. Describe the present research

- In the present study we performed. . .
- In this paper we present. . .
- In this report we test the hypothesis that. . .
- The aim of this present paper is to. . .
- The approach we have used in this study aims to. . .
- The objective of this paper is to. . .
- The paper is structured as follows.
- The present paper examines. . .

- The purpose of this study is to. . .
- The remainder of the article is organized as follows.
- This paper focuses on. . .
- This paper introduces. . .
- This paper is organized as follows: . . .
- This study investigated the use of. . .

IV. Sample analysis

In this part, you will read an authentic Introduction section published in an academic journal. Read it carefully and pay attention to the useful sentence patterns highlighted in bold. Then complete the task after the sample.

<blockquote>

Successful Social Entrepreneurial Business Models in the Context of

Developing Economies An Explorative Study

Johanna Mair and Oliver Schoen

(Published in *International Journal of Emerging Markets*, 2007)

Introduction

①As societies search for more innovative, cost-effective, and sustainable ways to address social problems, "social ventures"—typically led by inspired individuals known as "social entrepreneurs"—**have attracted increasing attention.** ②By combining a social purpose with a for-profit mindset these initiatives provide an effective means to cater to largely unsatisfied social needs (Seelos & Mair, 2005), especially as traditional social sector activities are often seen as inefficient, ineffective, and unresponsive (Dees, 2001).

③**Research conducted in recent years has shed light on** many interesting aspects of social entrepreneurs and their initiatives, for example, the social entrepreneur as a change agent (Dees, 2001); and the role of the founder, his or her vision and individual traits (Drayton, 2002; Bornstein, 2004). ④**However, previous research has not examined** how social entrepreneurs, in setting up self-sustained organizations, actually combine social and economic value creation. ⑤The structures created by these social entrepreneurs, the co-operations and partnerships they enable, the way they not only position themselves within, but also actively shape the value chains of their respective industries, **have rarely been taken into account.** ⑥**As a result, a number of questions remain open.** ⑦**We still have a limited understanding for instance, of** how specific strategies of network building and resource procurement facilitate the creation of social and economic value. ⑧**In addition, we know relatively little about** how to ensure that the right target group captures the created value.

⑨**The objective of this paper is to** address these questions. ⑩To do this, we chose to focus our analysis on three initiatives: Grameen Bank (GB) in Bangladesh; Mondrago'n Corporacion Cooperativa (MCC) in Spain, and Sekem in Egypt. ⑪All three started as social ventures and were led by extraordinary, visionary individuals; and all three developed into self-sustained organizations.

</blockquote>

⑫Moreover, they have been widely recognized as both socially and economically successful (Wahid, 1994; Whyte & Whyte, 1991). ⑬**By examining these organizations, we aim to** identify common patterns in their approaches and to derive propositions on how the organizational set-up and the business model can facilitate the creation and appropriation of social value. ⑭The organizations were selected to reflect a wide spectrum of social ventures addressing quite different social needs. ⑮Furthermore, they originated in different geographical regions, have different product and market scopes, and also vary in size (see Table II for an overview of the selected organizations). ⑯This diversity allows us, despite the small sample, to develop first propositions on the common features of social ventures that are successful in supplying to social needs and bringing about social change. ⑰Importantly, they can do so in a sustainable manner by having developed into self-sustained organizations.

⑱**The paper is structured as follows.** ⑲First, we clarify terminology and introduce the research methodology. ⑳We then introduce the three organizations and closely examine their business models to distill the shared features that have enabled them to create social value sustainably. ㉑To conclude we discuss the implications of this study for research and practice.

Task: *Read the sample carefully and identify its sub-moves. Note down the sentence numbers of each sub-move in the table below.*

Moves	Sub-moves	Sentence numbers
1. Introduce the research area		
2. Establish the motivation of the research		
3. Describe the present research		

V. Summary of the chapter

This chapter illustrates the main structure of research report writing. Then it focuses on how to write an effective Introduction for a research report. Research-based writing generally realizes three functions in the Introduction: introducing the research area, establishing the motivation of the research and describing the present research. Language patterns that can help realize these functions are provided as well in this chapter.

Chapter 11

Write Literature Review

文献综述部分具有为读者提供背景知识信息以及为研究提供研究理据的双重功能。本章讲述文献综述部分的功能、结构、语言特征,以及其他有效修辞手段的使用。

Learning objectives

When learning this chapter, you are expected:

● to learn the functions and structure of the Literature Review section,

● to learn the language features of the Literature Review section, and

● to be able to produce effective Literature Review writing.

The Literature Review section is a very important part in a research report, which relates your work to a larger research area. A literature review can be incorporated in the Introduction section, or structured as a separate section in a research report. A literature review is a thorough and critical analysis of the existing literature relevant to a particular research topic. A literature review is not just a simple description of previous research findings, but rather a well-organized piece of work that involves summarizing, categorizing, synthesizing, evaluating, and comparing previous research. So, it is very difficult to write. Through the critical analysis of various sources, a literature review shows previous work that has been done by other scholars, and presents the most recent work in a research field. More importantly, it reveals what remains to be done and provides important insights into your own research.

I. Functions of a Literature Review section

The Literature Review section has the following functions: serving as a solid background for your research; showing how your research is connected to a larger research field; unfolding the history of the development of a research area; demonstrating your knowledge of a particular research topic; providing theoretical framework or empirical basis for your research hypotheses; indicating gaps in the existing research and thereby justifying the contributions of your research.

II. Structural features of a Literature Review section

This section is focused on the structure of a Literature Review section presented as a separate part in the report. In general, a stand-alone Literature Review section includes four moves, as is shown below.

---

1. Give an overview of the literature review
1.1   Introduce the purpose of the literature review
1.2   Introduce the main topic to be discussed
1.3   Make comments on the overall literature
2. Summarize the existing literature
2.1   Synthesize previous research and present the main points
2.2   Review individual research
2.3   Make comparison and contrast between different researches
3. Evaluate the existing literature
3.1   Critique the previous research (e. g., strengths, inadequacies, inconsistencies, conflicts, problems)
3.2   Identify a research gap
4. Link the exiting literature to the present research
4.1   Indicate the need to fill the research gap/the need for further research
4.2   Present the aim of the present research
4.3   Propose research questions/conceptual framework/research hypotheses

---

It should be noted that the structure of the Literature Review section is not fixed. A few sub-moves in the afore-mentioned structure might not be presented in the Literature Review section, such as Move 1.1, Move 1.3, and Move 4.3. In addition, the above-mentioned moves can be intertwined, especially Move 2 and Move 3, and the order of the sub-moves might be changed. And in a Literature Review section, Move 2 and Move 3 usually appear cyclically.

Read the following excerpt of a Literature Review taken from a published research report. Numbers are added in front of the sentences to facilitate the analysis, and useful sentence patterns and phrases are highlighted in bold.

Exploring the Internationalization Strategies of Turkish Multinationals: A Multi-perspective Analysis

Yuksel Ayden, Ekrem Tatoglu, Keith W. Glaister, and Mehmet Demirbag

(Published in *Journal of International Management*, 2020)

Literature Review

①The internationalization of EC MNEs (Emerging Country Multi-national Enterprises) **has long been studied in the** IB **field as** firms from various emerging economies **have become prominent** in the global business environment. ②**The increasing number of studies of** EC MNEs **has initiated a discussion in** IB **research about** whether these firms represent a new kind of MNE and whether mainstream IB theories, such as the OLI paradigm (Dunning, 1988) and the Uppsala model (Johanson and Vahlne, 1977, 2009), are adequate to explain their behavior (Gammeltoft et al., 2010; Jormanainen and Koveshnikov, 2012; Luo and Tung, 2018; Madhok and Keyhani, 2012; Mathews, 2006, 2017; Narula, 2006; Ramamurti, 2012; Wilkinson et al., 2014). ③**Some scholars argue that** these firms represent a novel type of MNE due to their divergent behaviors and characteristics, such as lack of competitive advantages, aggressive asset-seeking behaviors and the rapid pace of their internationalization, which necessitates the development of new lenses to comprehend their international expansion (Luo and Tung, 2007; Mathews, 2006). ④**Other scholars claim that** extant theoretical views are sufficient to explain EC MNEs' behaviors and that research should seek to refute these perspectives before offering novel theories (Dunning, 2006; Narula, 2006). ⑤**Another view proposes that** EC MNEs provide opportunities for IB scholars to study the early stages of MNE development because classic IB theories were built on research conducted in the 1970s, when many developed country firms had, to a large extent, already established themselves as MNEs (Hernandez and Guillén, 2018; Jormanainen and Koveshnikov, 2012; Meyer and Thaijongrak, 2013; Ramamurti, 2012).

⑥**Consequently, a growing body of research on** EC MNEs **has been built, which primarily focuses on** the distinguishing characteristics of their internationalization processes, such as the role of weak institutional environments in their home countries (Peng et al., 2008; Wu and Chen, 2014), and the lack of traditional competitive assets, such as advanced technologies and well-known brands (Cui et al., 2014; Elia and Santangelo, 2017). ⑦**The latter research stream mainly focuses on** the potential sources of competitiveness of EC MNEs and highlights their low-cost advantages (Kotabe and Kothari, 2016), entrepreneurial behaviors (Yamakawa et al., 2007) and networks (Eren-Erdogmus et al., 2010; Yaprak and Karademir, 2010; Yiu et al., 2007). ⑧**Since** EC MNEs **are traditionally viewed as having limited resource bases, a substantial amount of research has been undertaken to reveal** how these firms also use internationalization as a way of upgrading their resources through asset-seeking behavior (Cui et al., 2017; Elia and Santangelo, 2017; Lu et al., 2011; Luo and Tung, 2007).

⑨**To shed light upon their strategic behaviors,** IB **scholars have attempted to develop** typologies of EC MNEs **and to identify** the different paths to internationalization (Child and Rodrigues, 2005; Chittoor and Ray, 2007; Wang and Suh, 2009). ⑩**For instance,** Child and Rodrigues (2005) **report that** Chinese firms pursue three internationalization paths, which are inward internationalization, aggressive acquisitions, and organic expansion. ⑪Chittoor and Ray (2007) **identify** four internationalization routes for Indian pharmaceutical companies **through** a strategic group analysis along the dimensions of markets and products. ⑫**Building on** their R&D and marketing investments, Tsai and Eisingerich (2010) **examined** the internationalization strategies of MNEs from ROK and India, and categorized them into six strategy groups labeled as regional exporters, global niche players, global exporters and importers, OEM/ODM technology leaders, OEM/ODM fast followers and multinational challengers. ⑬**In addition,** Luo et al. (2011) **proposed** a typology of emerging country copycats (i. e., emerging economy firms that begin with imitation and later progress towards innovation) and examined the transformation of four emerging economy firms from duplicative imitators to novel innovators **with a specific focus on** their imitative behaviors. ⑭Ramamurti (2009) **proposed several** generic internationalization strategies, **namely** local optimizers, low-cost partners, natural resource integrators, global consolidators, and global first movers. ⑮**Using** Ramamurti's (2009) five generic internationalization strategies of EC MNEs, Gaffney et al. (2013) **adopted a** resource-dependence **perspective** and **examined** EC MNEs' motivations to invest abroad, their strategic focus and entry mode choices. ⑯**The idea that** EC MNEs provide a suitable context for theoretical extensions **has accelerated conceptual studies, which put a special emphasis on** the behaviors of EC MNEs, examining how different learning mechanisms operate within and between MNE networks and resulted in learning-based typologies of MNE internationalization (Li, 2010; Wang and Suh, 2009). ⑰**Previous research has also attempted to extend the existing conceptualizations to investigate** the EC MNEs' behaviors. ⑱**In this regard, for example,** Luo and Rui (2009) **extended** the use of the ambidexterity concept and **presented** four different strategic behaviors by which an EC MNE can achieve ambidexterity, **namely** co-orientation, co-opetition, co-competence, and co-evolution. ⑲**Focusing on** a firm-level theoretical framework (i. e., the value chain), Moghaddam et al. (2014) **presented** a modified typology of strategic motivations of cross-border investments consisting of six categories: end-customer-market seeking, natural resource seeking, downstream and upstream knowledge seeking, efficiency seeking, global value consolidation seeking, and geopolitical influence seeking.

⑳**Although previous research offers valuable insights into** the plurality of EC MNEs' strategic behaviors, **the literature tends to assume that** firms follow one uniform strategy towards internationalization, **by overlooking the fact that** companies can behave differently in different market conditions, or else does not examine the adaptive mechanisms enabling the realization of these specific strategies, usually emphasizing the drivers of specific strategies. ㉑**In particular, the literature provides limited insights into** the dynamic interaction between foreign market conditions and firm resources, as well as the role of firm capabilities in shaping and enabling the execution of strategies in the internationalization process. ㉒**Despite the prior research on** the internationalization of EC MNEs, **questions remain regarding** what is really new about EC MNEs, and how studies on EC MNEs can extend what is already known about firm internationalization (Hernandez and Guillén, 2018). ㉓**In this regard,** Luo and Zhang (2016) **point out the necessity to** embrace the variety in the observed phenomenon and further explore the diversity and plurality in EC MNEs' strategic behaviors by developing typologies or taxonomies. ㉔**Other scholars have argued that** the literature should move beyond comparing EC MNEs and DC MNEs and focus on more fruitful issues, such as the genesis and evolution of MNEs' capabilities (Hernandez and Guillén, 2018) and how EC MNEs deploy and leverage their resources for internationalization (Buckley et al., 2017). ㉕**Consequently, examining** the internationalization strategies of EC MNEs within a more dynamic perspective, **addressing not only** "why they internationalize" **but also** "how they expand successfully", **will beneficially enhance research on** EC MNEs (Deng et al., 2018). ㉖ **In this study, we integrate** the DCV (The dynamic capabilities view), the RBV (The resource-based view), and the IBV (The industry-based view) **to develop a multi-perspective framework to explore** the internationalization strategies of firms as an outcome of the interaction between their existing resources and the level of competitiveness in target markets. ㉗ **We then reveal** how firms utilize their sensing, seizing, and reconfiguring capacities (Teece, 2007) to induce changes in their resource bases to adapt to the foreign market conditions at the different stages of their internationalization while pursuing different strategic trajectories.

Move 1: Sentence ① is Move 1.2, which introduces the main topic to be discussed in the Literature Review Section. Sentences ②~⑤ are Move 1.3, which are comments on the overall literature.

Move 2: Sentence ⑥ is Move 2.1, which synthesizes previous research and presents the main point. Sentences ⑦~⑧ are Move 2.2, which contrast sentence ⑥ by presenting main points of a different stream of research. Sentences ⑨ and ⑰ are Move 2.1, which summarize previous research. Sentences ⑩~⑯ and Sentences ⑱~⑲ are Move 2.2, which are reviews of individual research.

Move 3: Sentences ⑳~㉑ are Move 3.1, which critique the existing literature. Sentence ㉒ is Move 3.2, which identifies a research gap.

Move 4: Sentences ㉓~㉕ are Move 4.1, which demonstrate the need to fill the research gap. Sentence ㉖ is Move 4.2, which presents the aim of the present research.

III. Language features

The Literature Review Section should be presented comprehensively and logically. The following sentence patterns and phrases are commonly used as signals of different moves.

1. Introduce the purpose/contents of the literature review

- A brief overview of... is presented in this section as background to the rest of the paper.
- In line with the objectives of this study, the literature review focuses on...
- In this section below, we provide a literature review of...
- In this section, we first review... then discuss...
- This literature review intends to analyze...

- This paper begins with a review of the literature regarding the...
- This section is intended to provide a review of...
- This section presents a review of recent literature on...
- This section reviews...

2. Introduce the main topic to be discussed in the literature review

- A number of authors have recognized that...
- A survey of the literature on...indicates a question as to...
- During the past...years, research on...has grown significantly.
- The effects of...have been studied recently in the empirical literature.
- The importance of...has gained attention due to...
- There is a growing interest in...
- There is a wide recognition of...as...
- There is an increasing body of research on...
- Over the past few decades,...is gradually becoming one of the hottest topics.
- Since..., there has been a wide interest in...
- Studies about...have attracted an increasing attention over the past few years.
- When it comes to...
- ...has become a new social phenomenon recently.
- ...is an area of research that has received a longstanding interest.

3. Comment on the overall literature

- A substantial body of literature has investigated...
- Although...only limited research to date has explored...
- Despite the vast amount of studies on...few have addressed...
- However, to date, very few papers have focused on...
- Relatively little attention has been paid to...
- Studies of...are well documented.
- Studies on...has received considerable attention.
- The examination of... has been the focus of much research interest in... literature/field.
- The...literature contains extensive research and theory on...
- There have been numerous studies to investigate...
- There have been only a very limited number of...studies.
- Very few researchers appear to have linked...and...

4. Summarize the previous research

- As has been previously reported in the literature...
- As noted in previous research,...
- Cumulatively, these results suggest that...
- In sum, the findings summarized above indicate...
- Most researchers agree that...
- Overall, the literature highlights the importance of...
- Previous studies have shown/demonstrated/revealed that...
- Research has focused on...
- Research related to...suggests/indicates/emphasizes that...
- Researchers have recently emphasized the need to...
- Some studies have hypothesized that...
- The dominant view on...is...
- The literature on...covers various research topics: ...
- The research on...mainly focus on...
- ...is seen by many researchers as...

5. Discuss main points of individual research

- A recent study by...concluded that...
- A more comprehensive description can be found in the study of...
- In a review of...argues that...
- In examining...argued that...
- One recent study attempted to...
- This has also been explored in prior studies by...
- ...also postulated that...
- ...claims/argues that...
- ...found that...can positively impact...
- ...proposed/maintained/stated that...

6. Indicate a specific area of research

- Adopting a...approach,...
- From a...perspective,...
- From the view of...
- In terms of...
- In this regard,...
- The research on/as to...

- With regard to/With respect to/Regarding...
- Within...research...

7. Indicate similarities between different research

- Consistent with...finds that...
- Like X, Y...
- Likewise...argues that...
- Similarly, research of...suggests...
- ...is similar to...

8. Indicate contrast between different researches

- Another line of research focuses on...
- Different from/Contrary to...
- From a different point of view, an empirical study examined...
- In contrast/Instead...
- In spite of...
- On the other hand/However/Nonetheless...
- Other studies have confirmed...
- Researchers pay relatively more attention to...
- Some studies supported...whereas/while others suggested that...
- Unlike most...this study...

9. Critique the strengths/inadequacies/inconsistencies/conflicts/problems of previous researches

- However, scant evidence exists that...
- It is less clear that...
- Nevertheless, the results are far from conclusive.
- One reason that these findings are so mixed may be because...
- Scholars have found inconsistent evidence regarding...
- The research has deepened our understanding of...
- Their seminar/pioneering study provides...
- There is limited clarity and agreement about...
- These studies provide a rich and solid foundation for...
- Yet these results contradict views of...

10. Identify a research gap

- Although..., only a limited number of studies have focused on...

- A number of questions regarding...remain to be addressed
- Despite the progress made, there is still a lack of...
- However, only a few studies have explored...
- However, since...there is a need to...
- However...has not been examined/addressed yet.
- Recent studies have overlooked...
- Scholars have mainly focused on...they have neglected...
- Studies examining...from the perspective of...are limited.
- The major limitation of the literature is...
- There are...main gaps or limitations. First...Second,...
- There is also a lack of sufficient empirical evidence that investigates
- To our knowledge, no prior studies have examined...
- While...only limited research to date has explored...

11. Indicate the need to fill the research gap/the need for further research

- Bridging this gap is important, not only for...but also for...
- Filling this gap will advance our understanding of...
- Nevertheless...deserves further research.
- Researchers call for a greater focus on...
- There is a need to fill a research gap on the understanding of...
- Therefore, it is essential to carry out an analysis of...
- Thus, a...approach is required to...
- Thus,...requires further investigation.

12. Present the aim of the present research

- Building upon...this paper studies...
- In doing so, we also seek to...
- In this study, we attempt to contribute to the existing work on...
- The central aim of the study is to examine...
- Therefore, in this study we attempted to...
- Therefore, this research sought to...
- This study aims to add to existing research on...
- To advance the research on...we need to...
- To fill this literature gap, this paper aims to explore...
- To overcome limitations of past studies, this study sought to...

13. Propose research questions/conceptual framework/research hypotheses

- An analytical framework of. . . was proposed.
- Based on the previous literature, the following hypotheses are proposed. . .
- Specifically, we examined the following research questions. . .
- The associated research questions are as follows. . .
- Therefore, these theories provide the theoretical framework for. . .
- Therefore, we hypothesized that. . .
- This paper uses. . . to address two questions. . .
- Thus, there arises the following question: . . .
- To sum up, we formulated/proposed/postulated the following hypotheses. . .
- We thus pose the research question: . . .

IV. Verb tenses in Literature Review

When you write your literature review, you should pay attention to the use of appropriate tenses of verbs. Below are a few guidelines.

When you describe the work done by other researchers, past tense or present perfect tense are often used.

Examples:

- Genc et al. (2019) studied. . .
- Lee and Watkins (2016) have demonstrated. . .
- Earlier studies have addressed the influences of knowledge sharing dynamics on SME performance at the firm level (e. g. Maes & Sels, 2014; Soto-Acosta, Popa, & Palacios-Marqués, 2017).

When you describe commonly known knowledge or generally accepted facts, the present tense is used.

Example:

By deploying international R&D teams, firms are in a better position to generate novel knowledge which in turn improves innovation (Paruchuri & Eisenman, 2012).

When you describe research results that are limited to the specific study, past tense is used.

Example:

Bradford et al. (2019) reported a positive relationship between internal networking and effectiveness in obtaining internal support.

V. Sample analysis

In this part, you will read an excerpt of a Literature Review published in an academic journal. Read it carefully and pay attention to the useful sentence patterns highlighted in bold. Then complete the task after the sample.

Negotiation Beliefs: Comparing Americans and the Chinese
Zhi-Xue Zhang, Leigh Anne Liu, and Li Ma
(Published in *International Business Review*, 2021)

Literature Review

Culture and negotiation

①**Negotiation research has provided insight into** the effects of culture on the outcomes, inputs and processes of negotiation (Gunia, Brett, & Gelfand, 2016; Liu, Adair, Tjosvold, & Poliakova, 2018). ②Negotiation **studies** in cultural contexts **have usually adopted two approaches:** the cross-cultural approach and the monocultural approach. ③The cross-cultural **approach focuses on** comparisons across cultures, **whereas the** monocultural **approach highlights** culturally unique knowledge of how negotiators in a certain culture behave.

④**The literature has demonstrated** significant cross-cultural differences in negotiation (e. g., Adair & Brett, 2004, 2005; Adair et al., 2004; Brett, 2007; Tinsley & Brett, 2001; Tinsley & Pillutla, 1998). ⑤Negotiators who have grown up in different cultures possess differences in their behaviors such as initial offers, the approaches, the concept of time, and the objectives of the negotiation (Ott, 2011). ⑥**For example,** American negotiators exchange information directly and avoid influence, whereas Japanese negotiators exchange information indirectly and use influence but may adapt their behaviors when negotiating with American negotiators (Adair, Okumura, & Brett, 2001). ⑦**Furthermore,** Japanese negotiators were found to use offers earlier in the negotiation than American negotiators to gather information, and American negotiators were found to use offers later in the negotiation to consolidate information (Adair, Weingart, & Brett, 2007). ⑧**In a framework for** negotiating with and within different cultural groups, Ott (2011) **categorized** three activity-based cultures (linear-active, multi-active and reactive) and asked students to position themselves as a cultural type to negotiate a bargaining scenario between a buyer and a seller. ⑨Such effort can help international negotiators understand disagreements that arise due to different cultural mental programs.

⑩**Some scholars have specifically compared** the negotiating behaviors in North America and China.

⑪Tse, Francis, and Walls (1994) asked Canadian and Chinese executives to respond to scenarios involving joint project conflicts with potential partners from their own and the other culture. ⑫**They found that** neither group of executives altered its strategy when negotiating across cultures; also, the Chinese executives were more likely to avoid conflicts; but when conflicts did occur, the Chinese recommended more negative strategies such as negotiation discontinuation and withdrawal. ⑬**Scholars have found that** Chinese negotiators achieve higher joint gains than American negotiators (Arunachalam, Wall, & Chan, 1998). Probably because of the collectivist culture of China, negotiators values group goals more than individual goals. ⑭**In terms of** communication quality felt by negotiators, Americans felt less clarity and more comfort, but their Chinese counterparts felt more clarity and less comfort in cross-cultural negotiations (Adair, Buchan, Chen, & Liu, 2016). ⑮**Compared with** their US counterparts, Chinese negotiators make first offers that are more favorable for themselves, place more importance on competitive goals, engage in more actions directed at trying to gain at the expense of their counterpart and use more influencing tactics (Liu & Wilson, 2011; Rosette, Brett, Barsness, & Lytle, 2011). ⑯**In addition, similarities between** Chinese and American negotiators **also exist because** seeking a win-win solution requires negotiators to show openness and building trust (Adler, Braham, & Graham, 1992).

⑰**Using** monocultural research, **scholars have provided rich descriptions and conceptual analyses of** negotiation behaviors in single cultures (e. g., Blackman, 1997; Ghauri & Fang, 2001; Shenkar & Ronen, 1987). ⑱**For example,** Faure (1998: 140) **proposed that** Chinese people use either "mobile warfare" or "joint quest" to characterize negotiations depending on whether they define the other party as adversaries or "civilized people". ⑲Metcalf and Bird (2004) **offered rich descriptions of** six different countries' negotiation behaviors. ⑳**Whereas** Americans **are described as** market-oriented negotiators whose interests, best alternatives and bottom lines dominate negotiations, Germans **are considered as** having a legal-bureaucratic orientation characterized by following rules rigidly (Morris, Podolny, & Ariel, 2000; Thompson, 2001; Tinsley, 1998).

㉑**Both approaches summarized above have limitations despite the insightful findings.** ㉒Cross-cultural **research has provided explanations for** classic negotiation findings and **identified** boundary conditions for existing theories (Gelfand & Brett, 2004). ㉓**However, such research has posited too many variables to** determine the cultural patterns of negotiation behavior, **without a theoretically grounded framework to** provide an integrated explanation (Brett, Gunia, & Teucher, 2017). ㉔**The** mono-cultural **approach examines** the features of people's negotiation behaviors in a given culture, **but it is not parsimonious and does not address** what happens when negotiators from different cultures meet. ㉕**In this paper, we draw on the findings from the two research streams to** conceptualize and validate negotiation beliefs in the interest of providing a parsimonious account of negotiation behaviors in different cultures, with both culturally similar and different factors of negotiation beliefs.

Task: *Read the sample carefully and identify its sub-moves. Note down the sentence numbers of each sub-move in the table below.*

Moves	Sub-moves	Sentence numbers
1. Give an overview of the literature review		
2. Summarize the existing literature		
3. Evaluate the existing literature		
4. Link the existing literature to the present research		

VI. Summary of the chapter

This chapter focuses on how to write the literature review part. A complete literature review part includes four moves: giving an overview of the literature part, summarizing the existing literature, evaluating the existing literature and linking the existing literature to the present research. But not all writings follow these moves, and some writing may mix literature review with introduction part. It varies depending on the writing purpose or genre.

Chapter 12

Write Methodology

本章进入任务型研究性写作的主体部分——研究方法的写作,讲述研究方法写作要完成的功能和写作结构,学习语言特征以及其他有助于实现有效交际的修辞手段。

Learning objectives

In this chapter, you will learn how to write the Methodology section for a research report. When learning this chapter, you are expected:
- to learn the functions and structure of the Methodology section;
- to learn the language features of the Methodology section;
- to be able to produce effective Methodology writing.

The Methodology section is the first part of the central "report" section and it is like a roadmap leading to the core of the research, guiding the readers through the actual journey the researchers took to reach their destination. It describes actions taken to investigate a research problem and the rationale for the application of specific procedures or techniques used to identify, select, process, and analyze information applied to understanding the problem, thereby, allowing the reader to critically evaluate a study's overall validity and reliability. The writing of the Methodology section should be direct, precise and always in the past tense.

I. Functions of a Methodology section

The Methodology section is an essential element of a research report which answers two main questions: How was the data collected or generated? And, how was it analyzed? It describes clearly the set of approaches, procedures, and experimental materials followed or adopted by the researcher in conducting the research, with the aim of informing readers about the research design and specifically about what was done during the research, exactly how it was done, how results were analyzed and why those procedures were chosen as the most appropriate to achieve the objectives of the research, thus also making it possible for them to replicate the process.

II. Structural features of a Methodology section

The structure of Methodology section varies according to different disciplines, approaches, procedures, and subjects or materials employed in the research. Subheadings are often used to indicate different aspects contained in this section. The structure of the Methodology section is usually summarized into five moves, as is shown below, although not every Methodology section contains all these five moves or follows exactly the same order.

---

1. **Provide a general introduction and overview of the methods**
1.1　The rationale behind the methods
1.2　Relate methods to other studies
1.3　Justify choices made
2. **Restate research aims, questions, or hypotheses**
3. **Provide specific and precise details about the methods (procedures, subjects, materials, location, etc.)**
4. **Discuss the limitations**
5. **Introduce data analysis**

Read the following Methodology section taken from a published research report. Numbers are added in front of the sentences to facilitate the analysis, and useful sentence patterns and phrases are highlighted in bold.

Small Business Performance: A tourism Sector Focus

Alison Morrison and Rivanda Teixeira

(Published in *Journal of Small Business and Enterprise Development*, 2004)

Methodology

①**The empirical research undertaken in this study was of a** qualitative, exploratory and interpretative nature into the complex relationships between small tourism business owner-managers, their internal organization, external environment, and consequences for business performance and enterprise development. ②**It represents** an approach deemed appropriate by Goffee (1996) **and is supported by** Buick et al. (2000) and Frohlich and Pichler (1996). ③**This is on the basis that** it facilitates deeper analysis of more submerged variables, such as the owner-manager's orientation to business, their

---

management capabilities, personal qualities, and social/transactional relationships, representing a move into the "private" domain of the small business. ④**Hill and McGowan (1999) argue that** to fully comprehend these variables and the relationships between them it is imperative to embark on in-depth research, which not only is qualitative but also manifests much of the ethnographic tradition. ⑤Thus, while quantitative measurements have a place in comprehensive survey work such as that carried in the National Survey of Small Tourism and Hospitality Firms (Thomas et al., 2001), the findings can be limited in their communicative capacity in comparison to qualitative exploration (Gibb, 1997; Shaw and Conway, 2000). ⑥**Furthermore, a qualitative approach serves to** recognize the integration of the objective and subjective factors to guard against only partial insights (Gorton, 2000) **and aims to** yield a rich understanding of the key issues which actually affect and may even determine the small business's potential for enterprise development (Hill and McGowan, 1999).

⑦**The study focused on** the urban small tourism business sector. ⑧**A sampling frame was constructed from** the Greater Glasgow and Clyde Valley Area Tourist Board's (2002) directory of tourist accommodation with a total population of 66. ⑨All businesses that conformed to the sample selection criteria of the size of operation (4 – 50 bedrooms), independently owned and not part of a corporate group, and city center location were telephoned, to ascertain their willingness to participate in a face-to-face interview. ⑩**A sample of 22 was secured**, of which hotels accounted for 50 percent, guesthouses 45 percent and bed and breakfasts 5 percent of the sample, and 73 percent had 20 rooms or less. ⑪**The sample can be divided into two categories**: owner-managers who accounted for 86 percent; and 14 percent of employed managers. ⑫ **Thus, it can be said that a judgmental sampling method was adopted**, as random sampling was not possible given the relatively small size of the total population (Wright, 1996), **and the aim was to** obtain a robust sample from which inferences about the population could be drawn (Gummesson, 1991). ⑬**This approach is considered to be appropriate for** exploration and theory development, where **the research aims to** generate theory and a wider understanding of social processes or social actions. ⑭Thus, the representativeness of the sample may be of less importance and the best sampling strategy may be focused on judgmental sampling (Marshall and Rossman, 1989).

⑮**Semi-structured in-depth interviews involving closed and open-ended questions were administered** to each small business in the sample. ⑯In the majority of these businesses, there was either one owner-manager or a dominant owner-manager and this was the person interviewed. ⑰**Questions pertained to** their individual, social and economic contexts, within which they were encouraged to formulate their own responses. ⑱**This is recognized as having considerable advantages over quantitative surveys in** facilitating responses and data in-depth and overcoming individual interviewees' reservations concerning confidentiality (Wright, 1996). ⑲**Interviews were tape-recorded, fully transcribed and the content systematically analyzed**, interpreting patterns that revealed similarities and differences in meanings, actions and/or contexts from the grounded empirical data (Stenbacka, 2001). ⑳Thus, **data collection and analysis worked from an interpretative approach**, involving induction of research categories and frameworks from the interviews, and subsequent refinement until an informative comparative theory about small, urban tourism business performance emerged from the data (Hill and McGowan, 1999).

Move 1: Sentences ①∼⑥ provide an overview of the research method. Sentences ①∼③ are Move 1. 1 which explain the rationale behind the method. Sentences ④∼⑥ are Move 1. 2 and Move 1. 3 which relate methods to other studies and justify the choice made.

Move 2: Sentence ⑬ restates the research's aim.

Move 3: Sentences ⑦∼⑫ and ⑭∼⑲ provide specific and precise details about the method.

Move 5: Sentence ⑳ introduces data analysis.

III. Language features

The following sentence patterns and phrases are frequently and typically used as signals of different moves. The combinations of these patterns can often be found in Methodology sections.

1. Provide a general introduction and overview of the methods

- The empirical research undertaken in this study was of a...
- This research adopts a/an...approach.
- This study draws on data from...
- This study employed a/an...method.
- We deliberately opted for an explorative research approach.
- We apply a comparative case analysis design to...

2. Indicate research aims, questions, or hypotheses

- In an effort to examine..., this project...
- In order to investigate..., this study...
- The aim/objective of this research is...
- The research's aim is to...
- This study aims at...

3. Provide specific details about the method

- A random sample of participants was recruited from...
- A sample of 22 was secured,...
- A sampling frame was constructed from...
- After...had been done,...was conducted.
- Eligible women who matched the selection criteria were identified by...
- It can be said that a judgmental sampling method was adopted.

- Of the 156 participants, 70 were male and 86 were female.
- Prior to the study,... was obtained from...
- The final stage of the study comprised...
- The interview was conducted at...
- The sample can be divided into two categories: ...
- This study was carried out at...
- The subjects participating in this project were recruited from...
- To begin this process,...
- ... followed.
- ... was initially investigated.

4. Discuss the limitations

- Despite the..., this study is still limited in...
- It should be noted that this study only examined...
- The limitations of this experiment are...
- Unfortunately, we are unable to determine from this data...
- We acknowledge the limitations of...

5. Describe how the data was analyzed

- Data collection and analysis worked from an interpretative approach.
- Data were analyzed using...
- Data were computed by...
- The statistical interpretation of the results was performed by...

IV. Sample analysis

In this part, you will read an authentic Methods section published in an academic journal. Read it carefully and pay attention to the useful sentence patterns highlighted in bold. Then complete the task after the sample.

> **Successful social entrepreneurial business models in the context of developing economies:**
>
> **An explorative study**
>
> Johanna Mair and Oliver Schoen
>
> (Published in *International Journal of Emerging Markets*, 2007)
>
> **Methodology**
>
> ①**This paper aims at** identifying features and common patterns across the business models of successful social entrepreneurial organizations. ②**Given** the limited thrust of knowledge on social entrepreneurship, **we deliberately opted for an explorative research approach.** ③**Our focus lies in** gathering

propositions rather than testing hypotheses. ④ **Following** Miles and Huberman（1994）and **Yin** (1984)**, we apply a comparative case analysis design to** capture the complexity and richness of the underlying phenomenon and to detect patterns and regularities across cases.

⑤The selection of cases **was based on** the following criteria. ⑥First, the social entrepreneurial organization had to be widely recognized as successful and should have successfully mastered the transition from the venture stage to a self-sustained organization. ⑦Second, the cases had to reflect diverse regional realities. ⑧Special attention was given to organizations operating in emerging economies. ⑨By adopting a global approach we hoped to reveal patterns and features that hold across regional and national boundaries. ⑩Finally, priority was given to organizations, which had been previously described documented and were open for additional data gathering via interviews.

⑪**We gathered data from several sources**: existing case studies, published and unpublished reports and articles, personal interviews with the founders（GB and Sekem）, and organization members (GB, Sekem, and MCC), informed observations（Sekem）, and internet sources. ⑫**These data helped us to** identify patterns and compare them across cases. ⑬ **We acknowledge the limitations of** our sampling and data analysis approach, **however, we consider this study to be an important first step in** providing tentative propositions for a more inclusive empirical research agenda in the future.

Task: *Read the sample carefully and identify its sub-moves. Note down the sentence numbers of each sub-move in the table below.*

Moves	Sub-moves	Sentence numbers
1. Provide a general introduction and overview of the methods		
2. Restate research aims, questions, or hypotheses		
3. Provide specific and precise details about the methods (procedures, subjects, materials, location, etc.)		
4. Discuss the limitations		
5. Introduce data analysis		

V. Summary of the chapter

This chapter focuses on how to write the Methodology section. A complete Methodology section usually includes five moves: introducing the methods used, restating research aims, questions or hypotheses, providing specific and precise details about the methods, discussing the limitations and introducing data analysis. However, the structure of Methodology sections may vary according to different disciplines, approaches, etc., therefore, not every Methodology section contains all these five moves or follows exactly the same order.

Chapter 13

Write Results

结果部分承接研究方法部分,属于论文写作的核心。本章讲述结果部分的功能、结构、语言特征以及其他有助于实现有效交际的修辞手段。

Learning objectives

In this chapter, you will learn how to write the Results section for a research report. When learning this chapter, you are expected:

● to learn the functions and structure of the Results section;

● to learn the language features of the Results section;

● to be able to produce effective Results writing.

The Results section of a research report represents the core findings of a study derived from the methods applied to gather and analyze information. It presents these findings in a logical sequence without bias or interpretation from the author, preparing for later interpretation and evaluation in the Discussion section. A major purpose of the Results section is to break down the data into sentences that show its significance to the research question(s).

I. Functions of a Results section

In most cases, the results of your research can be given in graphs, tables, equations or images. Why, then, should you bother to write a Results section? Thinking about this question is a good way to begin to understand the functions of this section. Since a

Results section can be found in almost all research reports, it is clear that some things cannot be achieved by just using tables, graphs or other images of your results. They can be achieved only by using words. A Results section usually serves the following functions. First, it enables you to communicate some of your results which are more interesting or significant than others. Second, it enables you to relate your results to the aim(s) of the research. Third, it enables you to offer some background information to explain why a particular result occurred, or to compare your results with those of other researchers. Besides, your results may be problematic and you want to suggest possible reasons for this. Results do not speak for themselves, therefore, we need to write a Results section.

II. Structural features

Although variations exist, most Results sections follow a three-move structure with more or fewer sub-moves, as shown below.

---

1. Provide context information
1.1　Revisiting the research aim/existing research
1.2　Revisiting/Expanding methodology
1.3　General overview of results
2. Present results in text forms
2.1　Invitation to view results
2.2　Provide specific/key results in detail, with or without explanations
2.3　Compare results with model predictions or results in other research
3. Problems with results
4. Possible implications of results

Read the following Results section taken from a published research report. Numbers are added in front of the sentences to facilitate the analysis, and useful sentence patterns and phrases are highlighted in bold.

Research Rigor and the Gap Between Academic Journals and Business Practitioners

Eva Perea and Malcolm Brady

(Published in *Journal of Management Development*, 2017)

Findings

①**Practically all the persons who participated in the survey declared that** they read some sort of publication with only two out of 156 not reading any professional publication at all. ② The most popular publications are "Daily newspapers" and "Sector-specific newsletters", with about 56 – 57 percent of the respondents. ③ They are followed by "Magazines" (half of the respondents) and "Management books" with 38 percent (see Figure 3).

④**Regarding** the frequency with which respondents read business articles, **most persons declared**

---

that they read "Once a week" (44 percent) and "Daily" (33 percent), **which shows that** professionals are very interested in reading contents about business (see Figure 4). ⑤**It can be stated therefore that** business people do read and are keen on business knowledge: 78 percent of them actually read at least on a weekly basis.

⑥Respondents are afterwards asked whether they are familiar or not with academic journals related to their sector of activity. ⑦**Only 40 percent declare** to be familiar, **while 60 percent** do not know them at all (see Figure 5), **which shows that** academic journals are not very popular amongst business professionals, even when they have a high level of studies and several years of working experience. ⑧**Moreover**, in many respondents' minds, there appears to be a certain confusion as to what an academic journal actually is, and many would consider a professional publication (e.g. "Pulp and Paper International" or "Moneday Crédito") to be an academic journal.

⑨Having established a low level of familiarity with academic journals, respondents are asked to explain what that ideal journal would be for them. ⑩**According to** the business practitioners **who were surveyed**, the characteristics of ideal academic journals should be: accessible online, written by experienced business people, and should contain business cases: those are very clear the three main requirement journals should satisfy according to practitioners (Figure 6). ⑪They may focus on sector specifics or cover general business knowledge: there is less agreement on this point.

⑫On the other hand, the three factors that practitioners value the least are that: they are free of charge (so apparently, they would be willing to pay for practical knowledge); they contain theoretical research; and they are written by renowned academics (Figure 6). ⑬**There seems to be a very clear preference toward** practical experience rather than theoretical knowledge.

⑭Respondents were asked what, from a practitioner viewpoint, the ideal focus of an academic journal should be on. ⑮**The findings showed that** the most important areas of focus are: practical cases, best practice sharing, and dissemination of new management ideas (see Figure 7). ⑯The least focus should be placed on student education and academic research. ⑰However, practitioners also regarded building bridges between academia and practice as an important focus of academic journals.

⑱**Summarizing, the majority of respondents expressed** a wish to have "free and easy access to practical, simply written, 'best practice sharing' papers that can help them be more efficient in their jobs." ⑲In many respondents' minds, there appears to be confusion as to what an academic journal actually is, and many would consider a professional publication to be an academic journal. ⑳**The majority are not aware of** the existence of academic journals related to their sector of activity.

㉑At the end of the interviews, several general questions were asked of business professionals regarding their opinion on academic journals. ㉒**From their answers, it can be stated that** academic journals are not very well known by these professionals (only about 20 percent know them well or very well). ㉓**Only one-third of the respondents believe that** academic journals offer relevant or very relevant information for business leaders. ㉔While this seems to be certainly quite negative, there is hope: **almost 60 percent of the respondents would like to** know more about academic journals.

㉕**More detailed findings show that** more women than men believe that journals should focus on best practice sharing; more young people below 40 years old than people over 40 would be interested in seeing Finance and Accounting topics; top managers prefer academic journals to focus on best practice sharing and dissemination of new management ideas, more so than middle managers or employees; managers with higher education levels prefer that academic journals are written by renowned academics (which is not the case in lower education levels). ㉖**Apart from the ones mentioned above, no significant differences have been found** between independent variables (gender, age, number of years at work, education level and position in the company) and the preferences for academic journals. ㉗Here are a few key selected quotes from respondents' comments:

- "should be readable by the layman";
- "accessible online";
- "case studies";
- "partner with experienced business leaders";
- "should apply to business";
- "exec summary free of charge, full article on per event fee"; and
- "available as 'app'".

㉘**One interesting observation is that** the existence of Google Scholar is not mentioned once by any respondent. ㉙Leaving aside the pricing aspect and the issue of adapting the writing style to a business readership, tools such as Google Scholar would appear to answer all other requirements regarding accessibility. ㉚**One possible additional issue which does not appear as clearly identifiable from the survey results is that** business people often expect reading material to "land" on their desks, rather than have to look for it. ㉛Availability of information does not mean access to, and use of, information.

Move 1: Sentences ①~③ are Move 1.3, which gives a general overview of the results.

Move 2: Sentences ④~㉗ are Move 2.2, which provides a systematic textual description of key findings in a logical order, with or without explanations.

Move 3: Sentences ㉘~㉛ point out some problems with the results.

III. Language features

The Results section should be written concisely and objectively. The following sentence patterns and phrases are frequently and typically used as signals of different moves.

1. Revisiting the research aim/existing research

- As mentioned previously, the aim of the study was to...
- In earlier studies attempts were made to...
- In order to..., this study investigated...
- In order to..., we examined...
- It is important to reiterate that...
- Since..., ...was investigated experimentally.
- The main purpose of this work was to...
- To..., this paper examined...

- To investigate..., we needed to...
- We reasoned/predicted that...

2. Revisiting/Expanding methodology

- In order to evaluate..., we adopted...
- In order to examine..., we employed...
- In order to investigate..., we used...
- Simple statistical analysis was used to...
- The correlation between X and Y was tested using...

3. General overview of results

- Generally speaking,...
- In most/all cases,...
- In this section, we compare/evaluate/present...
- It is apparent that in all/most/the majority of cases,...
- It is evident from the results that...
- On the whole...
- The overall response was...
- The results are divided into two parts as follows:
- Using the method described above, we obtained...

4. Invitation to view results

- As detailed in Table 1/Figure 1,...
- As evident from/in Table 1/Figure 1,...
- As illustrated by Table 1/Figure 1,...
- As indicated/listed/shown in Table 1/Figure 1,...
- As we can see from/in Table 1/Figure 1,...
- Comparing Figs. 1 and 4 show that...
- Data in Table 1/Figure 1 suggest that...
- Evidence for this is in Table 1/Figure 1...
- From Table 1/Figure 1 it can be seen that...
- In Table 1/Figure 1 we compare/present etc....
- Inspection of Table 1/Figure 1 indicates...
- Results are given in Table 1/Figure 1.
- Table 1/Figure 1 displays the summary statistics for...
- Table 1/Figure 1 offers a breakdown...
- Table 1/Figure 1 provides an overview of...

- Table 1/Figure 1 shows/illustrates/indicates...
- Table 1/Figure 1 summarizes the results obtained from...
- We observe from Table 1/Figure 1 that...
- ...can be found in Table 1/Figure 1.
- ...can be identified from/in Table 1/Figure 1.
- ...can be observed in Table 1/Figure 1.
- ...can be seen from/in Table 1/Figure 1.
- ...is/are given in Table 1/Figure 1.
- ...is/are represented in Table 1/Figure 1.
- ...is/are visible in Table 1/Figure 1.

5. Provide specific/key results in detail, with or without explanations

- A total of...(number or percentage) of participants/subjects reported that...
- All...(number) of the participants stated that...
- Of the...(number) participants,...(number/percentage) reported that...
- Of the...(number) respondents to the survey,...(number) indicated that...
- Practically all the persons who participated in the survey declared that...

6. Compare results with model predictions or results in other research

- ...are almost identical in both cases.
- ...are parallel to the experimental data from corresponding tests.
- As expected,...is consistent with...
- As mentioned earlier,...is in line with...
- Contrary to earlier speculation (Shaw, 1996), this survey indicated that...
- In contrast,...this survey found...
- It is evident that the results obtained here are in exceptionally good agreement with...
- This contrasts with...
- This is comparable to Collins and Wartick (1995)...

7. Problems with results

- Although this was not obtained experimentally, it...
- Future work should therefore...
- It is difficult to...
- It should, however, be noted that...
- Nevertheless,...is only...
- Reasonable results were obtained...
- ...is of no significance.

8. Possible implications of results

- It could be assumed that...
- It could be concluded that...
- It could be inferred therefore that...may...
- It is conceivable that...
- It is evident that...
- It is, therefore, speculated that...
- It seems plausible that...
- This indicates that...
- This suggests that...
- We have confidence that...

IV. Sample analysis

In this part, you will read an authentic Results section published in an academic journal. Read it carefully and pay attention to the useful sentence patterns highlighted in bold. Then complete the task after the sample.

> **Getting Ready for the Young Generation to Join the Workforce: A Comparative Analysis of the Work Values of Chinese and Slovenian business students**
>
> Nada Zupan
>
> (Published in *East European Management*, 2001)
>
> **Results**
>
> ① **Table 2 presents** the six most and least important work values for both student samples. ② *Advancement* is the most important work value among the Chinese and Slovenia business students. ③ Further, *achievement and friendly co-workers* are two other factors that rank among the top six work values in both countries. ④ Among the bottom six work values, *influence*, *authority* and *impact* are the same for both countries. ⑤ **Interestingly, all of them relate to** prestige work values.

Table 2 Work values of the Slovenian and Chinese business students

Top six work values		Bottom six work values	
Slovenia	China	Slovenia	China
Advancement	Advancement	Influence	Authority
Interesting work	Continuously learn	Prestigious job	Impact
Salary	Co-workers	Social interaction	Use abilities
Achievement	Fun	Impact	Help people
Information	Achievement	Variety	Freedom
Co-workers	Job security	Authority	Influence

⑥We performed a multivariate test to determine if the means of the four work values are significantly different between the two student samples. ⑦Pillai's Trace value of 0.66 was significant (F = 15.38; df = 4; p = 0.000), indicating the centroids of the mean vectors of the two groups were different. ⑧**This offers initial support for Hypothesis 1**, generally indicating significant differences in work values between the Chinese and Slovenian business students.

⑨**Figure 1 shows** a detailed comparison between female and male students in both countries. ⑩Slovenian female students stand out with the highest score for instrumental work values, while Slovenian male students stand out with the lowest score for social-altruistic work values. ⑪**Overall, the results presented in Figure 1 show that**, although national culture is an important factor in shaping work values, gender also plays a very important role.

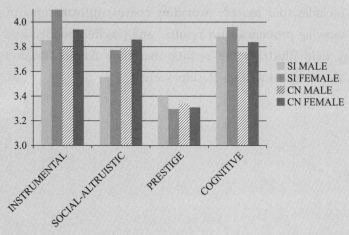

Figure 1　Comparison of work value dimensions for the Slovenian and Chinese students

⑫We also controlled for the effect of work experience. ⑬Multivariate results were significant for both factors and the covariate (Pillai's Trace was 0.02 for work experience, 0.067 for national culture, 0.068 for gender and 0.013 for interaction between national culture and gender; all $p <$ 0.05). ⑭**A more detailed examination reveals that** work experience significantly affects prestige (p = 0.002) and cognitive (p = 0.022) work values. ⑮Even after introducing work experience as a covariate, gender still significantly affects social-altruistic (p = 0.001), cognitive (p = 0.034) and instrumental (p = 0.000) work values. ⑯However, national culture now significantly affects only social-altruistic (p = 0.000) and instrumental (p = 0.002) work values. ⑰**These results offer further support for Hypotheses 1.1 and 1.2, as well as Hypothesis 2**. ⑱Therefore, while some variability in the work values of business students can be attributed to the national culture, the latter is not the only demographic factor shaping the work values of business students, let alone the most salient one.

Task: Read the sample carefully and identify its sub-moves. Note down the sentence numbers of each sub-move in the table below.

Moves	Sub-moves	Sentence numbers
1. Provide context information		
2. Present findings in text forms		
3. Problems with results		
4. Possible implications of results		

V. Summary of the chapter

This chapter focuses on how to write the Results section. A complete Results section usually includes four moves: providing context information, presenting results in text forms, showing problems with results, and possible implications of the results. Visual aids may help illustrate the results, but they do not speak for themselves. Therefore, it's necessary to write a Results section.

Chapter 14

Write Discussion

讨论部分与结果部分的差异在于,前者是基于后者客观事实基础上的主观诠释。讨论部分要完成研究结果的理论探讨和实践价值的延伸。本章讲述讨论部分的功能、结构、语言特征和其他实现交际目的的修辞手段。

Learning objectives

In this chapter, you will learn how to write the Discussion section for a research report. When learning this chapter, you are expected:
- to learn the functions and structure of the Discussion section,
- to learn the language features of the Discussion section, and
- to be able to produce effective Discussion writing.

The Discussion section is regarded as the core section of a research report. In this section, you will discuss how the research questions or the hypotheses have been demonstrated by the new research and then show how the field's knowledge has been changed by the addition of this new data. While the Introduction starts generally and narrows down to the specific research questions or hypotheses, the Discussion section starts with the interpretation of the results, then moves outwards to contextualize these findings in the general field.

In the shorter version of a research report, the Discussion section also serves as a conclusion. In the longer version of a report, where there are multiple findings, the Discussion is usually a separate section, and a separate conclusion section is provided to summarize the findings.

I. Functions of a Discussion section

The Discussion section has very clear functions, that is to answer the research questions posed in the Introduction section by stating what the results mean and how they fit with your theoretical framework and the literature you reviewed earlier. It serves as a bridge between the current research and the previous related research, and helps to find and claim a position. It also makes suggestions for future research.

II. Structural Features of a Discussion section

---

1. Revisit previous sections
1.1　Revisit the Introduction or Methodology section
1.2　Summarize and report key results
2. Discuss the key results
Make claims, explain the results, compare the new work with previous studies, offer alternative explanations.
3. State the achievements or contributions and refine the implications
4. State the limitations of the study
5. Make recommendations for future implementation and/or for future research

---

Read the following Discussion section taken from a published research report. Numbers are added in front of the sentences to facilitate the analysis, and useful sentence patterns and phrases are highlighted in bold.

Economic Value for University Services Modelling and Heterogeneity Analysis

Raquel Sánchez-Fernández, David Jiménez-Castillo, Angeles Iniesta-Bonillo

(Published in *International Journal of Market Research*, 2017)

Discussion and implications

①**This research shows that** perceived economic value in higher education is a complex concept that can be explained by several sources or dimensions. ②**Our findings also demonstrate that** these dimensions generate economic value for alumni and increase their satisfaction, and in turn their organizational identification and perceived image. ③**Furthermore, the results show** the existence of heterogeneity in alumni response to all of the relationships in the model. ④**We have identified** at least two different segments in which the sources of economic value and organizational identification differed. ⑤Those aspects are crucial for universities to be successful in their differentiation strategies.

⑥Regarding the relationship between perceived economic value and satisfaction, **our study provides additional insight to** previous research by confirming this relationship using a multidimensional structure of economic value adapted to the particular context of higher education. ⑦Accordingly, universities might overcome the traditional definition of economic value as a cost, adopt a more contemporary view based on its use as a management tool to fulfill market needs, and enhance their understanding of the dimensions that compose it. ⑧These organizations in turn should acknowledge the relevance of this concept and seek to improve alumni perceptions of economic value to ensure satisfaction by enhancing student-professor interaction quality, university facilities and services, and academic education. ⑨**Several studies have highlighted** the critical role of alumni satisfaction in institutional management. ⑩**As Sung and Yang (2009) have pointed out**, the use of scarce resources for the common practice of persuading the entire alumni population to make donations, or investing considerable resources in maintaining a good reputation through media or external ranking programs, may be inefficient. ⑪The single strongest determinant of an intention of support by current students is good relational outcomes based on active communication and satisfaction with their experience. ⑫Satisfied alumni will help educational institutions financially, provide positive word-of-mouth communication and provide jobs for graduates (see Hartman & Schmidt, 1995).

⑬**This study contributes to** the literature on organizational identification by demonstrating that the more satisfied alumni are with their university's service offerings, the greater is their identification. ⑭**Therefore, our results could help** professionals in institutions of higher education understand alumni's rationale for maintaining long-lasting relationships and respond accordingly. ⑮That response could eventually improve their perceived economic value and create satisfaction, which in turn affects organizational identification. ⑯**It is important to note that** alumni organizational identification could be a determinant for future behaviors, such as increased funding or promotion of the university (e. g. Porter et al. , 2011).

⑰**Despite** the trend towards stronger market orientation and commercial focus in universities, building up brand image in universities and other educational institutions **is likely to remain a challenge**. ⑱**This paper contributes to** this topic by demonstrating the role of satisfaction in constructing perceived organizational image. ⑲A favorable evaluation of satisfaction creates alumni's positive university image. ⑳This is important to universities as it provides insight into how to counter competitors' offerings. ㉑**This study confirms that** organizational identification also depends on the internal evaluation of image. ㉒Therefore, positive perceived image would not only contribute to university differentiation in the market, but also have a positive influence on alumni organizational identification.

㉓**Concerning the second objective of our study**, uncovering unobserved heterogeneity, **the paper contributes to** the literature on segmentation in the context of higher education. ㉔**We used** perceptual variables and evaluative judgements in a structural model **to** identify segments, going beyond the traditional individual descriptive characteristics or behaviors as segmentation bases. ㉕Thus **this study uncovered** unobserved heterogeneity in the alumni market through a nomological network of relationships between unobserved variables using FIMIX-PLS. ㉖**It provides an innovative view of** how higher educational institutions can improve market orientation by segmenting the alumni market to create and/or add value for the resulting groups. ㉗In particular, **it is important to note that** the different behaviors of the two groups found are due to their distinct perceptual and evaluative patterns. ㉘The first segment (78.4%), alumni highly receptive to university services, is composed of alumni who attach considerable importance to the value generated by their academic education, though the quality of student-professor interaction and perception of university facilities and services are also significant sources of economic value. ㉙Whether or not a university aims to create a stronger and more durable attachment with its alumni, it should attempt to enhance satisfaction in this segment through services based on the three dimensions of economic value. ㉚ In this segment, achieving higher levels of satisfaction also leads to a highly favorable image towards universities, which in turn increases organizational identification. ㉛**These results suggest that** this segment is formed by individuals who are more open and receptive to marketing actions related to university services, which provides universities with several alternatives for achieving their alumni's satisfaction and identification.

㉜The second segment (21.6%), alumni less receptive to university services, comprises a large number of alumni whose perceived economic value is influenced only by the academic education received. ㉝Thus, teaching methodologies and training programs would be critical for targeting this audience. ㉞It is also logical for the lack of significance of the value source related to university facilities and services in the overall model to be determined by the behavior of economic value in this segment. ㉟Identification of these alumni with the university is not affected by their satisfaction, but only by university image. ㊱**These results lead us to think that**, for this segment, sources other than economic value, such as social or hedonic (Holbrook, 1999), could improve satisfaction, and ultimately perceived image and organizational identification.

㊲**To summarize**, the proposed perceived economic value model and heterogeneity detected among alumni provide useful insights for universities. ㊳Differentiation from competitors, as one of the main strategies of universities, can be achieved not only by reinforcing image-oriented communication tools, but also through service-related economic value provided by these institutions. ㊴Differentiation would be even more successful if universities explored the potential existence of segments first, using models of relationships among unobserved variables as the segmentation basis. ㊵**The identification of these segments or subgroups would help** universities to design and develop suitable positioning strategies.

Limitations and future research

㊶**This study has several limitations** that should be considered in further research. ㊷First, as our model focused on economic value, a potential extension of this study could investigate whether the results vary when other specific dimensions of perceived value, such as social, altruistic or hedonic values, are analyzed. ㊸Second, a comparative analysis with other universities could make our findings more generalizable. ㊹For example, replication studies could use techniques such as FIMIX-PLS to explore unobserved heterogeneity in public or private universities and universities in other countries. ㊺Third, the cross-sectional nature of this research raises the need to conduct a longitudinal study to test potential variations in the results of the model and segment behaviors. ㊻Finally, **it may be interesting for further research to** test the effects of other variables in the model, such as trust, commitment or switching costs, or even the phenomenon of reverse causality in the relationship between value and satisfaction, identification and image. ㊼Moreover, **in the future, new insights into** the role of value in the development and improvement of decisions involving service design, strategic positioning, and value co-creation **must be sought**.

Move 1: Sentence ① forms Move 1.1 which revisits the research problem. Sentences ②~⑤ form Move 1.2 which summarizes and reports the key results.

Move 2: Sentences ⑥~⑫ discuss the key results.

Move 3: Sentences ⑬~⑳ state the contributions and implications of the research.

Move 4: Sentences ㊶~㊺ state the limitations of the research.

Move 5: Sentences ㊻~㊼ make recommendations for future research.

III. Language features

The following sentence patterns and phrases are frequently and typically used as signals of different moves. The combinations of these patterns can often be found in Discussion sections.

1. Revisit the research problems, purposes, theory, or methodology of the study

- In this paper, we examined...
- In this paper, we used...to evaluate...
- The aim of the study is to...
- This paper aims at...
- This paper explored...
- This study adopts...approach to...
- This study employs...method to...
- This study examined...
- This study showed...

2. Summarize and report the key results

- An increase was observed.
- As indicated by the data...
- As shown in the findings...
- The findings demonstrated that...
- The findings suggested...
- The number of...dropped.
- The number of...peaked at...
- The number of...remained unchanged.
- The number of...went up.
- The results indicated...
- The results showed...

3. Make claims based on the results

- According to some earlier studies,...
- According to this preliminary study,...
- Based on previous surveys,...
- Based on the limited data available,...
- In the view of many scholars,...
- It is rather clear that...
- It seems that...has a positive/negative impact on...
- The results are compatible with...
- The results confirm the theory of...
- The results correspond to the idea that...
- The results offer support/no support for the idea that...
- The results provide/show clear evidence of...
- The results revealed that...
- The results suggest that...
- There is a definite possibility that...
- There is a slight possibility that...
- This study discovered that...

4. Explain the results

- Because of...
- Due to...
- Since...
- ...may/might be caused by...
- ...may/might be one of the reasons that...
- ...may/might be the reason that...
- ...may/might explain...
- ...may/might help explain...
- ...may/might provide an explanation for...
- ...may/might result in...

5. Compare the new work with the previous studies

- Compared with the previous studies, the current study...
- Contrary to the results in the previous studies, the current study...
- In agreement with the previous studies, the current study...
- In consistent with the results in the previous studies, the current study...

- In contrast to the results in the previous studies, the current study...
- The findings challenge the theory that...
- The findings confirm the theory...
- The findings support the idea that...
- The results are congruent with those from previous research.
- The results are consistent with those from previous studies.
- The results are in agreement with those from previous studies.
- The results contrast with those from previous studies.
- The results correspond to those from previous research.

6. State the achievements or contributions and refine the implications

- ...is a novel finding.
- Our data rule out the possibility that...
- Our results provide a clear distinction between...
- Our results provide compelling evidence that...
- Our study provides the framework for...
- This paper contributes to...
- We have derived exact...
- We have made the surprising observation that...
- We identify dramatically...

7. State the limitations of the study

- Due to..., this study has not been able to...
- It should be noted that the outcome of this study cannot be taken as evidence for...
- It should be noted that this study only examined...
- Our methods are restricted to...
- The lack of...means that we cannot be certain...
- The results cannot be used to determine...
- There are a number of limitations in this study.
- This study has some limitations.
- This study only addressed the question of...
- We have ignored...

8. Make recommendations for future implementation and/or for future research

- Further studies involving...are expected to...
- Future studies using...would be worthwhile.
- Future work should...

- In future, care should be taken...
- In future, it is advised that...
- It is expected that further analysis of...will be significant in...
- It remains to be proved that...
- It would be beneficial that...
- Replication of this study using...may further elaborate...
- ...proves to be a fruitful direction for future research.
- ...remains to be further studied.
- ...should be replicated.
- ...warrants further investigation.

IV. Sample analysis

In this part, you will read an authentic Discussion section published in an academic journal. Read it carefully and pay attention to the useful sentence patterns highlighted in bold. Then complete the task after the sample.

Exploring Business Ethics Research in the Context of International Business
Christopher J. Robertson and Nicholas Athanassiou
(Published in *Management Research News*, 2009)

Discussion

①**Our results suggest that** variation in the number of articles and themes published in the top international business journals appears to exist. ②**Further, we have identified** thematic clusters that will help future international business ethics researchers clarify both well-received topics in these journals as well as gaps in topical coverage. ③A firm's success in international business depends greatly on the quality of the firm's strategy conceptualization and execution overseas across national borders. ④A major component of strategy implementation is the successful integration of activities across borders while achieving an appropriate local responsiveness (Prahalad and Doz, 1987; Bartlett and Ghoshal, 1989). ⑤Ethical behavior is a key element of such implementation. ⑥Ethics are culturally constrained and a firm must understand the impact of ethical behavior differences among national cultures and among the firm's corporate culture and such environmental imperatives. ⑦**This suggestion is supported by** research that tells us that a primary means of integration across borders is "normative integration", i.e. integration that depends on creating a set of accepted norms across the multinational corporation's activities (Edström and Galbraith, 1977; Boyacigiller, 1990; Roth et al., 1991). ⑧Such norms have ethics underpinnings.

⑨**Research that examines** ethical dimensions of international business practices at the organizational and managerial levels of analysis **has focused on** aspects of understanding the ethical theory explanations of managerial decisions, the risks involved in breaking laws and moral norms, the corporate efforts to establish rules to minimise such risks, the firm's ability to take care of workers' needs, and, more recently, in the past decade, environmental issues. ⑩**There is still a long way to go, however, for us to** understand how managers apply ethical norms to particular situations and how they can be sensitized and trained to bridge cultural gaps in ethical perceptions. ⑪**More importantly, there appears to be a need to** establish how ethical behavior can be related to positive international business performance. ⑫**This latter aspect can become very important given** global point-to-point competition among MNCs that draw on very different cultural backgrounds to establish their overseas strategies and their implementation processes.

⑬Although **our intention in this meta-analysis was to examine** the state of business ethics research published in top international business journals, we recognize that international business ethics research is also published in a variety of other outlets, such as *Journal of Business Ethics, Journal of Business Research, Academy of Management Journal, and Business Ethics Quarterly.* ⑭ *Journal of Business Ethics,* although primarily a target of ethics researchers rather than international business researchers, does have an International Management section and is the only ethics journal to appear on the *Financial Times* 40 journal list. ⑮Therefore **we decided to perform a follow up analysis of** all articles published during the same ten-year period (1996 – 2005) for comparative purposes. ⑯**In Table VII the results of this endeavor are presented.** ⑰**It should be noted** that *Journal of Business Ethics* (JBE) published more issues per year than JWB, JIBS or MIR.

⑱**An examination of** the *Journal of Business Ethics* data **reveals** a few interesting patterns. ⑲First, during our analysis new topics were identified and we had to determine what constitutes international research. ⑳Second, **partly due to** the publication of more articles per year than JIBS, MIR and JWB combined, a higher total number of international business ethics articles with cross-border implications were published over the review period (62 in JBE versus 42 in the three IB journals). ㉑**We identified** 48 different ethics themes in the published international business ethics articles in JBE during the review period, and many that were not represented in the three IB journals such as buying counterfeit products, receiving and giving of gifts, ethical perceptions of expatriates and employee trust. ㉒**We also noted that** JBE published 123 single-country, non-US, studies of ethical topics during the ten-year time frame. ㉓**Interestingly, the percentage of** multi-nation articles in JBE (3.70 percent) **was below that of** MIR (4.29 percent) and JWB (7.35 percent) during the period. ㉔Multi-nation studies are the primary focus of international business journals. ㉕Thus, **we are confident that this study** that is based on JIBS, MIR and JWB **produces conclusions on** international business ethics research that is broadly representative of this field's inquiry.

Managerial implications

㉖**A number of implications for** managers and international marketers **can be discerned from this research.** ㉗First, obtaining a more detailed understanding of which topics are the most salient in the academic literature can help practitioners better ascertain not only the frequently studied topics but also the topics that have been overlooked by scholars. ㉘This gap can potentially be bridged based on feedback from managers related to their actual real-world experiences with diverse ethical issues in international business. ㉙Second, our efforts related to the creation of ethical themes (as presented in Table VI) can help practitioners in their efforts to deliver focused and clustered ethical training programs. ㉚It is quite challenging to collapse the multitude of plausible moral dilemmas into sub-categories, yet we hope that our attempt has added value. ㉛And third, our research has yielded a total of 42 key articles over a ten-year period that address a wide array of ethical issues in international business. ㉜This synthesis should save both managers and practitioner-focused journals interested in these topics a significant amount of time and effort when searching for specific information related to a content area covered by our meta-analysis.

㉝From a corporate code of ethics perspective **our research can also be utilized by** managers and corporate governance teams charged with developing policies related to employee behavior in different national contexts. ㉞Indeed, many firms take into account local cultural norms and laws when developing policies for foreign subsidiaries or contract manufacturers. ㉟Some of the topics that we have identified, such as compliance, computer ethics, and ethical beliefs, vary substantially from country to country and **the research that we have identified can prove useful in future policy development.**

Future research directions and limitations

㊱The seven thematic areas identified in our analysis can be seen as a template for international business ethics research topics. ㊲Within the seven clusters the areas of corporate governance, fair treatment of workers, corporate social responsibility and environmental degradation **appear to have been less examined by** researchers when compared to the three most prominent topics. ㊳Yet **the narrow sample of** journals included in our analysis, **and the intentional avoidance of** mainstream management and ethics journals, **may have led to a less than comprehensive identification of** the total population of international ethics research over the review period.

㊴**Future research in the area of** international business ethics **may fall into different clusters or topical categories**. ㊵**Further researchers may** elect to bridge two or more areas in their research endeavors, such as studying the intersection between ethical judgment analysis and environmental degradation. ㊶International economic and political patterns experienced in recent years, such as falling trade barriers and the global war on terrorism, **may also result in** additional topics that have been either overlooked or deemed less significant historically.

㊷**One limitation in this line of research is the lack of** a formal guideline related to what constitutes "ethics focused" research. ㊸Indeed, some element of subjectivity will always find its way into moral debates in the literature. ㊹**Another limitation is the lack of** empirical data that exists related to determining thematic ethics clusters. ㊺**We encourage future researchers to** collect data and test how ethical variables and themes hang together so that we can collectively work toward more defined constructs.

㊻**This research paper has been a first step at** understanding how international business researchers have started grappling with the challenge of understanding ethical strategies in the international business arena. ㊼**Based on** our resulting summaries of publication patterns and themes, **it can be deduced that** a very low percentage of articles with an explicit focus on ethical behavior across borders have been published in mainstream international business journals. ㊽Starting with the template of articles summarized in this study, **future researchers in the field can** assess what needs to be further studied and how to build on work concluded to date.

Task: *Read the sample carefully and identify its sub-moves. Note down the sentence numbers of each sub-move in the table below.*

Moves	Sub-moves	Sentence numbers
1. Revisit previous sections		
2. Discuss the key results		
3. State the achievements or contributions and refine the implications		
4. State the limitations of the study		
5. Make recommendations for future implementation and/or for future research		

V. Summary of the chapter

This chapter focuses on how to write the Discussion section. This section usually includes five moves: revisiting previous sections, discussing key results, stating the contributions and refining the implications, stating the limitations, and making recommendations for future research. The language style in this section should be clear and concise. Appropriate stance markers which help qualify or moderate a claim should be used.

Chapter 15

Write Conclusion

结论部分是对全文的回顾。本章讲述结论部分的功能、结构、语言特征和其他实现有效交际的修辞策略。

Learning objectives

When learning this chapter, you are expected:

- to learn the functions and structure of the Conclusion section,
- to learn the language features of the Conclusion section, and
- to be able to produce effective Conclusion writing.

A research report usually ends with an overall conclusion, though it may not necessarily be headed as such. Sometimes it can stand independently, or it can be a merging part of Discussion and Conclusions, or Conclusions and Suggestions. Sometimes, it is also headed as "Limitations and Future Direction". In contrast to the Introduction section which goes from general to specific in terms of information flow, the Conclusion section is characterized by running from specific to general and therefore places the research in a larger context. So the focus of this section should be on what you have found and, especially, on what your findings mean.

I. Functions of a Conclusion section

The Conclusion section provides a generalized review and evaluation of the research. It guides the reader to move from the concise summary of the principal findings to more theoretical or abstract comment of the research. It is also inclined to provide implications or applications of the investigation.

II. Structural Features of a Conclusion section

There is not a standard structure of the Conclusion section, but the following four moves frequently appear in separate Conclusion sections.

---

1. Summarize the present research
1.1　Restate the motivation of the research
1.2　Review the objective of the research
1.3　Highlight the major or overall findings
2. Evaluate the present research positively
2.1　Contrast the present and previous studies
2.2　Highlight the merits of the present study
3. Discuss the limitations of the present research
3.1　Indicate the limitations
3.2　Give a justification or explanation
4. Provide a deduction
4.1　Indicate research implications and/or possible applications
4.2　Recommend future research

Read the following Conclusion section taken from a published research report. Numbers are added in front of the sentences to facilitate the analysis, and useful sentence patterns and phrases are highlighted in bold.

Business Ethics, Corporate Social Responsibility, and Brand Attitudes: An Exploratory Study

O. C. Ferrella, Dana E. Harrisonb, Linda Ferrellc, Joe F. Haird

(Published in *Journal of Business Research*, 2018)

Conclusions

①Business ethics and CSR are often defined as "doing good" and not damaging others. ②**This research has examined** scenarios of business ethics and CSR that are used to measure consumer attitudes toward brands. ③**The results provide evidence that** business ethics has more impact on brand attitude than CSR activities. ④This finding should not diminish the value of CSR, because CSR is important to firms and society beyond its impact on brand attitudes. ⑤CSR has been related to the reputation of the firm and can influence hiring opportunities, employee loyalty, as well as relationships with regulatory groups (Russell, Russell, & Honea, 2016). ⑥**Our findings are that** ethical conduct is more aligned with brand attitude, **thus suggesting an opportunity for future research to determine** why consumers are more concerned about business ethics as it relates to brand attitudes. ⑦**Peloza et al. (2013) found that** consumers were more concerned with performance of the brand than CSR. ⑧Possible business ethics transgressions could decrease expectations related to brand performance ⑨CSR may be viewed as incremental and not required, but business ethics is required by established

---

rules that are mandatory or essential before purchasing the brand.

⑩**Future research should focus on** moderators that can explain the strength of the relationship between expectations of business ethics and CSR related to band attitude. ⑪How does loyalty, trust, and experience with a brand influence reactions to business ethics conduct and CSR activities? ⑫**This research provides a solid foundation for** a new direction in business ethics and CSR research. ⑬Viewing these two areas as different related to attitudes toward brands can extend and change the direction of academic research and managerial focus. ⑭**The opportunity to expand insights and knowledge in this important topic is compelling.**

Move 1: Sentences ①～③ summarize the present research.

Move 2: Sentences ④～⑨ are Move 2.1, which contrast the present and previous studies.

Move 4: Sentences ⑩～⑭ are Move 4, which both indicate research implications and recommend future research.

III. Language features

The following sentence patterns and phrases are frequently and typically used as signals of different moves. The combinations of these patterns can often be found in Conclusion sections.

1. Revisit previous sections

- In this paper, we have successfully examined...
- It has been shown that...
- It is confirmed that...
- It was hypothesized...
- Our results show that...
- The analysis presented in this study shows that...
- The current work focused on...
- The examination revealed that...
- The purpose of this study is to...
- This study has explored...

2. Evaluate the present research positively

- A note of interest is...
- A promising application is...
- Based on..., ...can be managed easily.
- Based on...we can effectively...

- The results add to the growing literature on...
- The results are expected to help...
- The results present a useful technique for...
- The results will be extremely beneficial for...
- The study of...confirms that...
- The study of...contributes new insight to...
- The study of...extends prior evidence that...
- The study of...fills a gap in...
- The study of...highlights the efforts of...
- The study of...is a first step to...
- The study of...is among the first to...
- The study of...provides a novel...
- The study of...suggests that...
- This paper makes several contributions to...
- ...can be well used in...
- ...has succeeded in improving...

3. Discuss the limitations of the present research

- Much work needs to be done to...
- One limitation should be taken into account.
- One possible limitation lies in...
- The problem of...remains wide open.
- ...is difficult to apply to...
- ...needs a better understanding.

4. Give recommendations for the future research

- Future research on...is needed to...
- Future research should focus on...
- Future studies might benefit from...
- Future work on...should develop...
- It is advisable that future research should...
- It is to be hoped that future research should...
- It would be an interesting point that future research...
- One direction of future research is to...
- The approach could also be extended to...
- The future research needs to replicate this study by...
- The results of our study should encourage future research in several directions.

● We recommend that. . . should be studied.

IV. Sample analysis

In this part, you will read an authentic Conclusion section published in an academic journal. Read it carefully and pay attention to the useful sentence patterns highlighted in bold. Then complete the task after the sample.

An Exploratory Study of Innovation Strategies of the Internet of Things SMEs in South Korea

Dong-Il Shin

(Published in *Asia Pacific Journal of Innovation and Entrepreneurship*, 2017)

Conclusion

①**The primary focus of this study was on** the survival of the Korean IoT-SMEs and the path of driving innovation for growth. ②Korean SMEs have been achieving innovation and growth in the traditional manufacturing sectors. ③However, as industries such as ICT, Big Data, IoT and Industry 4.0 have emerged recently, not only manufacturing SMEs but also IT-related companies are in the critical needs of adapting to changes. ④As such, **the main motivation behind this study** of dealing with the survival and innovative growth of IoT-SMEs **lies in** the fact that these companies are an important part of the infrastructure for building the ecosystem of the future industry.

⑤**In this study, we presented** the factors for the IoT-SMEs facing the new environmental change to consider in making a strategic choice of the innovation-driving path type for their survival and sustainable growth. ⑥**We found that** the IoT has inherent disruptive and open innovation attributes. ⑦**We also discovered that** a successful IoT-SME has followed an innovation-driving and growth path consisting of self-evolution, aligned cooperation and their mix.

⑧The IoT-SMEs in Korea are facing challenges in global market entry. ⑨The first obstacle is the lack of information to sense and judge the market situation. ⑩The lack of diverse information, which hinders decision-making, makes it difficult for them to accommodate market needs. ⑪The second is the lack of capability to find a suitable BM. ⑫The IoT can lead to great results if synergy is created through close linkages with the intra or across the value chain companies. ⑬Those companies that produce chips, sensors, terminals, networks, equipment and platforms are playing key roles in the IoT value chain. ⑭It is important for companies to understand their role in the value chain and cooperate with the partners within and across the value chain. ⑮It is also critical for the companies without global market entry experience to create a partnership and establish communication environment with experienced companies in the global market. ⑯This is the very sector where government support policy is needed in identifying environmental changes and global market trends and deriving a suitable BM for new markets. ⑰The support that enables creating more synergistic results does not have to be for companies with a certain size, but for the companies within and across the value chain.

⑱**This study has its meaningful merit in that** it suggested a new point of view to establish an innovation-driving path to enter overseas markets by linking IoT innovation attributes. ⑲**However, the limitation** in this research is in using a single case study for the analysis to find an innovation-driving path. ⑳Future research needs to replicate this study by investigating multiple cases of IoT-SMEs, for validating and enhancing these study findings. ㉑This study can be applied to large IoT companies to see whether there is a difference in the innovation-driving path. ㉒Finally, it will be desirable to conduct studies for other emerging industries involving AI, big data, industry 4.0 and product-service convergence of XaaS (Everything as a Service).

Task: Read the sample carefully and identify its sub-moves. Note down the sentence numbers of each sub-move in the table below.

Moves	Sub-moves	Sentence numbers
1. Summarize the present research		
2. Evaluate the present research positively		
3. Discuss the limitations of the present research		
4. Provide a deduction		

V. Summary of the chapter

This chapter focuses on how to write the Conclusion section. This section usually includes four moves: summarizing the research, evaluating the present research positively, discussing the limitations and providing a deduction. Although not all Conclusion sections include these four moves or follow exactly the same order, the end of the Conclusion section always places the research in a larger context, thus emphasizing the value of the research.

Chapter 16

Write Abstract

摘要是浓缩全文主要信息的部分,摘要用最简洁的语言表现报告的研究问题、方法、结论和价值。本章讲述摘要写作的结构、语言、功能和修辞手段的使用。

Learning objectives

In this chapter, you will learn how to write the Abstract for a research report. When learning this chapter, you are expected:

- to learn the functions and structure of the Abstract section;
- to learn the language features of the Abstract section;
- to be able to produce effective Abstract writing.

Abstract is an important part of academic assignments, most often, reports and research papers. An abstract is a self-contained, short informative or descriptive summary of a larger work. It is the last item that you write, but the first thing people read when they want to have a quick overview of the whole work. The format and components included vary according to disciplines. However, all abstracts share several mandatory components, and there are also some optional parts that you can decide to include or not.

It's also worth remembering that an abstract is not a review, nor does it evaluate the work being abstracted. While it contains keywords found in the larger work, the abstract is an original document rather than an excerpted passage.

I. Functions of an Abstract section

An abstract has two main functions: selecting and indexing. Abstracts allow readers who may be interested in a longer work to quickly decide whether it is relevant to their study and whether it is worth their time to read it. The other main purpose of the abstract is for large database indexing. Many search engines and bibliographic databases use abstracts to index larger works. Therefore, abstracts should contain keywords and phrases that allow for easy searching. Also, a well-written abstract can also increase the impact of your work in your field, so words and contents must be carefully chosen for the abstract.

II. Structural Features of an Abstract section

There are two types of abstracts: descriptive/indicative abstracts and informative abstracts. They serve different purposes and therefore have different components and styles.

A descriptive/indicative abstract indicates the type of information found in the work. It makes no judgments about the work, nor does it provide results or conclusions of the research. It does incorporate keywords found in the text and may include the purpose, methods, and scope of the research. Essentially, the descriptive/indicative abstract briefly describes the work being abstracted, and therefore, it is often considered an outline of the work, rather than a summary. Descriptive/indicative abstracts are usually very short—100 words or less.

The majority of abstracts are informative. A good informative abstract can act as a surrogate for the work itself because all the main arguments, important results and evidence are presented and explained in it. An informative abstract includes the information that can be found in a descriptive/indicative abstract (purpose, methods, scope) but also includes the results and conclusions of the research and the recommendations of the author. The length varies according to disciplines, but an informative abstract is rarely more than 10% of the length of the entire work.

The format of an abstract depends on the work being abstracted. An abstract of a scientific research paper will contain elements not found in an abstract of a literature article, and vice versa. However, all abstracts share several mandatory components and five moves are generally employed in abstracts, especially informative abstracts.

1. **Provide the background of the research**
2. **Present the research purpose**
3. **Introduce the methodology**
4. **Report the results**
5. **Provide the contributions/limitations/implications/recommendations**

Read the following Abstract taken from a published research report. Numbers are added in front of the sentences to facilitate the analysis, and useful sentence patterns and phrases are highlighted in bold.

Successful Social Entrepreneurial Business Models in the Context of
Developing Economies An Explorative Study

Johanna Mair and Oliver Schoen

(Published in *International Journal of Emerging Markets*, 2007)

Abstract

①Social entrepreneurial organizations **have gained in awareness and interest among researchers, yet we know relatively little about** how these organizations can create social and economic value. ②**This paper seeks to understand** how such organizations have managed to achieve scale and sustainability in developing economies—often lacking the institutions, networks and resources required to support their growth—whilst also maintaining their focus on a social mission. ③**The paper presents a comparative case analysis of** three social entrepreneurial organizations based in Bangladesh, Egypt and Spain that have been widely recognized as successful. ④**It utilizes an explorative research approach** with data gathered from many sources including published and unpublished articles, existing case studies, personal interviews and internet sources. ⑤**Analysis of** these three business models **reveals common patterns in** the use of strategic resources, in their value networks, and in the customer interface. ⑥**The findings suggest that** successful social entrepreneurial organizations: proactively create their own value networks of companies that share their social vision; develop resource strategies as an integral part of the business model; and integrate their target groups into the social value network. ⑦**There are limitations in** the sampling and data analysis approach, **however, this study provides the first step towards** a more inclusive empirical research agenda in the future. ⑧**The paper offers interesting insights for** existing for-profit multi-business companies to rethink their business models, particularly for developing country contexts. ⑨**This paper encourages** managers to think beyond the creation of economic value and demonstrates how social entrepreneurs achieve sustainable growth based on building complementary networks of stakeholders and resources integrated into the value chain. ⑩**It provides propositions regarding** the business models of successful social entrepreneurial organizations and hopes to stimulate managerial interest in alternative business models and future empirical research which builds on these qualitative findings.

Move 1: Sentence ① states the background of the research.

Move 2: Sentence ② presents the research purpose.

Move 3: Sentences ③~④ introduce the research method.

Move 4: Sentences ⑤~⑥ report the main findings.

Move 5: Sentences ⑦~⑩ provide the limitations, contributions and implications of the research.

III. Language features

The following sentence patterns and phrases are frequently and typically used as signals of different moves. The combinations of these patterns can often be found in Abstract sections.

1. Provide the background of the research

- A number of studies have been focused on...
- It is known that...
- It is widely accepted that...
- There has been a growing interest in...
- There is an increasing demand for...
- ...have long been interested in...

2. Present the research purpose

- In order to..., this paper discusses...
- In order to..., this study proposes...
- The aim of this study is to explore...
- The main objective of this study is to investigate...
- The primary goal of this study is to examine...
- This paper seeks to understand...

3. Introduce the methods

- This study developed a strategy for...
- This study presents a quantitative method using...
- Using data drawn from..., this paper investigated...
- Using data from..., we examined...
- ...was examined using...
- ...was formulated using...
- ...was investigated using...
- ...was observed using...

4. Report the results

- It was noted that...
- It was observed that...
- The data provide supporting evidence for...
- The data show...
- The results reveal that...
- The results suggest that...
- There are three major findings. First,... Second,... Third,...

5. Provide the limitations/implications/recommendations

- Further research should focus on...
- Further studies are necessary to...
- More attention needs to be given to...
- The implications of these findings are discussed in terms of...
- There are limitations in...
- These findings contribute to...
- These findings suggest a need to reconsider...
- These results demonstrate the feasibility of...
- These results serve as a basis for further research into...
- We conclude by suggesting that...

IV. Sample analysis

In this part, you will read an authentic Abstract taken from a published research report. Read it carefully and pay attention to the useful sentence patterns highlighted in bold. Then complete the task after the sample.

From Selling to Managing Strategic Customers—A Competency Analysis

Sylvie Lacoste

(Published in *Journal of Personal Selling & Sales Management*, 2018)

①An increasing number of companies select strategic customers, who are then treated differently from standard customers. ②Thus, the customer-facing function has been divided into two separate functions: traditional selling and strategic account management. ③**This article seeks to provide** a comprehensive overview that compares the competencies of salespeople with the competencies of strategic account managers. ④**The article's objective is to** highlight a competency path that can lead salespeople to transition successfully into strategic account managers. ⑤Leveraging the two distinct competency classifications, **we identify** the key skills that traditional salespeople must be trained in or "unlearn" to successfully transition. ⑥ From a theoretical perspective, **this article bridges the gap between** the literature on sales and the literature on strategic account management and pinpoints the major differences between those two customer-facing dimensions. ⑦ From a managerial perspective, **the article helps** practitioners draw a competency grid to assess both salespeople's ability to succeed in their role transition and the training required to support this transition.

Task: Read the sample carefully and identify its sub-moves. Note down the sentence numbers of each sub-move in the table below.

Moves	Sub-moves	Sentence numbers
1. Provide the background of the research		
2. Present the research purpose		
3. Introduce the methodology		
4. Report the results		
5. Provide the limitations/implications/recommendations		

V. Summary of the chapter

This chapter focuses on how to write an Abstract for a research report. This section usually includes five moves: providing the background of the research, presenting the research purpose, introducing the methodology, reporting the results, and providing the limitations, implications and recommendations. Abstracts should be written in a concise manner and state the major elements of the research.

Chapter 17

Write Titles

好的写作题目画龙点睛,是吸引读者注意力的重要部分。本章讲述社会科学中标题写作的常用结构。

Learning objectives

When learning this chapter, you are expected:
- to write a proper title for your paper.

The title of academic articles and business reports summarizes the main idea and indicates the research topic and scope with as few possible words as possible. But compared to popular writings, it tends to be long, detailed, and sort of colorless. This does not reflect a lack of creativity; it is simply a convenience. A good title encourages readers to read on, and thus increases the chance of retrieval from large online databases. At the early stage of writing, the title is tentative, subject to change and refinement as your understanding of the topic goes deeper. The following gives a brief introduction to the structural features and language features of academic articles and business reports.

I. Structural features

Titles are usually classified into five categories: nominal titles, compound titles, full-sentence titles, participle phrase titles, and prepositional phrase titles, with the last two less popular.

1. Nominal titles

Nominal titles are a chief favor of engineering articles. They tend to be as explicit as possible without (m)any embellishments. There are usually two main types.

1) Noun phrase (+ noun phrase)

e. g.

● Emotional intelligence, cognitive intelligence, and job performance.

● Museums and tourist expectations

2) Noun phrase + prepositional phrase

e. g.

● Developments in trait emotional intelligence research

● A meta-analytic study of general mental ability validity for different occupations in the European Community

● Differences in the metacognitive awareness of reading strategies among native and non-native readers

Among the above two forms of nominal titles, the combination of a noun phrase and prepositional phrase is the most popular form, as prepositional phrases could indicate research topic, scope, context, even method and other information in a brief manner. Commonly used prepositions are *in, of, for, by, on, from, with, among, between*, etc.

The noun phrase (+ noun phrase) title focuses on the theme of the research, but it is less informative because of its structural restrictions.

2. Compound titles

Compound titles are often found in the humanities and social sciences, trying to combine color and thoroughness. They consist of a main title and a subtitle, which are separated by a colon, a dash, or a question mark. The main title will tend toward the snappy or engaging, indicating the paper's specific subject, while the subtitle does the actual business of labeling the contents, providing such additional information as research type, context, geographic or temporal scope.

Compound titles can be roughly classified into four types: general-specific, topic-method, problem-solution, and major-minor, with the first two more commonly used.

Table 17.1   Four types of compound titles

Types	Samples
general-specific	● A kiss is just a kiss: heterosexuality and its consolations in Sir Gawain and the Green Knight ● Unsettled moments in settled discourse: Women superintendents' experiences of inequality ● Personality and Intelligence: Gender, the Big Five, Self Estimated and Psychometric Intelligence International

(Continued)

Types	Samples
topic-method	● Accommodating English language learners in mainstream secondary classes: A comparative study of professional development delivery methods ● Overlap between the general factor of personality and emotional intelligence: A meta-analysis
problem-solution	● Who interacts on the Web? The intersection of users' personality and social media use ● Superintendents' perspectives on the involuntary departure of public school principals: the most frequent reasons why principals lose their jobs
major-minor	● Public school spending and student achievement: The case of New Jersey ● Welfare effects of milk commercialization: Evidence from smallholder producers in Georgia

3. Full-sentence titles

Full-sentence titles are increasingly common in biology and medicine, as they tend to be more specific or assertive about the discovery of the study, thus making the paper more eye-catching.

e. g.

- How do peers shape mental health clinicians' attitudes toward new treatments?
- The dual-diagnosis problem is the case-management problem in disguise
- Release of iC3b from apoptotic pancreatic tumor cells induces tolerance by binding to immature dendritic cells
- Caldesmon regulates the motility of vascular smooth muscle cells by modulating the actin cytoskeleton stability

4. Participle phrase titles

Participle phrase titles usually begin with a present participle, which shows the research action or process and is followed by prepositional phrases or infinitive clauses. They are not commonly found in academic papers.

e. g.

- Measuring brand associations for museums and galleries using repertory grid analysis
- Making sense out of degree completion rates
- Exploring the principal's contribution to school effectiveness
- Using balanced scales to control acquiescence

5. Prepositional phrase titles

Prepositional phrase titles usually emphasize the research scope, and are less favored by academic writers.

 e. g.

- From a literature review to a conceptual framework for sustainable development of new energy vehicles
- Toward a cognitive approach to second language teacher training

II. Language features

The following are some common language features of academic titles.

1. Frequently used phrases and words

Frequently and typically employed phrases and words in titles:

- A critical/comparative/theoretical/initial/qualitative/systematic/diachronical/ synchronical/content-based/meta-based/review/analysis/study of. . .
- A critique/survey of. . .
- A framework/model for. . .
- Recent developments/advances/trends/changes/problems in. . .
- Applications/Exploration/Evaluation/Impact/Implementation/of. . .
- Evidence from. . .
- Research on. . .

2. Capitalization

Compound titles are often found in the humanities and social sciences, trying to combine color and thoroughness. There are two ways to capitalize a title. The choice of the ways must be in line with the citation system required by your tutor or the expected journal. One way is to capitalize the first letter of each notional word, that is to say, nouns, verbs, adjectives, adverbs. Functional words such as articles, prepositions, and conjunctions are not capitalized unless they are the first word of a title.

The other way is to capitalize just the first letter of the first word, leaving all the other words in the title in the lower case, with the exception of proper nouns, which must be capitalized in any case.

3. Abbreviations and acronyms

Abbreviations and acronyms are rarely used in academic titles unless they are widely accepted in the research field. But you may use a full name in the title with its abbreviations or acronyms in parenthesis.

III. Summary of the chapter

This chapter introduces structural features and language features of report titles. Compared with other structures, compound titles are more frequently used in the humanities and social sciences, because they can be attractive and concrete at the same time. When writing a title, you can capitalize the first letter of each notional word, or capitalize just the first letter of the first word. Avoid using abbreviations in the title, because your title is to invite readers' attention instead of frightening them back.

Chapter 18

Edit and Write Effectively

修改是过程性写作的重要环节,写作质量与修改策略密切相关。本章讲述如何对初稿进行修改,实现有效的书面交际。

Learning objectives

When learning this chapter, you are expected:
- to know how to revise your writing;
- to learn how to write effectively.

No matter how great the research ideas, methods or findings are, thin and wishy-washy writing will cover all the shining aspects with dust. Forget about a good grade if you do not polish the paper at the final stage.

Revising your paper is an important part of the process of writing. Your paper will be drafted and redrafted while you go along. With your first draft, we suggest revising from the biggest elements to the smallest elements.

Step 1: Major Revisions

Rethinking the writing focus and checking the flow of ideas.

Step 2: Minor Revisions

Revise a part of your paper, usually a couple of paragraphs, which are unsatisfactory (within a generally reasonable part).

Step 3: Editing

Write concisely and write in an academic style.

Step 4: Proofreading

Check grammatical errors.

I. How to do major revisions

Macrostructure revising involves big changes: moving paragraphs, adding examples, deleting sections, and rewriting pages. Daigley and Witte (1981) found that experienced writers made 22% deeper changes than inexperienced. They know what story is more impressive.

It takes a certain amount of courage to genuinely revise your work. You need to accept that parts of your work may be on completely the wrong lines and need to be abandoned altogether. You need to be in the right mood to manage drastic changes.

For research-based writing, major revisions are often made in the introduction part. These revisions are often caused by writing focuses that need to be readjusted to give the report a broader theoretical background or explain how the research may solve a more pertinent practical problem in reality.

Besides the introduction part, you should consider the necessity of every paragraph in the paper. If any paragraph is not related to the theme of the paper, delete it. Once again think about "moves" of different parts we learned in the book. Check your writing according to these moves.

II. How to do minor revisions

Minor revision includes write good paragraphs and use quotations properly.

Students tend to overlook paragraphs. They make a paragraph as short as one sentence, or as long as a page. The appropriate length is various and determined by the subject, but normally a paragraph is of more than 2 sentences and less than 15 sentences. Each paragraph should have a clear main point. After the exposition of the main point, provide an exemplar or quotation to support the idea. When turning to a new idea, begin a new paragraph.

When writing comparison or contrasting paragraphs, use linking words such as: however, although, but, alternatively; When using an example to support your point, use linking words such as: for example, in addition, similarly, to illustrate, moreover. The characteristics of a good paragraph are:
- Have one clear point, supported by evidence;
- Relevant to the argumentation;
- Be composed of a linked sentence;
- Connected to the previous and the following paragraphs;

- Be of proper length.

Quotations are also important elements when revising. Your writing should stand on the shoulder of great researchers, but too many quotations will cover your voice. Use quotations when they elucidate an idea, not just to add your word count. Some suggestions for effective quotation are given here:

- Be sure the quotation links to your idea well
- Do not use a quotation if you do not understand it
- Always reference fully and correctly

III. How to write succinctly and write in an academic style

Eliminate waffle words. They cannot enhance meaning, and waste readers' patience. Write only one word if one word can carry the meaning. Write directly what is necessary and stop. such as:

In ~~his book,~~ "Das Kapital" ~~Karl~~ Marx said. . .

~~It seems to me that~~ the simplest method is. . .

It is ~~a~~ valuable ~~experience~~ to have ~~a little~~ understanding of. . .

~~Last but not least, I suggest~~ internship should be. . .

Avoid colloquialism. Written language is different from spoken language, and formal style is mandatory.

- Do not contract verb forms: *don't, can't*. Use the full form: **Do not, cannot**.
- Do not use "like" for introducing examples. Use "such as" or "for instance".
- Do not use "get" phrases such as "get better/worse". Use "improve" and "deteriorate".
- "good/bad" are simplistic. Use "positive/negative", e. g. the changes had several positive aspects.
- Avoid phrases such as "about a hundred or hundreds of years ago". If it is necessary to estimate numbers use "approximately" rather than "about".
- Do not use "thing" and combinations, "nothing" or "something"; Use "factor" "issue" or "topic".
- Do not use question forms such as "Why did war break out in 1914?" Instead use statements: "There were three reasons for the outbreak of war. . . "
- When writing lists, avoid using "etc. " or "and so on". Insert "and" before the last item: "The main products were pharmaceuticals, electronic goods, and confectionery. "
- Avoid using two-word verbs such as "go on" or "bring up"; If there is a suitable

synonym, use "continue or raise".

Avoid vague expressions. Vague language shows you have not thought clearly about an issue. If you know the number of strategies to be taken, do not write "I will take several strategies". The following expressions are frequently used unbearably vague language:

- With the development of human society...
- It is generally thought that...
- Most students think that...
- In recent years people begin to...
- My research is based on several theories...

Use assertive but not arrogant language. Research done by undergraduates in social science disciplines are often confined by small scale, or unsophisticated method and your tutor knows its limitation. This means your work needs more tests before being safely believed. Accordingly, *tentative language* should be used, but without too much humility. Expressions as "*it is a fact that...*" or "*all people think that...*" are seldom used, instead, academic writing more frequently uses expressions as follows:

- Evidence shows that...
- Research suggests...
- Generally, it is thought that...
- Not all findings support this, but...
- We may conclude that...

With the above expressions, your thoughts about an idea are shown with some reservations, because you are aware of the contradictory ideas, or the limitation of evidence.

IV. Avoid the language in literature such as novels or poems.

Good research language is precise, clear and brief. Nothing could let your writing tutor down more than using flowery or ornate prose.

The good news is that if you are a precise, clear and brief writer, then you do not have to conform to any other specific rules to be a good academic writer. The style of research-based writing is as plain as that you use to speak to your colleagues.

It is understandable for researchers to choose the plain style of writing considering the complexity of terms, the theories, and the logical issues embedded in reports. The purpose of academic writing is to have as many people as possible to read it, understand it and be influenced by it. Considering this purpose, your status would not be ruined by using plain language.

V. Avoid typical grammatical mistakes

The common mistakes in writing include the following. Pay attention to avoid these mistakes when editing your paper:

- Shift in tense.
  - × Tea was taken out of a cup. Then water is injected.
  - √ Tea was taken out of a cup. Then water was injected.
- Missing capital letters.
  - × The english legal system is well developed.
  - √ The English legal system is well developed.
- Incorrect preposition.
  - × Students are bored of doing exercises.
  - √ Students are bored with doing exercises.
- Indistinct reference

People may misunderstand puerperia. To address this problem. (Here the reference of "this" is unclear. This may refer to "puerperia problem" or, "the problem of puerperia misunderstanding".)

- Missing commas (or "and"):
  - × The research project shows children teachers and parents were upset.
  - √ The research project shows children, teachers and parents were upset.
  - × Socrates was a Greek philosopher his ideas are influential today.
  - √ Socrates was a Greek philosopher *and* his ideas are influential today.
- Subject-verb disagreement:
  - × The data was useful. The media was to blame.
  - √ The data were useful. The media were to blame.
- Run-on sentences:
  - × The results of the study were inconclusive, therefore more research needs to be done on the topic.
  - √ The results of the study were inconclusive; therefore, more research needs to be done on the topic.

VI. Peer evaluation of drafts

Peer evaluation is very useful because no matter how good a writer you are, your readers' background knowledge might be different from your expectation, so that some information may be redundant while other ones should be added.

Just as the response from your peers may help you, so will your response help them. Moreover, reading others' writing eventually heighten your awareness of your writing strength and weakness.

Chinese students consider more about *face* and avoid giving an authentic response. Do you want to get a real critical response? Criticize your peers' writing objectively now with the following checklist. This checklist is revised from Reinking and Osten (2016) to suit report genre.

Peer Response Checklist
1. Is the research question clearly stated?
2. What are the biggest problems?
3. What is the biggest strength?
4. What material doesn't fit the writing purpose or the audience?
5. What questions has the author not answered?
6. Where should more details or reasoning be added? Why?
7. At what point does the paper fail to hold my interest? Why
8. Where is the organization confusing?
9. Where is the writing unclear or vague?

When giving a response to your classmate's writing, it is suggested that no wording or spelling problems are concerned. Focus more on macro aspects. Academic writing is the dance between the writer and the readers. Whether the readers are teachers or your classmates makes no difference. Your classmates' response is as valuable as that given by your tutor. Revise accordingly.

VII. Summary of the chapter

Revising and editing are a very important part of report writing. In this chapter, 4 steps of revising and editing are suggested. Your editing job may begin from major part revising, minor part revising, language style editing to grammar checking. Although you may feel impatient to hand in your paper now, revising work is most tightly related to writing score. Peer evaluation is valuable at this stage. Use the checklist provided to have a try.

Chapter 19

Write In-text Citations and References

APA 引用格式是社会科学中最常用的引用格式。本章讲述最新版的 APA 文内引用和文后引用的格式，以及文献编辑软件 Endnote 的使用。

Learning objectives

For chapter 19, you are expected:
- to learn the functions of APA style;
- to learn the format of in-text citations in APA style;
- to learn the format of references in APA style;
- to learn the functions and the use of Endnote in managing in-text citations and references.

APA is a shortened form of American Psychological Association, which is an organization that focuses on psychology. APA citation style (also called APA style) is used by many scholars and researchers in behavioral and social sciences, not just in psychology. There are other citation formats and styles such as MLA (Modern Language Association) and Chicago, but this one is the most popular in the science fields.

There are two types of citations: in-text citations and reference citations. In this chapter, we will introduce APA style in the following aspects: the functions of APA style, the format or structure of in-text citations and that of references. In addition, as Endnote has become a very important tool for managing citations and organizing references, we will introduce its basic functions and how to use it to facilitate the writing and publishing process.

I. Functions of APA style

Abiding by APA style as a writer will allow you to provide readers with clues so that they can use them to follow your ideas more efficiently and to locate information of interest to them. Besides, it can establish your credibility or authority in the field by demonstrating an awareness of your audience as fellow researchers. In the following two sections, we will provide some guidelines for formatting your in-text citations and after-text references according to the style of APA 7th edition (2020).

II. Format of in-text citations

In-text citations are found in the body of your paper and are used when adding a direct quote or paraphrase into your work.

The purpose of in-text citations is to give the reader a brief idea as to where you found your information, while they're in the middle of reading. You may include direct quotes in the body of your paper, which are word-for-word quotes from another source. Or, you may include a piece of information that you paraphrase in your own words. You also need to include the full citation for the source in the reference list.

APA style requires a certain format of in-text citations. The following sections provide detailed guidelines for in-text citations for different types of sources.

1. Placement of in-text citations

First and foremost, you need to know how and where you place the sources. In-text citations of APA style adopts the author-date format which appears in either narrative form or fully parenthetical form. Note the following guidelines for each form:

Narrative form

For this form, you need to include the author surname or surnames within the sentences. You can put the publication year of the source in parentheses after the author surname(s), or you can put it into a sentence using the phrase "in yyyy".

Example:

Martinor (2010) maintains that whenever society seems to be minimizing racism, "it comes back wearing different language, speaking an up-to-date lingo, while creating more of the 'same old' effects" (p. 2).

Parenthetical form

This form requires that you put both the author surname(s) and the publication year of the source in parentheses at the end of a sentence with a comma in between. Then, give a period to end the sentence.

Example:

Ethnic identity corresponds to that part of an individual's self-concept which concerns how he/she relates to the native ethnic group and other relevant ethnic groups (Phinney, 1990).

Note that if the parenthetical citation does not appear at the end of the sentence, you can use nonterminal punctuation such as comma or semicolon after it, or you don't need to use any punctuations.

Examples:

Whereas the personal self is defined as a unitary and continuous awareness of who one is (Baumeister 1998), it is less clear how we should conceive of the social self, which can be as varied as the groups to which we belong.

An important contribution to our understanding of these issues is provided by the social identity approach, subsuming both social identity theory (Tajfel, 1978; Tajfel & Turner, 1979) and self-categorization theory (Turner, 1987).

2.　In-text citations for direct quotes

The in-text citation for direct quotes in narrative form should include the surname(s) of the author(s), followed by the year of publication, and page number in parentheses after the quotes. Put a period to end the sentence.

Example:

Casmir (1984) defined cultural identity as "the image of the self and the culture intertwined in the individual's total conception of reality" (p. 2).

In a parenthetical form, put the author surname(s), the year of publication, and the page number in parentheses after the quote. Separate them with a comma.

Example:

Buck needed to adjust rather quickly upon his arrival in Canada. He states, "no lazy, sun-kissed life was this, with nothing to do but loaf and be bored. Here was neither peace, nor rest, nor a moment's safety" (London, 1903, p. 25).

Note: If the quotation is on a single page, use "p." to indicate the page number; if it appears on consecutive pages, use "pp." to indicate the page numbers.

Example:

"The recognition of this point is fundamental to our thinking about education because it frees us from the..., and helps us to focus on the real world of human actions, language, intentions, meanings, goals, values, practices, institutions and customs within which we are all born and develop" (Kazepides, 2012, pp. 90 – 91).

Note: If the date of publication can't be identified, use the abbreviation "n. d." for "no date".

Example:

"Attempts to establish a definitive link between television programming and children's eating habits have been problematic" (Magnus, n. d.).

3. A long (block) quotation

If you quote more than forty words from an article, do not enclose the quotation in quotation marks. Set it in indented "block". The parenthetical citation comes after the final period of the quotation.

Example:

Social capital is defined as:

those tangible substances [that] count for most in the daily lives of people: namely good will, fellowship, sympathy, and social intercourse among the individuals and families who make up a social unit... If [an individual comes] into contact with his neighbor, and they with other neighbors, there will be an accumulation of social capital, which may immediately satisfy his social needs and which may bear a social potentiality sufficient to the substantial improvement of living conditions in the whole community. (Hanifan, 1916, p. 130)

4. In-text citations for a summary or paraphrased information

If you include a summary or paraphrased information of a source in your text, indicate the author surname(s) and the year of publication.

Examples:

(1) Mori (2000) noted that international students might experience difficulty forming new support networks because of differences in cultural or social backgrounds.

(2) At the time, papyrus was used to create paper, but it was only grown and available in mass quantities in Egypt. This posed a problem for the Greeks and Romans, but they managed to have it exported to their civilizations. Papyrus thus remained the material of choice for paper creation (Casson, 2001).

5. Specific citations of different author types

The following table presents examples of citations of different types of authors.

Table 19.1 In-text citation of different author types

One author	Putnam (1963) explains this relationship between strong networks of citizen participation and positive institutional performance in terms of "social capital".
Two authors Notes: a. Indicate their first names in the order as they appear on their work; b. Use "and" between their first names in a sentence; Use an ampersand ("&") between their first names within parentheses.	Kanazawa and Still (2000) in their analysis of a large set of data show that the statistical likelihood of being divorced increases if one is male and a secondary school teacher or college professor. Conscientious individuals typically demonstrate thinking and reasoning, and thus can fully establish goals, be motivated, be sociable, and be adaptive (Costa & McCrae, 1992).
Three or more authors Note: Indicate the surname of the first author, then use "et al." to include the rest of them.	In the past thirty years of social network analysis, many attempts have been made to find valid indicators and predictors of tie-strength (Walker et al., 1993).
Organization as author Notes: a. Include the organization's name in full in the first in-text citation; b. Put its abbreviation (if any) in parentheses and then use its abbreviation in subsequent citations.	*1st-time citation*: The Organization for Economic Co-operation and Development (OECD, 2012) [narrative]; (The Organization for Economic Co-operation and Development [OECD], 2012) [parenthetical] *Subsequent citations*: OECD (2012) [narrative]; (OECD, 2012) [parenthetical]
No credited author Notes: a. Use the title of the work or the first one or two words of the title in your text; b. Titles of short works such as articles and book chapters are put in quotation marks; c. Titles of books, reports, and websites are in italic.	Children struggling to control their weight must also struggle with the pressures of television advertising that, on the one hand, encourages the consumption of junk food and, on the other, celebrates thin celebrities ("Television", 2002).

(Continued)

Different sources from first authors with the same surname Notes: a. Include their given-name initials in all citations even if the year of publication is different; b. For a single source from authors who share the same surname and given-name initials, their given-name initials are not needed.	Brian Smith (2019) [narrative]; (B. Smith, 2019) [parenthetical] (Bennett & Bennett, 1993).
Multiple sources within the same parentheses Notes: a. Present them by first author surnames in alphabetical order (including those shortened to "et al.") and separate them by semicolons; b. List two or more sources by the same author chronologically if any (earliest source comes first), but only give the author's name once; c. If they are cited in narrative form, you can list them in any order.	Criticisms of large-scale educational testing are anything but new. They have been appearing repeatedly for many years (Crouse & Trusheim, 1988; Naim, 1978, 1980; Raimes, 1990a, 1990b; Sacks, 2003).

6. One author with publications within the same year

In this case, you need to identify each work of the author with a lowercase letter "a" "b" "c" and so on after the publication year. Note that "a" refers to the earliest work within the year.

Example:

Pajares (1996a) demonstrated that the predictiveness of self-efficacy measures increases as a function of both their specificity and correspondence to a skill.

7. Citing specific parts of a source

You need to include information about the specific parts of a source when you cite them.
Examples:

(Cutler, 2011, Introduction)
(Robinson, 2012, Chapter 5)

8. Sources in an anthology

In your text, cite the author of the text, not the editor of the anthology. Include the information of the anthology in your reference list. In the following example, Geoffrey Lloyd was the author of the quotation.

Example:

Geoffrey Lloyd (2017) notes that *post-traumatic stress disorder* (PTSD) is usually defined as "a delayed and/or protracted response to a stressful event or situation of a threatening or catastrophic nature" (p. 73).

9. Indirect citation (Citing secondary source)

APA advises you to quote primary sources wherever possible. If you do use a secondary source, in your text first indicate the original author whom you are citing. After citing quoted or paraphrased material, put in parentheses the words "as cited in", followed by the name of the author of the work in which you found the material (the secondary source).

Example:

David Goldberg (2000, as cited in Martinot, 2010) calls this phenomenon the "inherently homogenizing logic of institutions" (p. 59).

Note: *Martinot* instead of *Goldberg* will appear in the reference list with details of the source.

10. Personal communication

For personal communication (telephone conversation, unarchived letter, unpublished interview, e-mail, or unarchived electronic discussion group, social media post, memo, etc.), cite only sources that have scholarly content. Indicate the initial(s) and the surname of the author first, then put the label "personal communication" and the complete date in parentheses. Do not include them in the reference list.

Example:

"Museums engage our spirit, help us understand the natural world, and frame our identities" (V. Sand, personal communication, February 7, 2012).

11. Citing websites

If you cite an entire website, include the name of the website and provide the URL in parentheses. Don't include it in the reference list.

Example:

The questionnaires were collected on SurveyMonkey (https://surveymonkey.com).

III. Format of references

At the end of your paper, on a new numbered page, include a list of the information about where you find the source you cited. It starts with the heading "References" (centered on the page in bold; without quotation marks; not in italics). List only the works you cited (quoted, summarized, paraphrased, or commented on) in the text of your paper, not every source you examined. Do not number the entries.

The structure for each reference varies depending on the type of source used. However, the basic elements of a reference entry include author, date, title, and source. The following is a detailed introduction of the formats for reference entries according to APA 7th edition (2020).

1. Placement and order of the Entry

First, you should place the reference entries in the right order. Note the basic rules for reference entries in APA style:

a. All references are listed in alphabetical order by the first author surname(s).

b. If there are references whose first authors have the same surnames, order them alphabetically by the first author's given-name initials.

c. Reference entries whose first authors have the same full names (including surnames and given-name initials) are ordered alphabetically by the subsequent author's surnames and given-name initials.

d. Sources from the same author(s) are listed chronologically by their publication dates ("no date" entry precedes dated entry and then "in press" entry).

e. For reference entries with the same full author lists, list them chronologically by their publication dates ("no date" entry precedes dated entry and then "in press" entry).

f. Reference entries with the same full author lists and the same publication dates are ordered alphabetically by their titles (ignore "A" "An" and "The"), and put lowercase letters (ignore "a" "b" "c", etc.) after their publication years.

g. When organizations serve as authors of the sources, order these reference entries alphabetically among the other entries by the name(s) of the organization(s) (ignore "A" "An" and "The").

h. When the reference entries have no credited authors, order them alphabetically among the other entries by titles of books, articles and so on (ignore "A" "An" and "The").

Below is an example of a reference list.

Table 19.2   An example of references

Arends-Tóth (2006).
Arends-Tóth, & van de Vijver, F.J.R. (2007).
Benet-Martínez, V. (2010).
Berry, J.W., Kim, U., Power, S., Young, M., & Bujaki, M. (1989).
Berry, J.W., Phinney, J.S., Sam, D.L., & Vedder, P. (2006).
Commonwealth Foundation. (2007).
Holliday, A. (2011).
Holliday, A. (2013).
Holliday, A., Hyde, M. & Kullman, J. (2004).
Kymlicka, W. (2003).
Kymlicka, W., & Norman, W. (2000).
Relationship Marketing. (2019).
Trompenaars, F., & Hampden-Turner, C. (2004).
WTO Council for Trade in Services (2000)
Zuckert, C. (1991).

2. Published articles in academic journals

Entry for articles and short works published in academic journals should follow a certain order and a few guidelines listed below:

a. **Name of the author.** The entry begins with the author's name, which is placed in inverted order. Indicate the author's surname first, followed by the first initial and then the middle initial. Use a comma to separate the author's surname and the initials.

b. **Year of publication.** Put the publication year of the work in parentheses immediately after the author's name.

c. **Title and subtitle of the article.** Capitalize only the first letter of the first word in the title and the subtitle. If the title contains proper nouns, capitalize them using the title case.

d. **Title of the journal.** Capitalize the title of the journal using the title case and italicize the journal-title.

e. **Volume number.** Indicate the volume number of the journal after the journal-title. Italicize the volume number. Separate it and the journal-title with a comma.

f. **Issue number.** Include the issue number if there are any. Put it in the parentheses after the volume number. Don't leave space between them. Don't italicize the issue number nor the parentheses.

Note: Unlike APA 6th edition, APA 7th edition requires an issue number even if the issues are paginated continuously through each volume.

g. **Page numbers.** Use a hyphen ("-") directly to join the first page and the last page of the article as they appear in the journal. Don't write "p." or "pp." for page numbers in academic journals.

The table below shows reference entries for journal articles of different author types.

Table 19.3　Reference entries for journal articles of different author types

One author	Banks, J. A. 2012. Ethnic studies, citizenship education, and the public good. *Intercultural Education, 23*(6),467 – 473.
Two authors Notes: a. Use an ampersand ("&") before the second author's name; b. Use a comma before "&" to separate their names.	Herz, L., & Gullone, E. (1999). The relationship between self-esteem and parenting style: A cross-cultural comparison of Australian and Vietnamese Australian adolescents. *Journal of Cross-Cultural Psychology, 30*(6),742 – 761.
Three to twenty authors Notes: a. List the names of all authors; b. Use an ampersand ("&") before the surname of the last author.	Knight, G. P., Bernal, M. E., Garzza, C. A., Cota, M. K., & Ocampo, K. A. (1993). Family socialization and the ethnic identity of Mexican—American children. *Journal of Cross-Cultural Psychology, 24*(1),99 – 114.
Twenty-one or more authors Notes: a. List first 19, an ellipse, then the last author; b. Use an ampersand ("&") before the surname of the last author.	Loannidis, N. M., Rothstein, J. H., Pejaver, V., Middha, S., McDonnell, S., Baheti, S. Musolf, A., Li, Q., Holzinger, E., Karyadi, D., Cannon-Albright, L., Teerlink, C. C., Stanford, J. L., Isaacs, W. B., Xu, J., Cooney, K., Lange, E., Schleutker, J., Carpten, J. D.,... Weiver, S. (2016). Revel: An ensemble method for predicting the pathogenicity of rare missense variants. *American Journal of Human Genetics, 99*(4),877 – 885.
Organization as author Note: Put the name of the organization in the place of the author.	The Observatory on Borderless Higher Education (OBHE). (2008, February). Model for success? Malaysia's recent initiatives to enhance the international competitiveness of its higher education system.
No credited author Note: Put the title and the subtitle of the article in the place of the author.	Physician oversight of specialized emergency medical services. (2019). *Prehospital Emergency Care, 23*(4),590 – 591.

3. Articles in magazines and newspapers

If you cite an article from a magazine or a newspaper, you need to include the date when it was printed.

Example:

Tumulty, K. (2006, April 2). Should they stay or should they go? *Time, 167*(15), 3 – 40.

Note: If the article is from an online magazine or newspaper, include the URL of the webpage.

Example:

Rosenberg, G. (1997, March 31). Electronic discovery proves an effective legal weapon. *The New York Times.* http://www.nytimes.com

4. Entry for books and other long works

The entry for a book and long works should follow a certain order and a few guidelines listed below:

a. **Name of the author.** The entry begins with the author's name. Put the author's surname first, followed by the first initial and then the middle initial. Use a comma to separate the author's surnames and the initials.

b. **Year of publication.** Put the publication year of the book in parentheses immediately after the author's name.

c. **Book title and subtitle.** Only capitalize the first letter of the first word of the book title and its subtitle. Capitalize the first letter for any proper nouns as well. Italicize this information. End it with a period.

d. **Publisher.** Indicate the publisher's name as it is shown in the book. You can omit the terms "Publishers" "Company" and "Incorporated" Keep "Books" and "Press" if it is part of the publisher's name. End this information with a period. Note: Unlike APA 6th edition, APA 7th edition does not require the location of the publisher.

The table below shows examples of different types of book entries.

Table 19.4   Reference entries for books

One author	Finney, J. (1970). *Time and again.* Simon and Schuster.
Two authors	Hage, P. , & Harary, F. (1983). *Structural methods in anthropology* Cambridge University Press.

(Continued)

Three or more authors	Baumol, W. J., Litan, R. E., & Schramm, C. J. (2007). *Good capitalism, bad capitalism, and the economics of growth and prosperity.* Yale University Press.
Chapter or article in anthology Notes: a. If there is only one editor, use "Ed.", and for two or more editors, use "Eds."; b. Italicize the title of the anthology; c. Add the page numbers with the abbreviation of "pp." in parentheses.	Berry, J. W. (2006). Stress perspective on acculturation. In D. L. Sam, & J. W. Berry (Eds.), *The Cambridge handbook of acculturation psychology* (pp. 43 – 57). Cambridge University Press.
Edited books Note: Use "Eds." for two or more editors.	Gupta, R. (Ed.). (2003). *Remote sensing geology.* Springer-Verlag. Carr, S. C., MacLachlan, M., & Furnham, A. (Eds.). (2012). *Humanitarian work psychology.* Palgrave Macmillan.
Introduction, preface, forewords Note: Cite as you would for an article from an edited book.	Zachary, L. J. (2012). Foreword. In L. A. Daloz, *Mentor: Guiding the journey of adult learners* (pp. v-vii). Jossey-Bass.
Translated book Notes: a. Put in parentheses the translator's give-name initials first and then the surnames; b. Put "Trans." after the translator's name.	Jung, C. G. (1960). *On the nature of the psyche* (R. F. C. Hull, Trans.). Princeton University Press.
Republished book Note: Indicate the original year of publication in parentheses at the end of entry.	Smith, A. (1976). *An inquiry into the nature and causes of the wealth of nations.* University of Chicago Press. (Original work published 1793)
Edition other than the first Note: Indicate the edition other than the first in parentheses following the title of the book with no intervening punctuation.	Raimes, A. (2013). *Pocket keys for writers* (4th ed.). Wadsworth.

5. Entry of dissertation or thesis

1) Unpublished dissertation or thesis

Add "unpublished doctoral dissertation" or "unpublished master's thesis" in square bracket, and the institution name. Separate them with a period.

Example:

Lee, D. L. (2003). *A cluster analysis of procrastination and coping* [Unpublished doctoral dissertation]. University of Missouri.

2) Doctoral dissertation/master's thesis published in a database

Put the words "Doctoral dissertation" or "Master's thesis" in the square bracket, together with the institutional name. Then indicate the database name.

Example:

Jerskey, M. (2006). *Writing handbooks, English language learners, and the selective tradition* [Doctoral dissertation, New York Univesity]. ProQuest Dissertation and Theses database.

Note: If you cite a dissertation/thesis published online but not from a database, add the URL as hyperlinks at the end of entry.

6. Paper presentation at a conference

Unpublished. Cite unpublished conference papers or symposium presentations by listing the presenter, date (year, month dd-dd). Italicize the title and subtitle of the paper. Put the words "paper presentation" in square brackets, followed by conference name, and conference location information (city, state or province, and country).

Example:

Schack, E. O., Dueber, D., Norris Thomas, J., Fisher, M. H., & Jong, C. (2019, April 5 – 9). *Computer-programmed decision trees for assessing teacher noticing* [Paper presentation]. American Educational Research Association Annual Meeting, Toronto, ON, Canada.

Note: If the paper presentation is an online one, put the URL in place of the conference location.

7. Report

1) Printed report

Put the name(s) of the author(s) first. Italicize the title of the report. Then put the report number ("Report No.") in parentheses if any. End the entry with the agency's name.

Example:

Lempert, R. J., Norling, P., Pernin, C. G., Resetar, S. A., & Mahnovski, S. (2003). *Next generation environmental technologies: Benefits and barriers* (Report No. MR – 1682 – OSTP). RAND.

Note: If the author is an organization, put the organization name in place of the author.

2) Online report

Indicate information of author(s), year, title, and the report number. Add the URL of the webpage at the end of the entry.

Example:

Chiswell, S. & Grant, B. (2019). *New Zealand coastal sea surface temperature* (Report No. CR388). National Institute of Water & Atmospheric Research. https://www.mfe.govt.nz/sites/default/files/media/Marine/nz-coastal-sea-surface-temperature.PDF

8. Use of URLs and DOIs

For a webpage or online source, you need to indicate its URL (uniform resource locator) at the end of the reference entry. APA 7th edition does not require indicating the retrieval data before the URL unless the online source is updated periodically. If there are updates of the online source, put the retrieval data before the URL.

Examples:

Clement, T. (2019, September 30). Adopt-a-book activity. OER Commons. Retrieved October 4, 2019, from https://www.oercommons.org/authoring/58499-adopt-a-book-activity/view

Ethnomethodology. (2006). In STS wiki. Retrieved December 15, 2012, from http://www.stswiki.org/index.php?title=Ethnomethodology

APA 7th edition requires that a DOI (digital object identifier) for all types of works be included in the reference if it is available whether they are online versions or printed ones, which helps you find the document directly online. Use DOI only when both DOI and URL are provided for online work. Present it as a hyperlink.

Examples:

Ward, C. & Rana-Deuba, A. (1999). Acculturation and adaptation revisited. *Journal of Cross-cultural Psychology, 30*(4), 422–442. http://www.10.1177/0022022199030004003

Berry, J. W. (2006). Stress perspective on acculturation. In D. L. Sam, & J. W. Berry (Eds.), *The Cambridge handbook of acculturation psychology* (pp. 43–57). Cambridge University Press. http://doi.org/10.1017/CBO9780511489891.007

IV. Use of Endnote in in-text citations and references

Writing and publishing are arduous work, especially when you are struggling with citing or referencing. There is a few software (e. g., RefWorks, Noteexpress, Mendeley, Zotero, etc.) designed to organize and manage references, among which Endnote is the most popular and powerful one. It provides desirable solutions for collecting and organizing your references, managing in-text citations, searching references from online databases, as well as formatting your reference list. In this way, it facilitates your writing and publishing process by saving you a lot of time and trouble. This section provides you with an introduction of the basic functions of Endnote software and how to use it in your writing.

1. Storing and Organizing references

A primary function of Endnote is to store and organize references. You can create your own Endnote library to store all your references of any type such as journal, book, legal document, website, etc. in one place, which avoids the unnecessary complexity of finding references from various profiles on your computer. Select "New" in the "File" menu in Endnote, then you can name your library and save your library on your computer (for simplicity, you can save it in the Endnote folder).

To do this, you need to start from getting references into Endnote. There are four ways: importing references directly from an online database; using Endnote to search references from online databases; importing PDFs from your computer files and then they will be added into your Endnote together with your references; and adding new references by typing manually or copying and pasting. Then, you can have your own library of references (See Figure 19.1).

More importantly, with the function of "Group" in Endnote, you can organize your references into customized groups or subgroups of various categories to suit your needs. It helps you easily switch among different parts or themes in your research project. After including your references in Endnote, you can use the command "Create Group" to sort out these documents into various groups or subgroups and name them (See Figure 19.2).

What's more, Endnote provides you with detailed information about the references. Click on one reference item, and you can view at "references" a few necessary details such as reference types (journal, book, etc.), author(s), year of publication, title, journal name, volume and issue number, page numbers, or preview the format of references (See Figure 19.3). You can also view the abstract of the article.

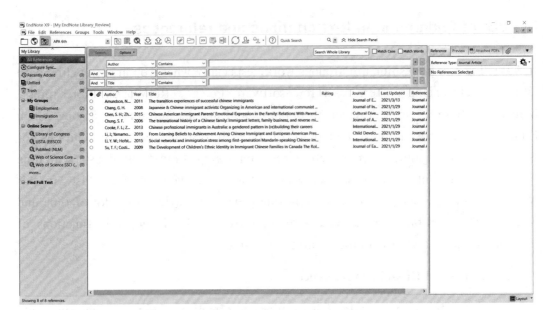

Figure 19.1　Library review window

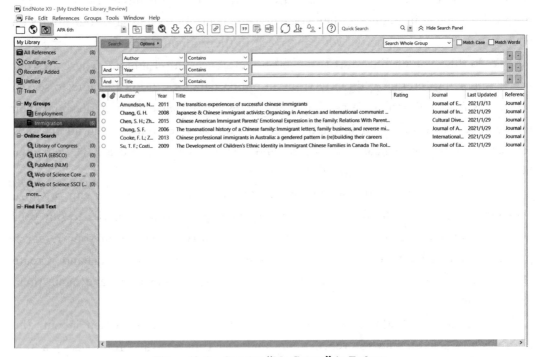

Figure 19.2　Creating "My Groups" in Endnote

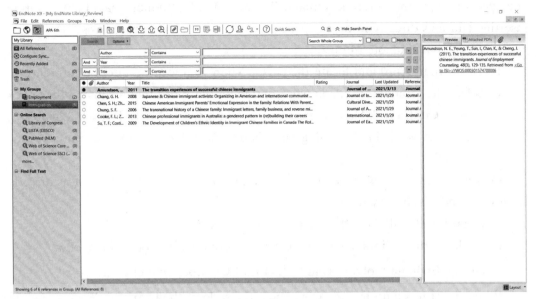

Figure 19.3　Previewing detailed bibliographic information

Figure 19.3　Previewing detailed bibliographic information

And if you want to view the text of a reference, you can use "attached PDFs" to add the text and link it to a specific reference.

2. Using Endnote as a search engine

Endnote can be used as an effective tool for searching online bibliographic databases. It provides access to some global library catalog and reference databases under an information retrieval protocol Z39.50.

To search references from online databases, you can start with the "Online Search" option on the Endnote toolbar. Click it and you will see "Connection Files" on a separate box with a collection of online databases listed in it. The databases that you have searched can be found in the "Groups Panel" list on the left side of the library review window. Or you can add your preferred databases to this panel. And once you have clicked on a database in the panel, you are connected to the database directly.

What you should do next is to enter in the search panel your request. When you begin to search, a list of references will appear on the screen. Then you can view the details of references and choose those relevant to your research, and include them into your Endnote library or into a temporary Endnote library.

3. Managing Citations

Experienced writers cite as they write. However, it will cost you a lot of time if you type or copy the references manually into Word. Endnote can help a lot in inserting citations directly into your paper. Note the following procedures:

a. Open your Endnote library

b. Go to your Word and locate the cursor where you want to cite the reference.

c. Select the "Endnote Version No." option on the Word tool menu and then click "Insert Citations." There appears the "Find & Insert My References" dialog.

d. Enter Keywords in the dialog and choose the reference(s) you want to cite. Then click "Insert."

Or you can use a simpler way when you want to insert selected references directly from your Endnote library to Word:

a. Open Word and place the cursor where you want to cite.

b. In the Endnote library screen, select the reference(s) you want to cite.

c. On the Endnote toolbar, find "｢"｣"(Insert Citation) and click it.

While inserting citations, you can choose the style of the format in Word. Click in the Word toolbar "Endnote" and then choose "Style" to select the style of references format (APA, Vancouver, etc.). If you want to customize the formats of your citation, choose "Edit & Manage Citation(s)" and you can change the citation style according to your needs. For example, you can choose to indicate both author and year of publication, omit either of them when necessary, or show them only in bibliography.

4. Creating and editing the reference list

Endnote also helps in creating and editing your reference list. While you use Endnote to insert a citation, the corresponding selected reference item from your Endnote library will appear at the end of the document. When you finish citing all the references, a complete list of the references will be created at the end of the document.

You can edit and format your reference list using Endnote. Choose "Formatting Bibliography" on the Endnote tab, and you can choose the output style of your references, or you can choose to link your in-text citations to the references (See Figure 19.4).

What's more, you can edit the layout of your references. Choose the "Layout" option and then you can edit the Font, Size, and Indent of the text. You can also edit the attributes of the bibliography title (See Figure 19.5).

EndNote X9 Configure Bibliography   ✕

Format Bibliography **Layout**

Format document: Chapter One Introduction.docx   ⌄

With output style: APA 6th   ⌄   **Browse...**

┌─ Temporary citation delimiters ──────────────────────┐
│   │
│   Left: {   Right: }   │
│   │
└───┘

☐ Link in-text citations to references in the bibliography

   ☐ Underline linked in-text citations

Figure 19.4   Format Bibliography in Endnote

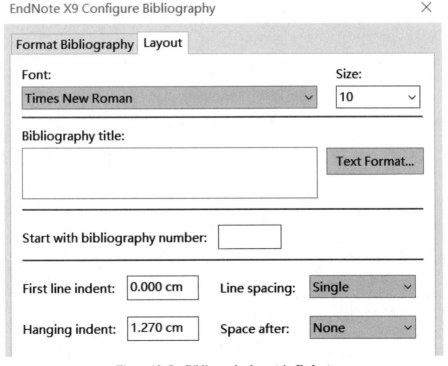

Figure 19.5   Bibliography layout in Endnote

V. Summary of the chapter

This chapter focuses on the functions of citation, how to write an in-text citation and after-text reference of APA style. You are suggested using Endnote or other tools to help to edit references. Some online websites, such as Scribbr (https://www.scribbr.com/apa-citation-generator), provide free editing as well. Have a try.

The Journey of

Presenting

Chapter 20

Plan Your Oral Presentation

在论文写作、修改到提交之间，研究者有很多机会参加面对面的学术交流，推广自己的研究。本章我们进入论文的展示环节，关注如何设计演讲的内容，选择陈述的要点并做书面语和口语之间的转换。

Learning objectives

After you have written up your academic paper, it may be still early to have it published, but to reach a wide audience, you may have to look for opportunities to present it in alternative forms. You may present it as a talk to your classmates or to the defense chair committee, or as a poster with other presenters at a large hallway. You may even present your research proposal in a large conference. In this chapter you are scheduled to learn how to present your research in these alternative forms. When learning this chapter, you are expected
● to plan an oral presentation for your research work.

Talks are superior to writing in the way that they can get immediate feedback from the audience during an oral presentation, especially in the question-and-answer period. Though responses may be less severely critical than they would be to your written work, good planning is the first step to save you from embarrassing moments and to ensure you a successful oral presentation. The following is a table of sample presentation outline.

Table 20.1　Sample presentation outline (Lunenburg & Irby, 2008)

I. Introduction
Greeting

(Continued)

Background of the study
Statement of the problem
Purpose of the study
Significance of the study
Operational definitions (list only)
Theoretical framework
Research questions (or hypotheses)
II. Literature Review
The literature review can be integrated with the elements above.
III. Method
Participants
Instrumentation
Validity
Reliability
Data Collection
Data Analysis
Limitations
Delimitations
Assumptions
IV. Results
V. Discussion, Implications, and Conclusions

All five sections constitute a formal oral presentation, but a presenter may not cover all of them and focus only on the results and discussion of those results, depending on the time allowed to the speaker.

I. Narrow your focus

For a class presentation, you may be allowed only 10 minutes. For a dissertation defense of bachelor degree, you may have 15 minutes to present it to the chair members. For a conference presentation, 20 minutes may be your targeted time. In whatever case, you have to boil down to its essence to suit your purpose. Here are some common tips:

- Start with a brief introduction. The introduction usually consists of these major parts: the problem, research purpose, brief literature review, theoretical framework, research questions or hypotheses. If the problem is new, highlight its originality.
- Describe all the other major aspects of your research: method, results, and interpretation.
- Focus less on the literature, rationale, and method of the study, but more on the results and interpretation of those results, since audiences are usually interested

only in conclusions and recommendations.

II.　Understand the difference between listeners and readers

Listeners are different from readers in that the former are usually passive while the latter can be very active. When we read, we can pause to reflect and puzzle over difficult passages. To keep track of organization, we can look at subheads and even paragraphs. If our mind wanders, we reread. But as listeners we can do none of those things. We must be motivated to pay attention, and we need help to follow a complicated line of thought. If we lose its thread, we may drift off into our own thoughts.

Presenters have endless ways to get listeners bored to death. Some of them may recite memorized sentences like a robot or hunch over notes reading every word, rarely making eye contact with their audience. Others may even turn sideways and read from the big screen, rambling through slides of data with no more than slide shows. So when speaking, be explicit about your purpose and your organization. Follow some tips:

- Don't read PPT. You may read without understanding the words, and send out complex information impossible for audiences to process.
- Tell out the message with your own understanding with the help of PPT and your notes.
- Have eye contact with your audiences, slow down or repeat if catching the sign of confusing.

III.　Understand the difference between written language and spoken language

Compare the following two texts: one is written language and the other is spoken language. Do you see their differences?

Written text: Protectionism refers to the imposition of barriers to international trade by government entities. These barriers usually involve either taxes on imports, that is tariffs, or quantitative restrictions limiting the volume of legally allowable imports of particular goods, or quotas, to achieve various economic and political targets.	**Spoken text:** Sometimes players in the government place barriers on international trade for economic or political reasons. There are two typical examples: the first is taxing, and the second is limiting imports. These taxes are called tariffs and the limitations are called quotas. And, when tariffs or quotas are imposed, it is called protectionism.

As can be seen, technical and complex nouns as "protectionism" "imposition" and noun phrases as "volume of legally allowable imports of particular goods" make the written text hard to understand without pause, reread and think. The term is complex and information is dense. But the spoken text is easy to understand with simplified sentence structure. Vocabulary and signposting as "the first, the second" is used to break longer sentences into sequential parts. Technical and complex vocabularies are explained in simpler, more accessible language. Less nouns and noun phrases are used so that information is communicated less densely, and therefore easy to understand. If a writer wants to emphasize some information, italics, bold, underlining are used for emphasis. If a speaker wants to emphasize, stress, pause and pace are used instead. These differences between the two styles are summarized in the following table.

Table 20.2　Differences between written texts and spoken texts

Categories	Written texts	Spoken texts
Grammatical structures	Complex grammatical structures are often used.	Complex grammatical structures are usually simplified to enhance understandability.
Vocabulary	Technical and/or complex vocabulary is often used.	Technical or complex vocabulary is explained in simpler and more accessible language.
Signposting	Information is often presented quite densely. The reader can choose the pace.	Information is less densely compressed to provide the listener with thinking time. Signposting is used to break up longer points, such as "the first/second/third point".
Emphasis	Italics, bold, and underlining are used for emphasis.	Stress/pause/pace are used for emphasis.
Audience	Academic audience for the sort of texts you read at university.	Your peers

Knowing the difference between written and spoken language, you can change written language into spoken language when giving presentation. Follow these tips:

- Make your sentence structure far simpler than that in a written report.
- Favor shorter sentences with subjects short and concrete.
- Avoid using complex terminology; use plain, clear language instead.
- But on some occasions, you will need to convince people of your knowledge of the subject by including some more complex terms. Make sure you understand the terminology thoroughly yourself.
- Use parallel structures a lot. What seems clumsily repetitive to readers is usually welcomed by listeners.
- Use *I, we,* and *you* a lot. They can shorten the distance between the presenter and listeners.
- Avoid complex statistics, keep it simple.

IV. Summary of the chapter

In this chapter we introduce commonly used presentation outline of how to choose presentation focus and how to adjust language from written to oral style. Keep in mind that listeners are different from readers; spoken language is not the same as written language.

Chapter 21

Design Your Oral Presentation

　　本章我们关注如何做会场的口头陈述。从演讲的姿态、语言、声音、焦虑、风格的管理方面提高学术演讲的水平。

Learning objectives

When learning this chapter, you are expected:

● to design an oral presentation for your research work.

To keep your listeners attentive, you must design your oral presentation carefully so that you do not seem to be lecturing at them, but rather amiably conversing with them. To achieve that purpose, you need to do a PowerPoint presentation with animation, artwork and diagrams. PowerPoint will make your presentation visually appealing, so listeners will focus on the screen, instead of you. For a ten-minute talk, do not exceed 10 slides. You are suggested making notes. Base the notes on the main points of the slides and prepare them well so that you can talk from notes to keep you on track.

I. Sketch your introduction

Prepare your introduction more carefully than any other part of the presentation to motivate your listeners at the start. Limit the time within one and a half minutes (if total time allotted is 10 minutes).

Use your notes to remind yourself of the major parts in one or two slides, not as a word-for-word script, but a sketch to remind yourself of the following:

(1) State the problem, purpose, rationale, research questions or hypotheses.

(2) Provide a forecast of the structure of your presentation (around ten seconds).

- The most useful forecast is the table of contents in oral form.
- Repeat that structure as you work through the body of your talk.

(3) Rehearse your introduction, until you are fluent enough to look at your audience in the eye as you present. You can look at your notes later.

II. Design notes for the body (method, results and interpretation)

(1) Avoid writing notes in complete sentences, since notes are cues for crucial points and help you recognize the structure of your talk instantly.

(2) Use a separate page for each main point. On it, you might add discourse markers such as *The first issue is...*, *Finally* and *However*.

(3) Visually highlight those main points so that you see them at a glance. Under them, make a list of the evidence that supports them. If there are numbers or quotations, write them out unless you know them well enough to cite them directly as evidence.

(4) Organize your points from the most important to the less important. If you run long (most people do), you can skip a later section or even jump to your conclusion without missing the most important ones.

III. Model your conclusion

Make your conclusion memorable. Present it without reading from notes while looking at your audience. Three parts should be covered:

(1) your research question or hypothesis, in more detail than in your introduction (if listeners are mostly interested in your reasons or data, summarize them as well);

(2) your answer to the question or hypothesis;

(3) suggestions for further future research.

Rehearse your conclusion so that you know exactly how long it takes (no more than a minute is preferred).

IV. Prepare for questions

The following tips may help you prepare for Q & A part.

(1) Prepare for questions about data or sources, especially if you didn't cover them in your talk.
- If you address matters associated with well-known researchers or schools of research, be ready to expand on how your work relates to theirs, especially if you contradict or replicate their results or approach.
- Be ready to answer questions about a source you never heard of. The best policy is to acknowledge that you haven't read it but that you'll check it out.
- If the question seems friendly, ask why the source is relevant.

(2) Don't prepare only defensive answers. Use answers to reemphasize your main points or cover matters that you may have left out.

(3) Listen to every question carefully, pause and think about it for a moment before you answer, just to be sure you fully understand it.

(4) If you don't understand the question, ask the questioner to rephrase it.

(5) Good questions are invaluable, even when they seem hostile. Use them to refine your thinking.

V. Editing your presentation slides

When making PowerPoint or PDF slides, keep the following points in mind:

(1) Pay attention to the font size so that it is large enough for the audience to read.

(2) Make sure the slides are not dense with text; they are to support rather than dominate your presentation.

(3) Avoid spelling and grammar mistakes.

(4) Present interesting visual information such as graphs, charts and tables in a format which can be viewed by everyone, but the number of them should not exceed three.

(5) Choose the most effective graphic to present data. The simplest and most common are tables, bars and pie charts, and line graphs, each of which has a distinctive rhetorical effect.
- To emphasize specific values, use a table.
- To emphasize comparisons that can be seen at a glance, use a bar or pie chart.
- To emphasize trends, use a line graph.

(6) Avoid inappropriate graphics, such as smiley faces and cartoon characters.

(7) Ask another student or your course tutor to check your slides before the presentation.

VI. Make the presentation: poise and confidence

To ensure a successful presentation, you should be poised and confident. To achieve this, keep the following points in mind:

(1) Arrive early, and make sure that the room is laid out in the way you want, all the equipment is available, and that you know how to work it.

(2) Start your presentation with a brief greeting, and make it clear from the outset whether you are happy to be interrupted or whether questions should be left for the end.

(3) Maintain eye contact

- Establish eye contact when you first stand before the audience: stand straight, smile, look directly at people in all locations, which should last for several seconds.

- Continue to maintain this eye contact during the presentation: hold the eye contact with each listener for several seconds, then shift it from one side of the room to the other, from the front to back, and at various points in the middle.

- Establish eye contact with the judges, who will be judging your ideas and your effectiveness as a speaker.

- Look frequently at the listeners who seem most interested and supportive of what you are saying. Their enthusiasm gives you extra energy and confidence.

(4) Pay attention to your body movement and gestures. Poised, natural use of your body and gestures contributes to an effective presentation.

(5) Keep audience interest by altering the pitch, volume and speed of your voice, and don't let your voice drop at the end of sentences.

(6) Manage stage fright.

Stage fright is often the nightmare of public speaking. A little bit stage fright may not be a bad thing, since emotion, if kept in control, can give the speaker extra charge to make an energetic, enthusiastic, and convincing presentation. Too much stage fright is counterproductive, but it can be avoided by the following strategies:

- Prepare well in advance and practice the presentation before other people. If possible, practice in the actual room you will be using for the presentation.

- Make good use of the last few minutes just before you speak by going over your notes one last time instead of thinking about how you're feeling.

- During the presentation, look directly at your audience with poise and confidence, and make frequent eye contact with most interested and receptive listeners. Their enthusiasm will contribute to your feelings of confidence.

VII. Other guidelines to follow

(1) Dress yourself in professional styles and colors.

(2) Create handouts which people can take away with them. These could be an outline of your main points with blank space for notes, short quotations or important data you read aloud for listeners, printed copies of slides and so on.

(3) Talk to people after the presentation and ask them how it went, whether there are any improvements they might suggest for future presentations.

VIII. Summary of the chapter

In this chapter we give detailed tips on how to give a successful presentation. Among all these tips, the most important ones are: motivate your listeners with a well-prepared introduction, design the body part clearly so that you know the contents at one glance, rehearse your presentation to know the length, prepare for questions with supporting data or sources and edit your presentation slides. When making the presentation, keep your poise and confidence by maintaining eye contact, managing your body language, voice and stage fright. Talk to your audiences after your presentation and ask for suggestions for improvement. Stay humble on the journey towards a public speaker.

Our suggestion to teachers is that to avoid stage anxiety, give students chance to practice speaking by small group exercise first. Let them tell their research to two small groups, listen to their classmates' suggestions, before presenting publicly.

Chapter 22

Plan Your Poster Oral Presentation

海报也是常用来展示研究成果的方式。本章中我们讲述海报的功能，对比传统的海报内容和广告效应更明显的海报设计方案。

Learning objectives

When learning this chapter, you are expected:

● to plan a poster oral presentation for your research work.

A poster is a large board (usually 3-foot by 5-foot) on which you lay out a summary of your research along with your most relevant evidence. Poster sessions are usually held in hallways or in a large room filled with other presenters. People move from poster to poster, read its contents, and discuss it with you if they wish.

Traditionally for a poster session, you prepare a visual layout of your research that parallels the content of an oral presentation, namely, the headings, Introduction, Materials and Methods, Results, Discussion and Conclusion. If there are only a small number of poster participants, say, one or two dozens of them, and each poster stand is allotted an equal period of time to address the delegates, you may follow the traditional formats to design and prepare your poster presentation.

But imagine delegates to a typical conference entering the poster hall to view and be informed by as many as 200 posters in no more than two hours. They would have an average of 36 seconds on each poster, which would clearly be impossible to carefully read every poster. Therefore, they have to choose to ignore some less interesting ones and focus on those highly appealing.

In this case, the traditional written format that includes headings, Introduction, Materials and Methods, Results, Discussion and Conclusion is almost invariably inappropriate for a poster. You can replace these headings with one or two sentences that best summarizes the whole section. And the order in which you present them can be quite flexible. In fact, what really interests the passing reader are usually the major results in summary form coupled with the major conclusions.

To ensure that your poster will be the lucky one to win a thorough exploration of a passer-by, it must fulfill the following four objectives. In sequence, they are:

I. Catching the eye of each delegate within 2 seconds

- Make sure that the layout of the poster is pleasing enough for a second look from most passers-by.
- Pay attention to the choice of colors, the distribution and content of photographs and figures, the use of attractive fonts of a variety of sizes and the imaginative use of diagrams.
- Avoid an oversupply of information which cannot be read in 30 – 60 seconds.
- Avoid presenting the poster in a font that is too small to read from further than about a meter or so.

II. Making a statement that stimulates the scientific interest within about 10 seconds

- Condense all of the scientifically important information in your presentation to about three sentences that will be prominent enough to be taken in during the reader's first scan of the poster
- The sentences do not have to provide full information, and they may be supported by other less prominent material to which the reader may return later.

III. Providing justification in the form of data within 30 – 60 seconds

- Once the poster has succeeded in winning the reader's interest, you can start to justify your few sentences of distilled wisdom that made your statement originally attractive. This justification and elaboration will come in the form of data (graphs or tables) or statements of detail that expand on the primary information.

- Differentiate clearly between the information that is used for attracting attention and that which is used for justification. The font for your supporting information does not have to be as large or prominent as the key information for arousing the scientific interest.
- Choose important data, only information that allows you to say something substantial about your hypothesis. Dump less important information ruthlessly.
- Keep it in mind that any justification that takes more than 60 – 70 seconds to read may simply not be read.

IV. Stimulating the onlooker to find out more by talking with the author(s)

A successful poster presentation means more than preparing an eye-catching, informative and imaginative poster. The conversational phase of the process of presenting posters is the real reason for preparing them. At this stage the poster will have successfully achieved its goals. There is virtually no time limit on discussions between interested readers and authors of posters. To do that well, pay attention to the following tips:

- Prepare written material that incorporates more detail than the poster and it can extend to new material that you would like an interested reader to have.
- Provide offprints from one or more of your recently published papers to enhance the story you wish to tell.
- Rehearse responses to likely questions and comments, such as questions about methodology, details of other work, planned or already done, prospects for employment or anything else imaginable.

In-class activity

Look at the following two samples, and discuss the following questions:
(1) Which one is relatively better and why?
(2) How to improve each of them based on the four objectives of a successful poster?

3 The Relationship Between College Students' Consumption Values and Brand Choices

Introduction

With the rapid development of China's economy, Chinese people's consumption concept is being updated day by day. Almost everyone would tend to choose a particular brand when he/she is buying a certain kind of product. Since little is known about the strength of the impact of consumption view on college students in Non-Western countries (Wang, 2010), or about limits only across luxury brand choices without other types of consumer products (Stathopoulou, Anastasia, Balabanis&George; 2019), we conducted the research about the relationship between college students' consumption values and brand choices.

Through exploring the relationship between college students' values and their brand choices, researchers can get a sense of someone or some groups' values to do something meaningful – boosting the development of the consumption market. More broadly, studying the group of college students' value and consumption tendency can help reflect the consumption tendency and consumption situation of the whole society, to some degree.

Research Questions

1)What are college students' main areas of consumption?
2)Which area do college students focus on brand selection?
3)Why do college students prefer to choose a certain brand?
4)What factors have greater influence on the formation of college students' consumption concept?

Research Methodology

This research is under the assumption that the values of Chinese college students and their mutual influence between consumer brand choice, carried out on the relationship of mutual shaping, the purpose of the research of the relationship between the two is to make China's college students better shape correct consumption values and based on the current see times making rational consumption choices.

The subjects of the study are college students, aged between 18-23 years old, most of which have distinctive personality traits and consumer decision-making styles. The survey was conducted in the form of an online questionnaire, with the help of SO JUMP(Wenjuanxing). It was a pity that due to the contagion of Novel Coronavirus Pneumonia, people have been restricted in their scope of action. And this current situation directly led to the fact that the survey could only be conducted through online questionnaires instead of face-to-face interviews or other offline methods. To get as much information as possible, the customized online questionnaires were sent to different Wechat groups, and it ended up with 100 feedback questionnaires. Meanwhile, when designing the questionnaire, the researchers referred to previous questionnaires about consumer psychology and try their best to quantify the questions asked in the questionnaire. The quantitative data provided by the research object helped the researchers to do a more detailed analysis.

Results

As illustrated by Fig.7, the main consumption areas are Clothes, for 71%,Cosmetics for 57% and Dating for 46%.

Besides, the focused consumption field of brand selection are Cosmetics, Clothes and Idol products, each for 76%,70% and 20%.

Obviously, the data for both coincide to a considerable extent.

It demonstrates that in the consumption fields that college students mainly need and pay close attention to, they usually lay great emphasis to brand selection.

This is because the consumer group of college students has a high level of consumer demand, and the main spending areas are mostly related to personal image and life quality, which is consistent with the several areas mentioned in the chart.

Fig.7

From Fig.9, only brands with good quality or word of mouth were chosen by more than half of the respondents, which meant these two were the main factors for college students to choose a particular brand.

And at the last of the questionnaire, there was an open-end problem asking respondents what were their favorite brands and why they preferred them.

Likewise, it verified the figure above.

These two analysis results prove that high quality and good reputation are indispensable and important factors at the present stage for brands that want to attract the consumption of college students with brand concept or brand image as their marketing advantages.

Fig.9

According to Fig.10,the tightness degree between college students' consumption values and brand choices was 58.4%.

In addition, as to another question surveying the degree of attention on brands when the respondents were shopping, the figure turned out to be a very consistent one——61.8%.

This result confirmed the factual correlation between the two subjects in the study by a majority and showed that brand concept was the dominant influence factor found in the study.If a brand can start from the integration of the concept of the brand and the values of college students, then the brand is likely to achieve a great success.

Fig.10

Contributions

This research project will provide some prospects on consuming of college students, as well as reference for the brand operators.

We suggest that college students should take the initiative to adjust their consumption structure to a rational state.

Once one of them achieves that, he/she will also be able to subtly affect the consumption structure of people around.

Besides, brand operators shall focus more on the cultivation of product quality and word-of-mouth advantages, and try to offer a reasonable price.

References:

Zhang, Lini& Zhao, Haidong. 2019. Personal value vs. luxury value:
What are Chinese luxury consumers shopping for when buying luxury fashion goods?
Journal of Retailing and Consumer Services.
Wang, Jing. 2010. An Empirical Study of Factors Influencing College Students' Brand Loyalty.
Zhang, Lan& Ma, Zichao. 2019. A Study of College Students' Consumption Psychology and Behavior under the Influence of Contemporary Consumerism. *Journal of Jinzhou Medical University(Social Science Edition).*
Stathopoulou, Anastasia, Balabanis, & George. 2019. The Effect of Cultural Value Orientation on Consumers' Perceptions of Luxury Value and Proclivity for Luxury Consumption.

12

tutor: 叶泉

Transformation of digital development mode of commercial banks in the post-pandemic era: the empowerment of financial technology to financial business

writers:

方艺淳　周逸甫
鲁缘情　黄翔宇

Introduction

—terrible infectious disease -- COVID-19
　　　　—decreasing aggregate demand
—commercial banks：fall in volume of business
　　　lower future revenue
　　　increase in the trading costs
—seek for new means to develop its own business

DIGITIZATION

Literature review

"Internet banking services can help to save cost"

"Electronic banking is a new option for customers"

"pressure of transformation on traditional commercial banks"

QUESTION&FINDINGS

Q1 impact of Covid-19 on economy and financial business\ challenge to commercial banks — global financial stability declined；a trend of online transformation

Q2 How can digitization achieved? Is it helpful? — online purchase of financial products；online financial management courses

Q3 What do transformation of digital development mode bring to the commercial bank in the long run? — in line with the future trend of digital economy

METHODOLOGY

O 'HOME RUN' BUSINESS
　　--PING AN BANK
　O FINANCIAL STATEMENT ANALYSIS
O QUESTIONNAIRE
　--E-S-QUAL MEASUREMENT

Both the posters are based on complete research. The first one provides detailed information about all the important elements: title, introduction, method, result and discussion. But we feel that the font is too small, information is densely presented and the whole poster impresses the audience as not so attractive as the second one. The second poster shows more interesting color and pattern, with bigger font size for more important information, and phrases rather than sentences to provide details. It also emphasizes research questions and findings by putting these two parts to the center of the poster. However, there is still some room for improvement in the second one, such as adjusting language to make it more related to the audience, and using more graphs to illustrate interesting findings.

V. Summary of the chapter

In this chapter, we provide advice on how to make a successful poster presentation. A poster should be eye-catching, arouse the scientific interest of onlookers, provide justification in the form of data, and stimulate onlookers to find out more by talking with the author.

To achieve the above-mentioned goals, the traditional format for an oral presentation with headings, Introduction, Materials and Methods, Results, Discussion and Conclusion, will probably not work effectively. You can replace each of the headings with one or two sentences that best summarize the whole section. And the order in which you present them can be quite flexible. The most important thing is that what you present in a poster board should not take the reader more than $60 \sim 70$ seconds to read.

Chapter 23

Plan Your Conference Proposal

学者参加国际会议之前,往往要提交一篇研究摘要,表明研究的领域。本章讲述会议论文摘要的写作功能和常见语篇结构。

Learning objectives

When learning this chapter, you are expected:

● to plan a conference proposal for your research work.

Conferences are good opportunities to share your work and reach a large audience, but to be invited to speak, you must submit a proposal in advance. Conference organizers usually have submission requirements which you have to follow when writing up your proposal. Generally speaking, a conference proposal should contain the following items:

- A brief introduction to the problem(s) you are interested in, your rationale, and research questions or hypotheses;
- a methodology section that explains the method(s) you employed, the instrumentation, procedure, data collection and analysis;
- a result section that describes your main findings;
- a concluding section that interprets the main findings and any recommendations for future research

About two-thirds of the proposal should describe the method and results. Conference reviewers will want to know the most important details of the study. They are less interested in your exact words than in why anyone should want to listen to them. You are expected to pose your research question and to answer the reviewer's So what? So focus on how your claim contributes to your field of research, especially on what's novel or controversial about it. If you address a question established by previous research, mention it, then highlight your new data or your new claim, depending on which is more original.

It is common that reviewers are often less knowledgeable about your topic than you are and may need help to see the significance of your question. Whether your role at a conference is to talk or only to listen depends not just on the quality of your research, but also on the significance of your question. So you need to be patient and explain the importance of your research to the reviewers, and convince them the value of your research.

The following is an example of a conference proposal and may serve as your model of a conference proposal.

Cultural Differences in Online Alcohol Marketing: Findings from Automated Attention Analysis

Wang Chunyan

Shanghai University of International Business and Economics

Wangchunyan8888@aliyun.com

Introduction

Alcohol is favored by both Chinese and Europeans. Evidence of drinking in China dated back for about 7000 years (Shen and Wang, 1998). Alcohol is considered an important aspect of the Chinese culture related to literature, art, music and social customs. In Europe average consumption of alcohol ranges from one liter in Czech Republic and Estonia to 10.5 l in Ukraine. Research on alcohol website marketing can not only show different cultures in the two areas, but also provide practical guidance to alcohol companies with international marketing aims.

The rise of the global consumers has prompted the theories which attempt to explain the differences between various markets (Maheswaran and Shavitt, 2000). Studies of cultural differences by Hall (1959), Hofstede (1984) or Trompenaars and Hampden-Turner (1995) have become classic academic literature, although several others have also investigated similar issues (Kluckhohn et al., 1961, Lewis, 2000) and the prominence of intercultural studies have survived and even grown in research interest (Engelen and Brettel, 2010). Discussions about cultural specificity affected all components in the marketing mix, including online marketing and e-commerce.

The online global environment takes into account local perspectives on the web design (Hsieh et al. 2009). The cultural impact on the user interface has been examined through extensive user testing (Cyr, 2008; Lee and Kozar 2009; Li et al. 2009), which is both costly and time consuming. A different approach to website analysis is expert-based assessment (Sinkovics et al., 2007; Ahmed et al., 2008). Experts might be familiar with technical and technological parameters, yet they usually come from a small number of cultural backgrounds.

In addition to user testing and expert testing, online behavior can be simulated via automated tools which can provide a more cost-efficient alternative. Pioneer study by Kincl and Štrach in 2013 showed the possibility of study cultural differences on website marketing with automatic analyzing software. They arrived at the conclusion that website difference was in line with Hall's high/low context theory. To give further study on the possibility of automatic test of culture by computer technology, we are to study other products besides beer for investigation.

Literature review

Cultural differences between web designers and users determine the success of web-based applications (Baack and Singh, 2007). The literature highlights the strong impact of high and low-context communication styles on web design and website content organization and similar effects have been attributed to Hofstede's individualism—collectivism and power distance (Usunier et al., 2009). Websites in high context cultures display fewer interactive features (Cho and Cheon 2005, Cyr, 2008), with less varied and more shallow content (Wurtz, 2005) and are less informative (Suh et al., 2007). High-context cultures usually prefer implied or indirect nonlinear messages with rich-context, which cannot be easily coded in the digital environment (Dafouz-Milne, 2008). Websites from more individualistic cultures often offer more opportunities for face-to-face communication, because viewers feel more comfortable with personal communication (Lim et al., 2004; Liao et al., 2008). Channels for mutual communication between clients and vendors are readily available in cultures with low power distance; the websites are rich in information as secretiveness would not be a source of advantage or power (Cho and Cheon, 2005). Evidence from studies focusing on the impact of uncertainty avoidance on web design is ambiguous: the evidence is either inconclusive (Baack and Singh, 2007) or partially supportive for overall website attractiveness, content depth and information richness (Usunier et al., 2009).

Research methodology

Eye-tracking testing monitors eye movements and those areas which the eye is focused on. Rapid website development has put eye-tracking at the forefront of website usability assessment (Wedel and Pieters, 2007). Eye-tracking studies help to assess websites and gain understanding of user behavior and perception. Issues connected with conducting eye-tracking studies encouraged the development of automated tools, which are able to simulate visual attention and produce heat maps similar to traditional eye-tracking outputs. These tools are based on neuro-science findings, visual attention studies, statistics from eye-tracking sessions, perception and cognition of humans and have been a recent phenomenon (Kondratova and Goldfarb, 2009).

Feng-Gui (http://www.feng-gui.com) and Attention Wizard (http://attentionwizard.com) are popular tools for eye-tracking simulation, reflecting the current state of knowledge in the field of Natural Vision Processing and Computational Attention. Outcomes from Feng-Gui are solid proxies and correspond to 70%–80% research evidence gathered through real users (Mancas 2007). Feng-Gui enables automated identification of areas of interest (AOI). Each AOI is a focal point of the user's visual attention. The advantage of automated tools is their inbuilt visual objectivity and independence from local conditions or target groups.

Data Choosing

In order to study if eye-tracking tool can be used to study website culture difference, we choose China and three countries in CEE. We choose the three CEE countries on two standards: one is that this country should have large alcohol production and consumption amount so that enough websites can be studied; the other is that the 3 CEE countries should have different cultural distance with China. In the 5 dimensions of Hofstede's theory, individual/collectism dimension is regarded as most reliable. Therefore we studied all the CEE countries in this dimension and chose one of the highest score, one of the lowest score, and one in the middle. At last Hungary, Czech Republic and Slovenia were chosen. Individual dimension scores for the three countries are $80, 58, 27$ respectively. China has the lowest distance with Slovenia in the dimension with low individual feature.

The next step is to choose alcohol product that can best represent local alcohol culture. In China spirits has the longest history and is loved by native people. Beer represents local culture and has the longest history compared with other beverages in Czech. In both Hungary and Slovenia wine is most consumed. For every country ten most famous companies' websites were studied.

Research Questions

1) Can eye-tracing tool be used to test differences of web-designs in different culture?

2) Does eye-tracing tool testing results go with 5 dimension scores in Hofstede's theory? Which one does the result go with and which one does the result go against?

3) If differences are found with eye-tracing tool, what suggestion can be provided for brewing companies with international marketing intentions?

Findings and contributions

The research is to find if there are cultural differences between China and CEEC countries in web designing based on eye-tracing tool. With the research, a new and less expensive method is found to judge cultural differences. The new method is easy to handle with, and efficient. On the other hand, the differences found out in web designing would work as guides to those brewing companies to enlarge their international markets in the two areas. As found by the research, China and other three CEEC countries were divided into two different groups. The conclusion was consistent with research done with eye-tracking software before. But little consistence was found with Hofstede's cultural theory.

Summary of the chapter

In this chapter, we provide advice on how to write your conference proposal supported by an example. The proposal should contain the following items: problem, theoretical (or conceptual) framework, method, results, and implications. Once the proposal is accepted as a paper presentation at a conference, you must prepare for the presentation. The suggestions we offer for oral presentation in Chapter 20 and 21 also apply here.

Part 4

Specialized Genres

Chapter 24

Case Study

案例分析是社会科学常用的调查研究方法。本章讲述案例分析写作的功能、结构和语言特征,并提供案例分析的样文。但是由于案例分析的写作目的差异性大,写作的时候,学习者应根据修辞目的进行语言和语篇的调整。

Learning objectives

When learning this chapter, you are expected:
- to learn the functions and structure of a case study,
- to learn the language features of a case study.

A case study confronts researchers with a real-life situation and engages their abilities to solve its challenges. The reader of the case should be provided with the information needed to form assumptions and make good decisions. A good case is fun; it creates a participatory learning process in which readers learn from one another. A well-written case compels readers to distill complex subject matter that helps them to get comfortable making decisions.

The functions, structural features, and language features of an effective case study will be learned in the chapter.

I. Functions of a case study

A good case study has the following advantages for research. It can be used for deep analysis of a new problem when there is no theoretical reference or large scale investigation available. A case study provides chances of studying a case from all aspects. For example, in the following table, Topic 1, Methods of teaching dyslexic children can be studied by Case study: An experimental approach to reading difficulties with under-8s in Singapore. Because a case study is concrete and interest to read, it is often welcomed by teachers and students in social science disciplines. These case topics came from Bailey (2020).

Table 24.1 Topics of case studies

Topics	Case studies Topics
1. *Methods of teaching dyslexic children* 2. *Improving crop yields in semi-deserts* 3. *Reducing infant mortality* 4. *Building earthquake-resistant bridges* 5. *Dealing with re-offending among prisoners* 6. *Improving recycling rates in large cities*	a. *An experimental approach to reading difficulties with under-8s in Singapore* b. *Using solar power to operate irrigation pumps in Ethiopia* c. *A program to cut smoking among pregnant women in a Greek clinic* d. *The lessons from Chile—how three structures withstood the 2010 quake* e. *Work and learning—how a Brazilian scheme encouraged convicts to stay out of jail* f. *The Berlin experiment: increasing public participation in collecting and sorting waste*

II. Structure and language features of a case study

A case study often includes the following parts: title, introduction, situational analysis, discussion of alternatives, presentation of recommendation and conclusion.

1. Title and Introduction

Title and introduction are very important and should be concise, easy to read, and free from academic jargon, as well as quickly capture the reader's attention.

Some guidelines: The title should clarify what is special about this particular case—in 10 words or less. It is important to keep the title short. The title should also contain the name of the featured company or organization so that faculty and students will know what to expect.

Within the first paragraph, **identify the protagonist**. Within the first few paragraphs, present—from the protagonist's point of view—the decision point. Identify other major players, if relevant. Provide the **context of the situation**. Include the situation's time, location, the purpose of the company or organization, relevant factors, and the goal of the protagonist. Frequently used expressions in the part are listed in the following table:

Table 24.2   Functions and expressions in the Introduction part of case studies

Functions	Expressions
Case background or information	• *Funded in 1952, Monarka Hotel Group is...* • *Monarka Hotels aim to...* • *The Monarka Hotels brand would now like to...* • *All factors mentioned above have relevance to the case of...*
Theoretical background or importance	• *New business models and processes should be identified...* • *Established firms should integrate the traditional strategy with the new technology in order to...* • *Most of the textbooks include....However, very few of them provide...*
Research object, aim or subject	• *This report consists of a detailed analysis...* • *A higher importance will be given to...* • *I would elaborate the above ethical dilemmas...* • *The purpose of this report is to...* • *This investigation concerns...*
Paper layout	• *This report outlines the recommendations...* • *The conclusions and recommendations are set out below.* • *A SWOT analysis of the project are presented and analyzed in this report.*

2. Situational Analysis

In this section, readers are given background information of the company and organization of the case. However, it is very important to avoid revealing what actually happened in the case. Following are frequently used expressions for this part.

Table 24.3   Functions and expressions in situational analysis

Key words	share, sale, environment, product, price, advertising, scenario, budge, value, profit, competitor, revenue, environmental
Expressions for internal performance	• *the company's Share Price Index stands at 1159* • *SUCK is currently in the growth stage* • *It is apparent that VUCK is in a position of 'decline* • *Kodak is one of the most established companies in the world* • *The company has been growing consistently since Period 1 to Period 7.*
Expressions For external condition	• *whereby sales are increasing but the emergence of competitors is evident* • *The matrix above shows that the VUCK brand is very badly placed.* • *This stage is to generate a set of factors which characterize the Kodak's external environment.*
Expressions for summarizing situational condition	*Concluding, one can say that Accor in general belongs to the pioneers, aiming to manipulate the market.*

3. Discussion of alternatives and recommendation

Based on the analysis in the above session, the writer should provide suggestions to solve the problem. In business case study, marketing strategies or managing strategies are frequently given by modal expressions such as: *should, must, need*. See the following expressions that are frequently used.

Table 24.4   Function and expressions in discussion

How to suggest	• *The only opportunities are therefore...* • *From the analysis given above, it would be advisable to...* • *Handling resistance to change can be assisted by...* • To address the issue of implementation I suggest... • Santa Clara alternative would not be recommended since... • ...is both unnecessary and highly inefficient with regards to this project.
Problem and solution	• *There have been previous problems due to...* • *Therefore, there will be many opportunities for employees to...* • *Despite evidence to suggest potential benefits of..., problems arise when...* • *It thus becomes important for most companies to...*
Balanced suggestion	• *Therefore, although it is relatively costly in both time and monetary terms, it is worth the investment as...*

4. Conclusion

In the Conclusion part, the case should draw the reader's attention back to the protagonist of the case and briefly revisit the case study's central problem. Generally, the author will reclaim its research aim, situation analysis method and main suggestions given. Sometimes importance of the research and limitation of it will be given. The frequently used expressions are as follows.

Table 24.5   Function and expressions in conclusion

Research aim and importance reclaimed	• *In applying... theory to Accor's strategy, the company will not only obtain a competitive edge, but also ensure consistent and continuous internal change.* • *This report has looked at the strategy development using the WBS scenario approach.* • *Although ultimately, each of these opportunities require thorough investigation that ought to be conducted with great care due to the risks involved.*
Situation analysis recovered	• Few simple rules, horizontal and vertical connectivity as well as external observation provide a solid base for future growth and development of the firm. • It has explored the key factors that affect the business environment. • ...scenarios have been developed using a deductive approach.

(Continued)

Suggestions summarized	• *A few strategies have been recognized using SWOT matrix and two of them have been identified as the possibility to be successful long-term strategies.* • *Of the options offered for consideration, it can be concluded that there are a number of feasible combinations available, each of them subject to certain limitations.*
Limitation of the study	• *Limitations to this solution have been identified.*

In-class activity

Activity 1: Read the following case study adapted from Bailey (2020): The experience of IKEA in China. What functions do you think different parts in the case have? Underline language expressions that help realize those functions.

Activity 2: Critical thinking questions

(1) What has IKEA done to adapt to the Chinese market?

(2) What are the problems the company has faced in this market?

(3) What recommendation has been given by the case?

(4) How do you think of the recommendation?

(5) How to improve the writing of the case?

The Experience of IKEA in China

Introduction

The Chinese economy has expanded at an annual rate of over 8 percent for the past 30 years. Parallel to this, the Chinese furniture industry has grown vigorously, with annual sales recently rising by over 20 percent a year. Legislation to privatize home ownership and rapidly rising income levels have created unprecedented growth in the home improvement market. According to estimates from the Credit Suisse group, China will be the world's second largest furniture market by 2015. This demand has boosted domestic production and also prompted international furniture manufacturers to enter this lucrative market.

IKEA, a Swedish furniture company, was one of the international companies to move into China. It is a major furniture retailer operating in over 40 countries around the world and has annual sales of over 21 billion euros (IKEA website). It entered the Chinese market in 1998 with its first store in Beijing. IKEA has found itself facing a number of challenges in terms of local differences in culture and business practices.

Marketing IKEA in China

Marketing management needs to be largely tailored to local contexts. IKEA has kept this notion in mind when designing marketing strategy around the world and has annual sales of over 21 billion euros (IKEA website). The company attempts to find the best possible compromise between standardization and adaptation to the local markets. Its product policy pays careful attention to Chinese style and integrates the set of product attributes effectively (Armstrong and Kotler, 2006).

The store layouts reflect the floor plan of many Chinese apartments, and since many of these have balconies, the stores include a balcony section. In contrast with traditional Chinese furniture, which is dark with much carving, IKEA introduces a lighter and simpler style. However, efforts have been made to adapt its products to Chinese taste. For instance, it has released a series of products just before each Chinese New Year. In 2008, the year of the rat, the series 'Fabler' was designed, using the color red, which is associated with good luck.

An important feature of a retailer is the services it offers. The Shanghai store, for instance, has a children's playground and a large restaurant, which make it distinctive. However, Chinese consumers expect free delivery and installation, and although IKEA has reduced its charges for these, it still compares unfavorably with its competitors.

Price

When the company first entered China its target market was couples with an income of 5,000~8,000 RMB per month. Following steady price reductions this has now been lowered to families with just over 3,000 RMB. Various strategies have been adopted to achieve these reductions; the most effective being to source locally. 70 percent of its products sold in China are now made in the country (Song, 2005). Furthermore, IKEA replaced its thick, annual catalogue with thinner brochures which now appear five times a year. These not only cut printing costs but also give greater flexibility to adjust prices.

Accessibility is also an important issue for the Chinese market. In most countries IKEA stores are sited near main roads, but as only 20 per cent of likely customers own cars in China, easy access to public transport is vital (Miller, 2004).

Advertising plays an important role in the total promotional mix. IKEA uses advertising effectively, with adverts in the local newspapers to keep customers informed of special offers. All TV commercials are produced locally with Chinese characters. Public relations are also vital to building a good corporate image. In China, IKEA co-operates with the Worldwide Fund for Nature (WWF) on forest projects. The company insists on using environmentally friendly and recyclable materials for the packaging of their products, as part of their efforts to build a good corporate image.

Discussion and conclusion

IKEA's product policy in China has been to successfully standardize products as much as possible, but also customize as much as needed. But it has learned that service is also vital: free delivery and installation are the perceived rules in the local market which it needs to follow. It has further found that it is better to locate in a downtown area, easily accessible with public transport, when free delivery is not provided.

International companies which operate in China, such as IKEA, face more complicated marketing decisions than local companies. They must become culture-conscious and thoroughly research local requirements rather than simply introduce a standard model of business.

III. Summary of the chapter

This chapter focuses on how to write a case study. A case study often includes title, introduction, situational analysis, discussion of alternatives, presentation of recommendation and conclusion. The title and introduction of it should be concise, easy to read, and can quickly capture the reader's attention. Situational Analysis should provide background information of the case. Then in the discussion part, the writer should illustrate the suggestions to solve the problem. In the conclusion part, the case should draw the reader's attention back to the protagonist of the case and briefly revisit the case study's central problem.

Chapter 25

Business Proposal

商务策划书是公司和个人请求出资人支持完成一个商业项目、提供一种服务的应用型报告写作。本章讲述商务策划书的写作目的、结构、语言和修辞策略，并提供参考范文。

Learning objectives

When learning this chapter, you are expected:
- to learn what a business proposal is;
- to learn the different categories of a business proposal;
- to learn the structure and language features of a business proposal;
- to learn the strategies of writing a successful business proposal.

A business proposal is a request by a business or individual to complete a specific job or project; to supply a service; or in some instances to be the vendor of a certain product.

It is not a business plan, although you might use your business plan to help inform your business proposal when you're writing it. In its simplest form, a **business plan** is a guide for your business, a roadmap that outlines goals and details how you plan to achieve those goals. A **business proposal**, however, is used to try to attract and acquire business, to build up a working relationship to make it happen. It pitches your business, product, or service to a potential client, vendor, or supplier. A business proposal can make or break your chances of securing a new client.

The categorization, the structure, the language features, and strategies of a successful business proposal will be learned in the chapter.

I. Categorization of a business proposal

Proposals can be classified into internal proposals and external proposals, depending on whether they are used internally or externally. Internal proposals are used within companies to plan or propose new projects or products. External proposals are used to offer services or products to clients outside the company.

Proposals are also classified as solicited or unsolicited, depending on whether they are requested or not. Solicited proposals are proposals requested by the readers. For example, your company's management might ask your team to submit a proposal for a new project. Or, your team might be asked to write a proposal sent out by an external client that answers a request for proposals (RFP), request for quotation (RFQ), request for information (RFI), or invitation for bid (IFB). Unsolicited proposals are proposals not requested by the readers. For example, your team might prepare an unsolicited internal proposal to pitch an innovative new idea to the company's management. Or, your team might use an unsolicited external proposal as a sales tool to offer your company's clients a product or service.

II. Structure and language features of a business proposal

A formal business proposal can range from several to two hundred pages, including the following parts: title page and introduction, statement of problem, recommendations or solution, areas of detail, conclusion, and appendices.

However, an informal proposal is short, usually excluding title page (with title included, of course) and appendix, written in the form of memos or letters.

1. Title page and Introduction

A formal complex business proposal, like a book, begins with a title page. This states the title of the proposal, the addressee's name and organization, the addresser's name and organization, and the date of submission, which is usually an indispensable part even in an informal business proposal. This page can also give the contact details of the addresser (which, if not here, must be somewhere else in the proposal). The title, similar to that in a case study, is usually a phrase, with no more than 10 words, clarifying what is special about this proposal.

Following this is a front sheet, that is, a table of contents, giving the contents and page numbers, depending on how long your business proposal is. It often makes it more interesting if there are headings and subheadings, which are descriptions of the functions and roles of the sections.

The proposal's introduction acts as a bridge to the next section, therefore, it should concentrate on essentials and be kept short. It should also command attention, establish interest, and lead to the main text, making people want to read on. A proposal's introduction will usually include up to five aspects: establishing the background, stating the purpose, stating the main point, stressing the importance of the subject, and forecasting the organization of the document.

Note that not all introductions contain all these six moves or follow exactly the same order as shown above.

Useful phrases and sentence patterns

---

1) Title

To...

From...

Date:

2) Establish the background[①]

In response to Request for Proposal dated..., and in accordance with the laws and regulations of The People's Republic of China, ABC Co. Ltd. Hereby proposes to...

The company is located in....

...is an organization that provides...services to...

We serve clients...

3) State the purpose

- The aim/purpose/objective/primary goal/intention of the proposal is...

- In this proposal, we attempt to/intend to...

- This proposal attempts to/intends to...

- This proposal is to...

- The proposal is intended/aimed to...

4) State the main point

- The main point/central point of the proposal is...

- Specifically, we propose that...

- It is proposed that...

---

① Phrases and sentence patterns for this part vary a lot according to the contexts, and in most cases, there are no definite phrases and sentence patterns, but a formal proposal may begin with the given phrases and sentence patterns.

5) Stress the importance of the subject
- This proposal will...
- Meanwhile, it will...
- This proposal will contribute to...
- An important contribution is to...
- This proposal will help to avoid/solve the problem of...

6) Forecast the organization of the document
- This proposal is organized as follows/is divided into...parts
- In this proposal, we will first discuss/present/describe/review/focus on...
- Second, we will offer a plan...
- Third, we will review...
- And finally, we will go over...
- In the first/final/next/following/conclusion section, we (will) discuss/present/suggest/review/propose...
- ...is/are presented/proposed/described/provided/discussed in...

2. Statement of problem

This section is also called statement of need, or statement of the current situation, and it can be incorporated into the introduction section. In this section, you should help clients or readers understand the current situation, by clearly stating the problem, its causes, and its effects. The length of the current situation section depends on the readers' familiarity with the problem. If readers are new to the subject, then several paragraphs or even pages might be required. However, if they fully understand the problem already, only one or two paragraphs may serve the purpose.

Useful phrases and sentence patterns

- Recently/Lately...
- There are a number of...
- This is due to...
- This may be due to...
- As a result of...
- Besides/Also/Furthermore/What is worse/In addition/What's more...
- A direct result of this is...
- There is a lack of...
- ...is one of the most...
- ...as a consequence of...

- ...to be one of the...
- ...have an impact/a negative effect on...
- ...be taken into account when...
- ...due to a lack of...
- ...can be attributed to...
- ...lead to an increase/decrease of...
- ...at the expense of...
- ...need to be taken into account...
- ...for a number of reasons...
- ...as a threat to...

3. Recommendations or solutions

After the statement of the problem comes the solution of it. This section is also called recommendations or describing the project plan, or execution plan. It is a step-by-step method for solving the problem, therefore, it may be the longest section and needs to be logically arranged and divided to make it manageable.

In this section, you should do the following: identifying the solution, stating the objectives of the plan, describing the plan's major and minor steps, and identifying the deliverables or benefits (goods and services you will provide when the project is implemented).

Note that this section needs to be set out in a way that is benefits-led, that has a focus on the customer's needs and individuality. Only when customers appreciate exactly what value and befits are being provided will they be willing to move on for the costs and other areas of detail.

Useful phrases and sentence patterns

- To/In order to solve the problem
- To/In order to reduce the/increase the level of...
- To/In order to achieve/meet these objectives,...
- In addition to this,...
- Furthermore/What's more,...
- The primary/chief/main/advantage of...
- Our plan will be implemented in four major phases...
- ...have a positive/significant effect/impact on...
- ...to improve the quality of...

- ...play a significant role in...
- First...Second...Third...And finally...
- In this phase/At this stage...
- Benefits/Rewards/Incentives/Privilege/Promotion...

4. Areas of detail

Exactly speaking, areas of detail such as costs, timing, logistics, technical specifications, qualifications, etc. can also be incorporated into the solution section. But if there are too many of them, it might be better to list them in an independent section to make the proposal more clearly and logically presented.

Note that matters such as costs and timing must be made completely clear and all possibilities of misunderstanding or omission avoided. Note also that some areas such as qualifications (description of personnel, description of the organization and past experience of the team or company) may also appear in the introduction section. Costs and timing may be listed in appendices, and benefits may be listed in this section. There is no fixed format in the writing of a business proposal.

Useful phrases and sentence patterns

- As shown in our budget,...will cost...
- We anticipate/estimate that the price/cost for...will be $3,550...
- The total cost/budget for...will be about/around/roughly...
- As for the timing/cost/logistics/our qualifications...
- In addition, money is also needed for...
- The implementation of the project may take...months...
- They will spend one week in...
- The length of...will be 3 months...
- ...will last six weeks, beginning in...and ending in...
- As shown in Appendix 2, implementation of our plan will cost an estimated $250...
- Cost is the most significant advantage of our plan...
- A detailed table for the cost/timing will be attached in appendix 2, page 33...
- Let us conclude by summarizing the costs and timing of our plan...

5. Conclusion

The conclusion section is also called closing statement or summary. It should be concise, perhaps only one or two paragraphs.

In this part, you should: ①restate the main point of your proposal one last time; ②thank your readers for their consideration of your ideas; ③leave your readers with a clear idea of what they should do when they finish reading your proposal, that is, link to action, action dates and people of contact (though this could equally be dealt with in the title page).

Useful phrases and sentence patterns

- To conclude/To summarize/To sum up/In summary/On the whole...
- The aim/purpose/overall objective/primary goal/intention of the proposal is...
- The main point/central point of the proposal is...
- Thank you for giving...the opportunity to...
- Thank you for your consideration of our ideas/for thinking of us...
- If you have any suggestions for improving our plan or you would like further information about..., Please contact/call Jean Miller, head of..., at 0086 – 21 – 67000000, or you can E-mail her at...
- If you have any questions on the above, I would be pleased to answer them.
- Should you have any doubts on the above, please don't hesitate to contact...

6. Appendices

For a short and/or informal proposal, this section is not an indispensable part. But for a proposal of any complexity, to ensure the smooth flow and logical arrangement of ideas, some ancillary materials in connection with the proposal are usually covered in appendices. These materials may include documents testifying the qualifications of the personnel in charge of the project, terms of reference, contract details, graphs and figures, tables and so on.

III. Strategies of writing a successful business proposal

The best policy for writing a successful business proposal is to be persuasive, that is, to persuade the client or readers to accept your proposal and turn down those of your competitors. To achieve this purpose, some strategies or techniques are to be followed:

- Obtain as much information about the client as possible, even about your competitors.
- Differentiate—make your proposal more powerful and distinctive than those of competitors and avoid stereotyped business proposal.
- Concentrate on facts. You want to seem serious, fair, objective and factual.
- Be clear and understandable even to a lay person and avoid jargons.
- Be error free. Check for typing, spelling, grammatical and technical errors.
- Print and bind. Print your document on good quality, heavy-bond paper, and

take it to an office service for backing and binding.

- Create visibility. Using logos, clip art, graphs, charts, tables and other visual elements will greatly enhance the visual appeal of your document and make it easier for people to read and comprehend.
- Use captions. While pictures, illustrations, photographs, and charts can often be regarded as speaking for themselves, they will have more impact if used with a caption.

As mentioned earlier, a business proposal can make or break your chances of securing a new client. If you follow the business proposal format and strategies above as a guide, you'll be well on your way to create a winning business proposal—and securing new clients.

In-class activity 1

Read an internal unsolicited business proposal: Internal Business English Training. What functions do you think different parts in the proposal have? Underline language expressions that help realize those functions.

In-class activity 2

(a) What is the main point of the proposal?

_____

(b) What are the problems the company has faced according to Lilian Pei?

_____

_____

(c) What recommendations have been given by Lilian Pei?

_____

_____

(d) What do you think of the recommendations? Can you give some other recommendations?

_____

_____

(e) How to improve the writing of the case?

_____

_____

Topic: International Business English Training

Project Proposal: International Business English Training

To: Daniel Robinson, CEO of Robinson Brothers Co., Ltd.

From: Lilian Pei, Training Department Manager of Robinson Brothers Co., Ltd.

Date: July 16th, 2017

1. Recently a number of department managers have told me that some employees' Business English is so poor that they cannot work effectively. Therefore, I am writing to inform you of this and to present my proposal to solve the problem.

The Problem

Some of the clerks of the sales department **are not able to** communicate in English with customers, which results in loss of orders. Besides, some employees in our marketing department, though they have passed Band 6 College English Test, are poor in Business English so that they did not perform well enough in the previous marketing presentations. In addition, some employees are not only poor at oral Business English but also at business writing. For example, they even don't know how to write a business report or proposal. What is worse, some of them write terrible sentences in daily memos or e-mails to our customers. Consequently, they fail in communicating with people, which lead to poor work.

A Solution to Solve the Problem

To solve the problem and to improve work efficiently, it is proposed that those employees should be trained in terms of International Business English.

Methods to Train the Employees

We are going to organize Business English training courses to train those who are poor at Business English. We have two ways to hold the training courses:

To hold in-service training courses: We are going to invite a well-known Business English expert, Professor Wang Ping from Shanghai Pudong International Business English Training Center to our company to teach International Business English. The in-service training courses, which are intended to last three months, are divided into two kinds: intermediate level and advanced level. The classes take place twice a week: on Tuesday and Friday from 16:00 to 18:00. There is a limitation to the size of each class. As to the minimum and maximum numbers of the limitation, we will decide on them to the actual situation. We are going to ask the department managers to hand in a name list of the participants.

The courses will last for a semester, namely, from September to January 2018. They are requested to take part in BEC Vantage examination. If they pass the exam, we suggest that the company pay the tuition for the courses. If they fail in it, they must pay half of the tuition, the other half being paid by the company.

We encourage all the department managers to improve their Business English. To train them, we suggest that they attend in-company Business English classes at weekend. We can also invite Prof. Wang to teach. If he is not available, some other Business English professors are to be invited to do the job. The participants are all requested to take part in the final examination: both written and oral examinations.

This kind of training courses will be held periodically. The length of the course is three months.

Those who do well in the examination or have passed the BEC examination enjoy the privilege of getting promoted in future. In this way, they will have incentive to learn Business English.

Textbooks and Materials

We will choose proper textbooks for participants at different levels. We are going to choose some imported textbooks and also some books published at home. Besides, some useful materials of International Business English will be provided by Prof. Wang, which are written by her.

We are considering inviting Prof. Wang to write some special materials for the courses, which are related to our company's business scope.

We intend to ask the Training Department at the London Headquarters to provide some professional materials of Business English.

Cost

The total budget will be about ¥150,000, which is to be used for teachers' pay, the tuition of the participants who will go out to attend training courses and buy course materials. We cannot work out the exact sum of money for each item for the moment. Details about the account will be reported to the Board of Directors after this proposal is granted.

Conclusion

It is very obvious that it is urgent to improve the employees' Business English. Now that it is not the business season of the year, employees can afford time to improve Business English. I think the training courses, if organized well enough, will be effective. The Trainees' Business English can be improved to some extent.

Should you have any good idea or suggestions about my proposal, please let me know as soon as possible. I'd like to meet you for a consultation at your convenience. Thank you for your consideration.

Looking forward to your answer.

Sincerely yours,

Lilian Pei

Training Department Manager

After-class activity

After class, write an unsolicited proposal according to the instructions given below, following the writing principles explained in this chapter.

You are the Managing Director of Smith Corporation and you are aware that the present premises are not enough for better development of the corporation. Write a proposal to the Board of Directors for the solution to the problem.

IV. Summary of the chapter

Proposals can be classified into internal and external proposals, and can also be classified as solicited or unsolicited ones. A formal business proposal includes title, introduction, statement of problem, recommendations or solution, conclusion and appendices. The title should clarify what is special about this proposal. Statement of problem is the part to help readers understand the current situation. Recommendations or solutions describes the project plan, or execution plan. Detail such as costs, timing, logistics, technical specifications, qualifications, etc. can also be incorporated into the solution section. The conclusion section should restate the main point of your proposal, thank your readers for their consideration of your ideas, and leave your readers with a clear idea of what they should do when they finish reading your proposal.

Chapter 26

Social Survey Reports

本章关注社会调查报告的写作过程、必要的修辞语步，并提供两个不同风格的样文：一个正式而完整；另一个简洁且明了。由于社会调查报告的写作目的和对象各不相同，没有统一的格式可以模仿，因此需要学习者根据写作目的进行判断取舍。

Learning objectives

When learning this chapter, you are expected:
- to learn steps in conducting a survey,
- to learn the structure of social survey reports.

Social surveys are one of the most widely used tools in social science. Through market research and opinion polling, they have become recognized as parts of our contemporary life. Properly conducted surveys are effective means of collecting data.

In social surveys, researchers collect mainly quantitative but also qualitative data from (usually representative) samples of people, by means of their verbal responses to uniform sets of systematic, structured questions presented either by interviewers or in self-completed questionnaires.

Social surveys can be conducted face to face, by telephone, or by use of a questionnaire. Many surveys today use multiple modes in order to obtain high response rates and honest reporting of sensitive topics.

I. Steps in conducting a survey

Social survey researchers always follow a systematic plan of actions. They start from identifying a theoretical or practical research problem and end with empirical measurement and data analysis. Figure 26.1 shows the basic steps in a survey research project (Neuman, 2010, p.277)

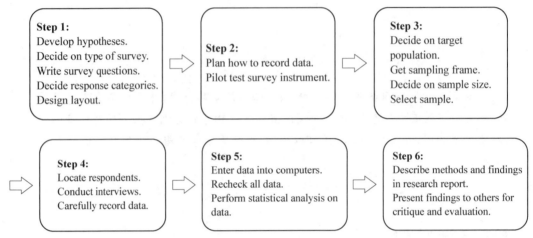

Figure 26.1   Steps in the Process of Survey Research

II. Structure of social survey reports

Once a survey has been conducted, and the data collected and analyzed, it is time to start drafting a report to present the results of the survey. The survey report aims to describe the survey, its results, and any patterns or trends found in it.

In survey reports, each section is given a heading. While there may be differences between reports, they usually include sections with the following headings (Wiltshire, n.d.):

- Title page (title of the report, name and institution of the researcher);
- Table of contents;
- Summary/Executive summary;
- Introduction/Background and objectives (what problems you are investigating & why);
- Method/Methodology (what procedures were employed?);
- Results/Findings;
- Conclusion;
- Recommendations;
- References/Bibliography (an alphabetical list of books and articles cited in the

report);

- Appendix/Appendices (copies of questionnaires, scales, etc.)—an optional part.

(**Note:** a survey report may include some, not all of the sections mentioned above.)

A survey **summary** comes at the very beginning of the report, after the table of contents. It should give the reader a condensed overview of the content, focusing on what matters, with less important findings filtered out. It includes methodology of the survey, key results, conclusions drawn from the results, and recommendations based on the survey results. For most surveys, a 1-page summary is enough to get the information across. They are sometimes called executive summaries because they are designed to be quickly digested by decision-makers.

In the **introduction** part, the researcher tells the readers why the survey was conducted, explains its hypothesis and goals. Some background information could be provided to the readers, explaining similar research and studies. This research can help you determine if your survey results support current beliefs on the topic or disagree with them.

The **method** section explains how the survey was conducted. Things to be covered in this part could be:

Whom did you ask? How can you define the gender, age, and other characteristics of these groups? Did you do the survey over e-mails, telephones, websites, or 1 – on – 1 interviews? Were participants randomly chosen or selected for a certain reason? How many people answered the survey? Were participants offered anything in exchange for filling out the survey?

Moreover, what types of questions were asked could be described in this part. Some common question types are multiple choices, interviews, and rating scales (referred to as Likert scales). The general theme of the questions should be mentioned too, with a few examples of questions (not all of the questions, which should be put in the first appendix).

The section of **results** presents what was discovered in the survey, i.e. the results of the survey. Here are some useful principles to follow.

- Break up the results into bullet points to make them easier to read.
- Report the results of each section separately, with a subheading for each section, if the survey was broken up into multiple sections.
- Avoid making any claims about the results in this section. Just objectively report the data, using statistics, sample answers, and quantitative data.
- Include graphs, charts, and other visual representations of the data in this section.

- Highlight the interesting patterns, trends, or observations, to help the readers understand the significance of the survey.

The **conclusion** starts with the implications of the survey. It could be a paragraph that summarizes the key takeaway points of the survey. It is like telling the readers what they should learn from it. Claims could be presented in this part. For example, the researcher might highlight how current policy is failing, or state how the survey demonstrates that current practices are succeeding. Thus, the tone of this part may be different from the objective one of the rest of the report, e. g. the necessary tone to be used when readers should be alarmed, concerned, or intrigued by something.

In the section of **recommendations**, suggestions are given about what needs to be done about the issue under discussion. Some common recommendations include:

- More research needs to be done on this topic.
- Current guidelines or policy need to be changed.
- The company or institution needs to take action.

The **appendices** include graphs, charts, surveys, and testimonies. The first appendix (Appendix A) should always be the survey questionnaire itself. The other appendices can be those showing statistical data, interview results, graphs of the data, and a glossary of technical terms.

Appendices are typically labeled with letters, such as Appendix A, Appendix B, Appendix C, and so on. They could be referred to throughout the report. For example, "Refer to Appendix A for the questionnaire" or "Participants were asked 30 questions (Appendix A)".

Sample survey report A (CIPD, 2015)

Notes: (1) Here are some extracts taken from a 20-page report.

(2) The following sections are not organized as what mentioned above, but they each do correspond to some of those main headings.

(3) The structure of the report and important functional expressions are noted or underlined to help analytical reading and writing.

(4) The full text of the report can be accessed from the following link: https://www. cipd. co. uk/Images/gender-diversity-boardroom _ 2015-reach-for-the-top_tcm18-10828. pdf

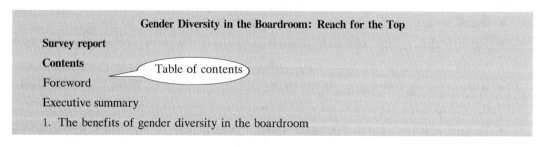

Gender Diversity in the Boardroom: Reach for the Top

Survey report

Contents   Table of contents

Foreword

Executive summary

1. The benefits of gender diversity in the boardroom

2. Voluntary targets for executive and non-executive directors

3. Mandatory quotas—yes or no?

4. Gender diversity in the workforce

5. Strategies for improving gender diversity in boardrooms

6. A broad perspective on boardroom gender diversity

Our research

References

Foreword — Background information

Gender diversity in the boardroom makes fundamental business sense. This survey report highlights some of the key benefits of having a good gender balance on boards, such as bringing different perspectives to decision-making, reflecting the wider diversity in society and improving business performance.

The common view is that concerted action is needed to breach the glass ceiling that persists at the top of most organizations. But it is more apt to highlight the challenge that most women face in climbing the glass slope to reach senior-level positions. Female progression to top roles is not sustainable unless organizations provide a strong and sustainable framework to recruit and develop women at every stage of their career.

The UK Government encourages a voluntary approach to improving the gender balance in company boardrooms but an EU initiative under negotiation in Brussels sets a minimum compulsory quota of 40% representation for each gender. These contrasting approaches raise crucial issues for female diversity: do we want or need compulsory quotas, and what are the most effective ways of improving the representation of women in senior roles?

In December 2014, the CIPD surveyed 452 HR professionals, the majority drawn from the CIPD's membership of more than 135,000 members. Through this sample we explore HR practitioners' perspectives on gender diversity in the boardroom and practical strategies for improving female representation at the top of organizations. The report also draws on the practical experiences and learning of leading diversity specialists belonging to the CIPD's Senior Diversity Network.

Rachel Suff and

Dianah Worman, OBE

CIPD Advisers

Executive summary

Three years on from the Lord Davies Review in the UK, by October 2014 women accounted for 22.8% of board directors of FTSE 100 and 17.4% of FTSE 250 companies (up from 12.5% and 7.8% respectively in February 2011) (BIS 2014). Progress has been made but much more is needed and the pace of change needs to accelerate. Some FTSE 100 companies will have to increase the pace of change to meet the initial 25% target set by Lord Davies for 2015 and this target still does not represent gender parity. We need to ensure that attention continues to focus on improving the level of female representation in the boardroom, or risk losing the momentum that the issue has started to generate.

Increasing the number of women at board level is starting to influence how companies view their talent pipeline and opening up new opportunities for women at work. However, our findings reveal that the proportion of female employees decreases with seniority in two-thirds (67%) of organizations and just three in ten (31%) have taken action to improve the gender diversity of their board. Improving the female balance of senior talent therefore remains a key challenge for organizations across the economy and not just for FTSE 350 companies.　　Significance of the survey

Finding 1 in brief

Greater awareness needed of the Women on Boards initiative

Over half of respondents (56%) are aware of the Lord Davies review of women on boards; however, a sizeable 44% are not. Just 17% of our survey respondents are aware of the Think, Act, Report (TAR) initiative that provides a simple step-by-step framework to help companies consider gender equality in their workforce.

The UK and EU initiatives to improve the gender diversity of boardrooms are understandably focused on a relatively small number of corporate companies but their underlying aim—to enhance senior female progression—is relevant to all organizations, big or small and regardless of sector. Awareness is the first step in the change process; therefore, wider promotion of the Women on Boards initiative and supporting guidance on how to build female talent pipelines could help to encourage a broader number of employers to foster a better gender balance in senior roles.

Realizing the full potential of a diverse boardroom and its impact on organizational performance relies on a wider perspective on diversity. Boardroom diversity is about more than achieving a certain ratio of female directors—our respondents strongly identify with the statement that boards should aim for a balance of many different elements including experience, gender, age, culture, background and perspective.

Finding 2 in brief

Voluntary targets are the way forward

The Brussels proposal to impose a mandatory quota system for female non-executive directors raises the real spectra of a rigid and compulsory approach to boardroom selection. The effectiveness of voluntary targets versus mandatory quotas prompted lively debate on the part of our survey respondents, but there is clear support for the UK Government's voluntary approach: six in ten respondents (60%) think that mandatory quotas should not be introduced.

The CIPD recognizes the frustration felt by some regarding the seemingly slow progress of gender equality in boardrooms, particularly in relation to the appointment of executive, as opposed to non-executive, directors. However, we believe that the introduction of a compulsory quota system would not be a sustainable and long-term solution to achieving greater gender parity at the top of organizations. The CIPD has always advocated a voluntary approach to increasing boardroom diversity, to enable organizations to develop an appropriate and sustainable range of responses in how they develop female talent and affect cultural change. This view is backed up by our panel of HR professionals: more than half (55%) feel that a voluntary approach to setting organizational targets is more helpful than a mandatory quota system, while 23% think that this approach is equally helpful, 15% less helpful and 7% unsure.

Legislating to ensure that a certain number of women are appointed to board positions will not solve the underlying reasons for failures in boardroom gender diversity. As many HR professionals told us, a quota imposition could be counter-productive and lead to a potential backlash towards those appointed as a result of what is often perceived as positive discrimination. People want to be seen as successful based on their own ability and not as a result of their identity. While voluntary targets—set by government or by organizations themselves—can be helpful to focus the mind and encourage greater gender diversity in the selection pool, the key criterion for boardroom appointments should be merit.

Looking ahead, more than half (53%) of the HR professionals taking part in our survey believe that the Government should set a more ambitious voluntary target to improve gender diversity in boardrooms post-2015. We asked respondents what they believe the new voluntary target for female representation on boards should be: a voluntary target of 50% was most popular, with 36% indicating this equal level of gender representation.

. . . (Note: brief findings 3 – 5 are omitted)

6. Building sustainable strategies to support female progression

As Lord Davies suggests, "strengthening the executive pipeline remains a longer-term task" and is a goal that needs sustained action. This raises crucial issues about how employers—whether private, public or voluntary sector—can build a strong and sustainable framework to encourage good female representation throughout the organization. Therefore, our research explores respondents' views about female progression at work and the kind of organizational practices considered most effective to promote gender diversity in senior roles.

An open and supportive culture that supports gender diversity is viewed as the most effective way of improving the gender diversity of boardroom executives (64% of respondents), followed by:

- unbiased recruitment and selection practices to attract diverse talent pools (56%)　　　　　　　　　　　　　　　　Findings in brief
- good work-life balance policies that support female staff with caring responsibilities (50%)
- clear career paths and promotional opportunities in middle and senior management roles (50%)

Our findings show that HR professionals think there is a whole raft of organizational approaches that have the potential to support the career progression of women at work. Coaching and mentoring for women, female sponsorship and advocacy schemes and leadership development programs aimed exclusively at female employees are all rated positively by respondents. This indicates that there is no quick fix to boosting senior female representation in organizations and that employers need to take a holistic approach to building a strong and sustainable female talent pipeline to secure future senior appointments for women. This means developing a number of supportive and inclusive strategies that reach out to women employees across the workforce. This may take time but it will be worth it in the long term.　　　　　　　　　　　　　　　　　　　　　Implications of the findings

Research method

Our research

This survey was conducted in December 2014. It was sent to a sample of UK-based HR professionals in the public, private and not-for-profit sectors. In total, 452 people responded to the survey.

The sample includes a mix of different-sized organizations, with a sizeable proportion (41%) from the SME category. Private sector services (49%) and the public sector (29%) are the largest two sector groups represented.

References

...

Sample survey report B

Notes: Report B seems to be a relatively new format of survey reports. The following sections all correspond to the parts of a typical survey report we talked about previously, but just in different order. Parts under such headings as "Internet Access and Ability in WV" "The Internet and Age in WV" "Education and the Internet" "Income and the Internet" present the findings to the readers. The "Data source" includes information about methods and objectives of the survey. Report B is downloaded with the following connection: https://survey.wvu.edu/files/d/2ecc6402-b338-46b5-9c06-2a881c72d1e8/internet-access-accessible.pdf

Internet Access in West Virginia

West Virginia Social Survey Report

WVSS-20-03 Issued on October 22, 2020 Prepared by Erin Hudnall, Katie E. Corcoran, and Christopher P. Scheitle

Background

In 2019, about 56% of the world's population had access to the internet with North America having one of the highest rates of access globally (94%).

Having access to the internet is most commonly impacted by level of education and income. This means that access is lower for disadvantaged groups. Similarly, older Americans report lower rates of access to the internet, which could be due to limited resources and ability to use technology.

In West Virginia, those with low income and those with lower educational attainment have the lowest rates of access to the internet. Reports of ability to use the internet follow similar patterns.

Highlights

- 83% of West Virginians have access to the Internet in their homes.
- Of those reporting that they do not have access to internet in their homes, 33% reported accessing the internet through an internet-enabled mobile device, like a smartphone or tablet.
- Access to the internet at home is most common among West Virginia residents who have high household incomes and education.
- Self-reported ratings of ability to use the internet are highest among residents with high incomes and education.
- Older residents report lower rates of access and ability to use the internet.

Internet Access and Ability in WV

Respondents were asked "Do you have access to the internet in your home?" Approximately 83 percent said yes. When asked "Do you have access to the internet through an internet-enabled mobile device like a smartphone, tablet, or watch?", roughly 81% of respondents said yes. Of those who said they did not have access to the internet in their home, 33% indicated that they had access to the internet through a mobile device.

Respondents were asked: "How would you rate your ability to use the internet?" and were given the options "very good" "good" "fair" "poor" "very poor". Most West Virginia residents rated their internet ability as "very good" or "good" (62.62%), 24% rated it as "fair,," and about 19% rated it as "poor" or "very poor".

Figure 1—Access to the Internet at Home by Age in West Virginia

. . .

The Internet and Age in WV

The lowest rates of access to home internet according to age were reported by those 60 and older. This reflects national trends showing internet use to be lower among those 65 and older.

In West Virginia, the lowest access rate was reported by those aged 80 or older. This is likely due to older populations having lower educational attainment and income, including those in West Virginia. Of respondents reporting access to the internet through a device only, about 33% were aged 50 – 69.

The highest rates of having access to the internet at home were reported by those 18 – 24(95%) and those 25 – 29(100%).

While rates of home internet access are lower among older West Virginians, another barrier to internet use is a lack of confidence in using technology, which is common among older populations.

In West Virginia, ratings of ability to use the internet were lowest among those 80 or older with 64% reporting "poor" or "very poor" ability.

In contrast, none of those aged 18 – 24 or 25 – 29 reported "poor" or "very poor" ability to use the internet. The highest ratings of ability to use the internet were reported by these respondents. This is likely due to a high percentage of students within these age groups who use the internet for their education as well as national trends that show faster technology adoption among younger populations.

Figure 2—Ability to Use the Internet by Age in West Virginia

. . .

Education and the Internet

Level of education influences access to the internet. In West Virginia, internet access is lowest among those with less than a high school education (48%). Access in the state is highest among those with professional or doctoral degrees (99% each).

The most dramatic increase of reports in having access to the internet at home occur between those with a high school diploma (78%) and those with some college education (94%). Those accessing the internet through a mobile device only are more commonly high school graduates (59%).

For ability to use the internet, ratings of "very good" and "good" are most common among those with a doctorate degree (98%). Ratings of "very good" or "good" ability to use the internet are high among those with a Bachelor's degree (88%), Master's degree (85%), and those with an Associate's degree (82%). Ratings of "very poor" or "poor" ability to use the internet are most common for those with less than a high school education (64%) and those with some high school education (62%).

Figure 3—Access to the Internet at Home and Ability to Use the
Internet by Education in West Virginia

. . .

Income and the Internet

Income also influences access to the internet. In West Virginia, those with a household income of $10,000 or less reported the lowest rates of access to the internet in their homes (57%). In contrast, those with a household income of between $35,001 – $50,000 report having access to the internet at rates of 90% or higher.

In contrast, those with a household income of between $35,001 – $50,000 report having access to the internet at rates of 90% or higher.

Those with the highest household income of $150,000 or more report the highest rate of home internet access (99%). Those who access the internet through a mobile device only more commonly have lower household incomes ($35,000 or less).

Among those in the lowest income categories, ratings of "very good" or "good" are the least common. Less than 50% of those with a household income below $35,000 rated their ability to use the internet in this way. More than 50% of those with a household income above $35,000 rated their internet ability as "very good" or "good".

Figure 4—Access to Home Internet by Income in West Virginia

. . .

Summary

As of 2018, WV was ranked 45th for access to broadband internet. There has been a push to increase access to quality internet in the state and other rural locations. Improved internet connectivity in the state could attract remote workers and improve access to virtual health services and remote education and employment in the altered social and economic environment of the COVID‑19 pandemic.

The 2020 West Virginia Social Survey finds that the majority of West Virginia residents have access to the internet in their homes or through an internet enabled mobile device.

However, access and self-reported ability to use the internet are also low among older West Virginians and residents with lower incomes and education.

Low access to the internet and lower ability to use the internet also inhibit opportunities for self-employment and small businesses as well as virtual healthcare and education.

Data Source

The WVSS is produced by the Survey Research Center at West Virginia University. The purpose of the WVSS is to gather information on the attitudes, concerns, and challenges facing WV residents.

The WVSS is a mail survey utilizing an address-based sample of nearly 5,000 households across the state.

The 2020 WVSS received nearly 1,900 responses for a response rate of 38.1% (American Association of Public Opinion Research Definition #3). Data are weighted to be representative of

the West Virginia adult population.
   Reference
   . . .

(**In-class activity**) --

What is the difference between social survey report and the other two genres in the book: research-based report and case study?

III. Summary of the chapter

In this chapter social survey reports are introduced by illustrating the research process, necessary rhetorical moves, and two samples. We have to say that there are no set survey structures to follow. Writing purpose and targets must be considered before deciding what form to take. The two samples are good illustration of the diversity of survey report: the first sample is quite formal and complex with the parts of "Forward", "Executive Summary" "Findings" "Methods" and "References"; while the second one is much briefer and simpler.

Conclusion

Chapter 27

Wrap up with Reflection

恭喜大家走到了学术报告写作的最后阶段,本章回顾整个的学习过程和收获,了解反思总结的重要性,写作反思日志,做自我评价。

Learning objectives

After you have learned the previous chapters, you have mastered essential knowledge and skills of academic report writing and presenting. It's necessary to have a review of the learning and writing process. When learning this chapter, you are expected:

- to learn the importance of reflection and self-assessment,
- to learn how to write a reflective journal, and
- to make self-assessment on your work.

Through the previous chapters, you have learned a lot about how to write an academic report and have obtained some experience in academic writing. Reflecting on your learning and writing process, as well as assessing the achievements you have made during this process, is an important stage but sometimes is neglected by both teachers and students. They are, however, fundamental and indispensable steps that help you learn from your experience and make you move forward. In this chapter, you will learn the importance of reflecting on your learning and writing experience and how to write a reflective journal. In addition, you will know the criteria of self-assessment on your learning and writing process.

I. Reflecting on your writing journey

Writing academic reports is like a journey. You may be excited when you get started and feel accomplished when you finish your first academic report. You may also encounter some problems during this long and complex process, and gain a lot of experience from each step of your writing, such as how to collect and analyze data. Therefore, you will have a lot of thoughts and feelings on your writing experience. This is a process of self-reflection, which should be encouraged to write down. It is not only valuable for developing your academic writing abilities but also your learning abilities, and will further be proved to be valuable in your lives. Just as Race (2006) points out that:

Reflection deepens learning. The act of reflecting is one which causes us to make sense of what we've learned, why we learned it, and how that particular increment of learning took place. Moreover, reflection is about linking one increment of learning to the wider perspective of learning—heading towards seeing the bigger picture. Reflection is equally useful when our learning has been unsuccessful—in such cases indeed reflection can often give us insights into what may have gone wrong with our learning, and how on a future occasion we might avoid now-known pitfalls. Most of all, however, it is increasingly recognized that reflection is an important transferable skill, and is much valued by all around us, in employment, as well as in life in general.

An important way to make self-reflection on learning and writing process is to write reflective journals. Next, we will introduce the importance of keeping reflective journals and how to write a reflective journal.

1. Why write reflective journals?

Reflection is a process through which people intentionally look back on their past experience, and consciously take down something to record and analyze what they did. One of the most commonly used ways of making self-reflection is to write reflective journals. A journal is like a diary, on which you can write anything about your thoughts and feelings. Reflective journals, which is also called "reflective learning journals", is to record and examine how you did your work and what you have achieved. What's more, you can add your thoughts and feelings into these processes and describe what you have gained from this experience. Reflective journals can provoke creative introspection in you, which will give you insights and enhance your learning and writing abilities. The following table shows some specific purposes of writing reflective journals.

Table 27.1   Purposes of writing reflective journals

- To deepen the quality of learning in the form of critical thinking or developing a questioning attitude
- To enable you to understand your own learning process
- To increase active involvement in learning and personal ownership of learning
- To enhance professional practice or the professional self in practice
- To enhance the personal valuing of the self toward self-empowerment
- To enhance creativity by making better use of intuitive understanding
- To free up writing and the representation of learning
- To provide an alternative "voice" to express yourself
- To foster reflective and creative interaction in a group

Source: Reale (2017, p.53)

In summary, keeping a reflective journal develops your habit of reflecting, as well as increases your learning and writing abilities. So, get started to write your reflective journals, and you will become an autonomous learner with strong commitment to professional development.

2. What do you write?

Before you start to write a reflective journal, you need to know what reflection involves. Reflection is a cyclic process. You can have a look of Figure 27.1 to learn about the reflection learning circle and the key elements involved in this process. According to Gibbs (1988), reflection begins from description of what happened, your feelings, evaluation, and analysis of the happenings, your conclusion and action plans for the future.

You should keep in mind that writing reflective journals includes more than just a record of some detailed stories of what happened in your writing process. More importantly, you should uncover how you feel about your experience, and how it influences you. In a broad sense, you can focus on the following three major parts when you write a reflective journal:

a. A critical review of your experience. In this part, you can look over your learning and writing activities and examine your performance throughout the process. It includes your strengths and weakness, the strategies you adopted, the problems you encountered, the outcomes you achieved, etc. Below is an example:

During term one I found myself inwardly questioning the reliability and validity of scientific journals, as I came across conflicting studies and contradictory data in our weekly research and feedback sessions.

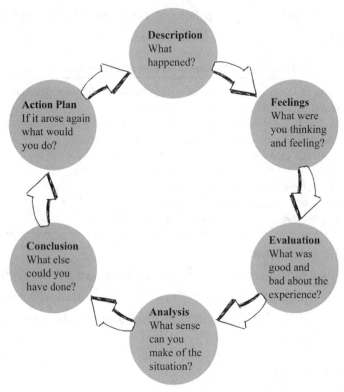

Figure 27.1   Reflection learning circle; Source: Gibbs (1988, p.9)

b. Your thoughts and feelings about your experience. Writing a reflective journal is more than simple story-telling. When you review your experience in your learning process, you should add your reflection into this process, e. g., how did you feel before you start your work, how did you comment on your performance. Below is an example:

Tasked with the overwhelming burden of writing my first ever reflective essay, I sat as still as a mouse as my fingers shakily hovered over the lifeless buttons of my laptop keyboard. Where would I begin? Where would I end? Thoughts frantically found their way through my mind as I envisaged the treacherous journey on which I was about to embark.

c. Your personal growth from your learning and writing process. The ultimate purpose of self-reflection is to help you learn from your past experience, to have a clearer self-concept and to enhance yourself. Therefore, a crucial component in your journal writing is to relate your experience to your personal growth. In this part, you can summarize the lessons you have learned from your experience, analyze the reasons of your success or failure, and elaborate on how your experience have stimulated or will promote your personal growth. Below is an example:

> This seminar has provided a wonderful structure within which I have been able to thoughtfully look back over my four years, reviewing, questioning, bringing to articulation a portrait in words of my experience here... Writing my Summary &Evaluation paper was a chance for me to come to a sense of completion with what I have accomplished at my college and to also see that I take with me much work still to be done.

These afore-mentioned contents are what you should focus on when you write reflective journals. There is one thing to note: these contents are not written separately or unfolded following strict linear steps. If there are multiple events, you had better weave your ideas, feelings, or comments into each specific event you are writing about.

Beside, Clandinin et al. (1986) argue that reflection is "reflection-in-action" rather than "reflection-on-action", meaning that one reflects while he is doing an activity but not after he finishes doing it. So, you can write reflective journals regularly, jotting down your thoughts, feelings while you are in your learning and writing process.

3. Specific reflective questions guiding your writing

When you write reflective journals, asking yourself some specific questions will help you review and reflect on the whole learning and writing process by structuring your writing and organizing your thoughts. Here are some reflective questions you can ask yourself at different stages of your writing process:

Questions asked before writing:

a. How did I feel before I start my writing my report? Why?

b. What are the challenges or difficulties I think I might encounter?

c. What preparations should I make to start my academic writing? How might they help in my writing?

d. Have I made a plan for writing? What are the specific steps in my plan?

Questions asked during writing:

a. Am I following the plans I set at the beginning?

b. Is my writing working out as I expected?

c. Am I doing well now with my writing?

d. What are my feelings about my writing now?

e. Is there anything interesting or exciting about my writing?

f. Which step am I in? What theories or research methods am I using in this step?

g. Am I stuck in a specific step of the writing process now?

h. Are there any problems happening during my writing process? What method am I using to solve these problems?

i. Have I successfully handled the difficulties?

j. Am I cooperating with my team members well? How do they help me?

Questions asked after writing:

a. What are my feelings about my writing experience in general?

b. What specific steps in my writing (e. g., collecting data, writing literature review, making conclusions) were the easiest for me?

c. What specific steps in academic writing (e. g., writing introduction, discussing research findings, reporting on a conference) were the most difficult?

d. What problems did I meet during my writing? How did I solve them?

e. What exactly did I learn from the whole writing process (e. g., writing format, presentation skills)?

f. How did my team mates help me? What did I learn from them?

g. Is there anything I would do differently if I were to restart my writing?

h. Did I succeed in the writing process? How will I comment on my performance during the whole process (e. g., teamwork, data collection, writing efficiency)?

i. How does my writing experience benefit me as a researcher, a writer, a presenter, or a team player?

j. How has my writing experience changed me in terms of my attitudes, beliefs, learning abilities, and so on?

k. How will I make use of what I learned in my writing in the future? Is there anything that needs to be done to improve my writing in the future?

4. How do you write?

Writing a reflective journal is personal, and you can use your own style to write it. However, a well-structured reflective journal with appropriate tone will make your writing more professional. There are certain guidelines you can follow:

The Structure. A reflective journal requires you to describe, analyze and summarize the events in a process. In general, it includes three parts: introduction, body, and conclusion.

Introduction. A reflective journal begins with an introduction. The introduction part aims to inform the reader what you are going to write about. Give an overview of the experience you are going to tell. You can focus on the essential elements to describe the experience: who, when, where, what, and how.

Body. This is the main part of your reflective journal. In this part, you should recall and elaborate on you learning and writing experience, describing and analyzing the whole process and adding your feelings to it. You can arrange the events in a chronological order. Following a chronological order helps you clearly recollect what has happened and organize your writing in a systematic and coherent way. In addition, it makes your reader follow your flow of thoughts easily.

Conclusion. In the conclusion part, you summarize your writing process and provide its implications. You can focus on how your writing experience has changed your attitudes or abilities, what achievements you have made, what improvements you would like to make, or how you will make use of what you have learned from this experience in your future learning or writing.

The Tone. When writing the reflective journal, you are the story-teller who unfolds your experience and guides the readers throughout your journey. Therefore, a first-person pattern in a narrative tone is always adopted in reflective journals. Below are two examples:

(1) I found the Self-assessment difficult to write. I've never had to do a self-evaluation before, so I hope they will get less difficult as I progress...

(2) During this quarter I realized that to accomplish something extraordinary you've got to step out and attempt something you're not comfortable with. That one insight is worth any length of time.

5. Writing samples

You can have a look of the reflective writing samples below. These samples were reflective thoughts from our students while they were learning academic writing.

Table 27.2　Reflection samples

Reflection on academic writing	Comments
I think the introduction section is to introduce clearly what you want to study and the general background, so as to give the readers a more concise perspective to understand the general problems discussed in the article; there is also a difficult problem for me, that is, how to use expressions as these writers? How to diversify vocabularies?	*The writer introduces the topic of his reflection and his main point: he has realized that he had met problems in choosing vocabulary and writing style.*
Literature has to be read one by one, and translation can be used as a reference. At this stage, we do not have any specific division of labor. We all read the literature by ourselves and communicate with each other in the group. The reason for last week's stagnation came from the disputes of some members. At that time, everyone was very upset to the extent that even normal life was disturbed, not to mention the progress of the research.	*The writer describes his learning experience of the past week and the feeling of the whole team.*

(Continued)

Reflection on academic writing	Comments
Description of difficulties encountered: 1. Some articles have a large number of rare nouns and proper nouns, which are difficult to understand. When reading, I need to constantly consult the dictionary and the Internet, which greatly reduces my reading comprehension. 2. Most papers are too long. It's hard to comb the logical connection between paragraphs. Because of the first contact with such requirements, it produces a kind of fear, and loss of self-confidence. Solutions: 1. I can start reading from the shorter and simpler articles, and then read the more complicated articles step by step. 2. In the process of reading, take some notes to facilitate subsequent review, and circle some important short sentences to facilitate understanding of the article.	*The writer tells the problems he encountered in reading and writing, and describes his feeling about them. He also analyzes in detail the reading strategies he will use to improve his ability to understand the literature and write the literature review.*
I would like to talk about the difficulties I encountered in the speed of reading literature. Reading has always been difficult for me. In fact, I analyzed the main reasons, which were my lack of vocabulary, reading amount and unfamiliarity with the structure and logic of the paper. In the past I would go back to Chinese literature with the excuse that I didn't have time. Now I force myself to read on. I control myself from using translation software. This week, my reading speed has greatly improved. I feel that I've gradually found the rhythm. I feel that I'm making progress...	*The writer summarizes his difficulties in reading speed and the measures taken to improve it. In addition, he tells his growth from his experience.*

II. Self-assessment on academic report writing

Self-assessment is a process whereby you examine yourself (e.g., your knowledge, skills, attitudes, personal traits, scholastic aptitudes) through a series of self-reported answers, rather than through external standardized tests. Self-assessment is an important component in learner-centered education, through which you gather evidence from your learning experience to discuss and judge whether you have known, understood, and can appropriately use the knowledge and skills acquired.

Self-assessment is adopted as an effective approach to measure your performance in academic report writing, as well as your learning outcomes. In general, it aims to find out whether you have achieved your goals set at the beginning of your writing journey, whether you have successfully gained essential knowledge and writing skills, and whether you have become a competent researcher and writer, etc.

1. Basic forms of self-assessment

Self-assessment requires you to respond to specific areas of your report, such as text organization, grammatical structure, etc. There are three basic forms of self-assessment:

Rubric. A rubric is a document containing statements about the assessment criteria for an assignment, as well as descriptions of the quality of the assignment and the levels of the quality (usually from excellent to poor). It is generally believed that using rubric as a tool of self-assessment increases your knowledge of the learning outcomes, helping you focus on the goals and improve the quality of your work.

Checklist. A checklist is a sheet which lists the description of specific assessment criteria which requires the students to make judgment by ticking in the box or choosing between "yes" and "no". A checklist helps you examine whether or not you have met all the requirements of an assignment.

Rating scale. A rating scale is the description of the assessment criteria with indicators (e. g., frequency, degree of agreement, level of competence) to assess student's performance. Common types include Likert response scale, numeric rating scale (NRS), verbal rating scale (VRS), graphic rating scale, etc.

2. Contents of self-assessment on academic report writing

As academic report writing is a complex process involving various steps, its assessment is multi-dimensional. Contents of self-assessment should be focused on the following two dimensions:

Quality of the academic report. First and foremost, the quality of your written product, i. e., your report, should be assessed. Here, we make a list of some dimensions of assessment criteria for writing, which serves as the basis for your self-assessment on the quality of the report.

Table 27.3   **Dimensions of assessment criteria on writing**

Saddler & Andrade (2004)	a. Ideas b. Organization c. Voice d. Word Choice e. Sentence Fluency f. Conventions
East (2009)	a. Cohesion, coherence and rhetorical organization b. Knowledge of lexis, idiomatic expressions; Functional knowledge c. Grammatical competence: syntax, sentence-grammar semantics d. "Mechanics": spelling and punctuation e. Knowledge of register and varieties of language; knowledge of cultural references (where appropriate)

(Continued)

Good et al. (2012)	a. Focus: discipline-based written product b. Content: idea development c. Organization d. Style e. English language conventions
Honsa (2013)	a. Organization b. Content c. Grammar and mechanics d. Content and discourse
Greenberg (2015)	a. Content b. Expression c. Formatting
Mazloomi & Khabiri (2016)	a. Content b. Organization c. Grammar and mechanics d. vocabulary and language use

From the above table, we can draw some commonalities of the assessment criteria for the written paper: showing disciplined-based knowledge or awareness of the audience, having clearly-stated ideas and sufficient supporting materials, having well-organized text, following academic format in writing, and accuracy of language use.

Research methods. Conducting a research project is a crucial step in academic report writing, without which you will not get your data and move forward. As a result, in addition to assessing your competence as a qualified writer, you should assess your competence as a qualified researcher.

In the previous chapters, you have learned some basic steps involved in conducting a research. When you assess whether you are a qualified researcher, you need to focus on the following aspects: choosing appropriate research methodology; appropriate ways of analyzing data, presenting and discussing research results.

3. A Self-assessment tool on academic report writing

Based on the above-mentioned contents of self-assessment for writing, we adapted a few existing writing assessment tools (East, 2009; Good, 2012; Honsa, 2013; Greenberg, 2015; Mazloomi & Khabiri, 2016) to develop a rating scale for you to assess your academic report writing. It contains six dimensions: focus (discipline-based product), ideas and content, organization, style, language conventions, and research methods. We have not included soft skills such as time management or team work ability in the rubric for fear that the rubric would be too complex. Items are put on a 5-point Likert scale. How good is your work in terms of the following aspects? Rate a score for each item. 1 = Undesirable; 2 = Not good enough; 3 = Acceptable; 4 = Good; 5 = Excellent. Higher scores indicate higher levels of competence in academic report writing.

Table 27.4　A Self-rating scale for self-assessment on academic report writing

Items	1	2	3	4	5
Focus: (discipline-based written product)					
I know the purpose of my writing.	1	2	3	4	5
I am thinking of my audience while I am writing, and I am trying to answer their questions.	1	2	3	4	5
My report has a focused and proper topic.	1	2	3	4	5
I show the focus clearly in the Introduction part.	1	2	3	4	5
Ideas and content					
My ideas are clearly presented in my paper.	1	2	3	4	5
I provide extensive explanations and illustrations of key ideas.	1	2	3	4	5
I give detailed reasons to support my ideas.	1	2	3	4	5
I provide relevant and accurate facts to support my ideas.	1	2	3	4	5
My ideas are convincing.	1	2	3	4	5
The contents of my report are sufficient.	1	2	3	4	5
Organization					
My paper has a well-structured introduction that gives a clear overview of my research.	1	2	3	4	5
I include a topic sentence and supporting ideas in all paragraphs.	1	2	3	4	5
I use effective transitions to join sentences and paragraphs.	1	2	3	4	5
The paragraphs are cohesive and are logically organized.	1	2	3	4	5
There is unity in each paragraph (one idea per paragraph).	1	2	3	4	5
The pronouns in my paper arc coherent.	1	2	3	4	5
The conclusion part clearly summarizes my research and presents implications and limitations of my research.	1	2	3	4	5
Style					
I use concise and precise language.	1	2	3	4	5
I omit extraneous information in my paper.	1	2	3	4	5

(Continued)

I use academic language to write the report.	1	2	3	4	5
I use discipline-based terminologies correctly in my paper.	1	2	3	4	5
I follow discipline-specific format (e.g., APA, MLA) for in-text citations.	1	2	3	4	5
I give complete bibliographic information in discipline-specific style.	1	2	3	4	5
English Language conventions					
The pages in my paper are numbered.	1	2	3	4	5
The grammatical structures of my sentences are correct.	1	2	3	4	5
The verb tenses in my sentences are correct.	1	2	3	4	5
The spellings in my paper report are accurate.	1	2	3	4	5
The punctuation and capitalization are correct.	1	2	3	4	5
My audience can understand my expressions.	1	2	3	4	5
Research methods					
I use appropriate methodology (e.g., case study, interview, action research, questionnaire) to conduct my research.	1	2	3	4	5
I put forward research hypotheses based on theories or existing empirical data.	1	2	3	4	5
I cite relevant sources to review literature on my research topic.	1	2	3	4	5
I use the correct way (e.g., random sampling, snowballs) to collect data.	1	2	3	4	5
My sample size is adequate for data analysis.	1	2	3	4	5
I use correct qualitative or quantitative methods to analyze the data.	1	2	3	4	5
I analyze the research results in detail.	1	2	3	4	5
I discuss the research results critically.	1	2	3	4	5

III. Summary of the chapter

We begin the book by making your writing plan and wrap up the book by reflection and self-assessment of the researching, writing and presenting journey. Do you remember the competences to be learned on the road? Reflect on the ups and downs of the journey, assess your competences, and wrap up the journey with a bigger stature of yourself.

❧ References ❧

[1] A Short Guide to reflective writing (n. d.). University of Birmingham. https://intranet. birmingham. ac. uk/as/libraryservices/library/asc/documents/public/Short-Guide-Reflective-Writing. pdf

[2] Agrawal, A. (2006). *EndNote 1 – 2 – 3 easy!*: *Reference management for the professional.* Springer Science + Business Media.

[3] American Psychological Association. (2020). Publication Manual of the American Psychological association (7th ed.).

[4] Anson, C. (2017). *A guide to college writing.* Pearson.

[5] Ayden, Y. , Tatoglu, E. , Glaister, K. W. , & Demirbag, M. (2020). Exploring the internationalization strategies of Turkish multinationals: A multi-perspective analysis. *Journal of International Management*. Advance Online publication. https://doi. org/10. 1016/j. intman. 2020. 100783

[6] Bailey, S. (2020). *Academic writing for international students of business and economics* (3rd ed.). Routledge.

[7] CIPD. (2015, February). *Gender diversity in the boardroom*: *Reach for the top.* https://www. cipd. co. uk/images/gender-diversity-boardroom_2015-reach-for-the-top_tcm18-10828. pdf.

[8] Clandinin, D. J. , Connelly, F. M. , & Schön, D. A. (1986). The reflective practitioner and practitioners' narrative unities. *Canadian Journal of Education*, *11*(2), 184 – 198.

[9] Dawson, C. (2009). *Introduction to research methods*. Little, Brown Book Group.

[10] East, M. (2009). Evaluating the reliability of a detailed analytic scoring rubric for foreign language writing. *Assessing Writing*, *14*(2), 88 – 115. https://doi. org/10. 1016/j. asw. 2009. 04. 001

[11] Fisher, C. , Buglear, J. , & Lowry, D (2010). *Researching and writing a dissertation*: *An essential guide for business students*. Prentice Hall.

[12] Furman, R. , Coyne, A. , & Negi, N. J. (2008). An international experience for social work students: Self-reflection through poetry and journal writing exercises. *Journal of Teaching in Social Work*, *28*(1), 71 – 85. https://doi. org/10. 1080/08841230802178946

[13] Gibaldi, J. (2003) *MLA handbook for writers of research papers* (6th ed.). Modern Language Assn of Amer.

[14] Gibbs, G. (1988). *Learning by doing*: *a guide to teaching and learning methods*. Further

Education Unit.

[15] Good, J. M., Osborne, K., & Birchfield, K. (2012). Placing data in the hands of discipline-specific decision makers: Campus-wide writing program assessment. *Assessing Writing*, *17*(3), 140 - 149. https://doi.org/10.1016/j.asw.2012.02.003

[16] Greenberg, K. P. (2015). Rubric use in formative assessment: A detailed behavioral rubric helps students improve their scientific writing skills. *Teaching of Psychology*, *42*(3), 211 - 217. https://doi.org/10.1177/0098628315587618

[17] Hacker, D, & Sommers, N. (2016). *A pocket style manual: APA version* (7th ed.). Bedford/St. Martin's.

[18] Hartley, J. (2008). *Academic writing and publishing: A practical handbook*. Routledge.

[19] Heard, S. B. (2016). *The scientist's guide to writing: How to write more easily and effectively throughout your scientific career*. Princeton University Press.

[20] Hofmann, A. H. (2019). *Scientific Writing and Communication: Papers, Proposals, and Presentations* (4th ed.). Oxford University Press.

[21] Honsa, S. (2013). Self-assessment in EFL writing: A study of intermediate EFL students at a Thai university. *Voices in Asia Journal*, *1*(1), 34 - 57.

[22] Hudnall, E. H., Corcoran, K. E., & Scheitle, C. P. (Eds.). (2020, October). West Virginia University. *Internet access in West Virginia University*. https://survey.wvu.edu/files/d/2ecc6402-b338-46b5-9c06-2a881c72d1e8/internet-access-accessible.pdf

[23] Klimova, B. (2015). Diary writing as a tool for students' self-reflection and teacher's feedback in the course of academic writing. *Procedia-Social and Behavioral Sciences*, *197*, 549 - 553. http://doi.org.10.1016/j.sbspro.2015.07.189

[24] Lindsay, D. (2011). *Scientific writing = thinking in words*. CSIRO Publishing.

[25] Lunenburg, F. C., & Irby, B. J. (2007). *Writing a successful thesis or dissertation: Tips and strategies for students in the social and behavioral sciences*. Corwin.

[26] May, C. B., & May, G. S. (2014). *Effective writing: A handbook for accountants* (10th ed.). Pearson.

[27] Mazloomi, S., & Khabiri, M. (2018). The impact of self-assessment on language learners' writing skill. *Innovations in Education and Teaching International*, *55*(1), 91 - 100. http://doi.org/10.1080/14703297.2016.1214078

[28] McCormack, J. & Slaght, J. (2015). *English for academic study: Extended writing & research skills*. Foreign Language Teaching and Research Press.

[29] McMahan, E., & Day, S. (1988). *The writer's rhetoric and handbook* (3rd ed.). McGraw-Hill College.

[30] Melzer, D. (2011). *Exploring college writing: Reading, writing and researching across the curriculum*. Equinox Publishing Limited.

[31] Neuman, W. L. (2010). *Social research methods: Qualitative and quantitative approaches* (6th ed.). Posts & Telecom Press.

[32] Oliver, p. (2010). *The student's guide to research ethics (open up study skills)* (2nd ed.). Open University Press.

[33] Race, P. (2006, November). *Evidencing reflection: Putting the "w" into reflection*. ESCalate. Retrieved March 27, 2021 from http://escalate.ac.uk/resources/reflection/02.html

[34] Reale, M. (2017). *Becoming a reflective librarian and teacher: strategies for mindful academic practice*. American Library Association.

[35] Reddy, Y. M. , & Andrade, H. (2010). A review of rubric use in higher education. *Assessment & Evaluation in Higher Education*, *35*(4), 435 – 448. https://doi. org/10. 1080/02602930902862859

[36] Rosenwasser, D. , & Stephen, J. (2005). *Writing analytically* (4th ed.). Cengage Learning.

[37] Rowntree, D. (2018). *Statistics without tears : An introduction for non-mathematicians*. Rowntree. Penguin UK.

[38] Saddler, B. , & Andrade, H. (2004). The writing rubric. *Educational Leadership*, *62*(2), 48 – 52.

[39] Saunders, M. N. K. , Lewis, P. , & Thornhill, A. (2015). *Research methods for business students* (7th ed.). Pearson.

[40] Slade, C. (2000). *Form and style : Research papers, reports, and theses*. Foreign Language Teaching and Research Press.

[41] Thomas, M. (2007). *Mastering people management : Build a Successful Team—Motivate, Empower and Lead People*. Thorogood Publishing.

[42] Turabian, K. L. (2018). *A manual for writers of research papers, theses, and dissertations : Chicago style for students and researchers* (9th ed.). University of Chicago Press.

[43] Widdowson, H. G. (1983). *Learning Purpose and Language Use*. Oxford University Press.

[44] Wiltshire Council. (n. d.). *Preferred ecological survey report headings*. Retrieved February 28, 2021, from https://www. wiltshire. gov. uk/media/996/-Preferred-ecological-survey-headings/pdf/Preferred-ecological-survey-headings-biodiversity. pdf?m = 637108844993170000

[45] Winstanley, C. (2012). *Writing a dissertation for dummies—UK Edition*. John Wiley & Sons.

[46] Zhang, Z. X. , Liu, L. A. , & Ma, L. (2021). Negotiation beliefs: Comparing Americans and the Chinese. *International Business Review*. Advance online publication. https://doi. org/10. 1016/j. ibusrev. 2021. 101849

[47] Zimmerman, B. J. , & Risemberg, R. (1997). Becoming a self-regulated writer: A social cognitive perspective. *Contemporary Educational Psychology*, *22*(1), 73 – 101. https://doi. org/10. 1006/ceps. 1997. 0919

[48] 黑玉琴,郭粉绒.(2013).英语学术论文写作.西安交通大学出版社.

[49] 卫乃兴.(2017).英语研究论文写作.上海交通大学出版社.

[50] 徐艳英,刘佳,吕蓓蓓.(2015).英语研究论文写作指导.北京理工大学出版社.